AF697570

INDONESIAN ECONOMIC DECOLONIZATION IN REGIONAL AND INTERNATIONAL PERSPECTIVE

Cover: Advertisement of the Dasaad Musin Concern stressing its role in constructing a new Indonesian economy under the Japanese military administration (*Djawa Baroe*, 15-4-1945; NIOD collection).

VERHANDELINGEN
VAN HET KONINKLIJK INSTITUUT
VOOR TAAL-, LAND- EN VOLKENKUNDE

267

INDONESIAN ECONOMIC DECOLONIZATION IN REGIONAL AND INTERNATIONAL PERSPECTIVE

Edited by

J. THOMAS LINDBLAD and PETER POST

KITLV Press
Leiden
2009

Published by:
KITLV Press
Koninklijk Instituut voor Taal-, Land- en Volkenkunde
(Royal Netherlands Institute of Southeast Asian and Caribbean Studies)
P.O. Box 9515
2300 RA Leiden
The Netherlands
website: www.kitlv.nl
e-mail: kitlvpress@kitlv.nl

KITLV is an institute of the Royal Netherlands Academy of Arts and Sciences (KNAW)

Cover: Creja ontwerpen, Leiderdorp

ISBN 978 90 6718 353 6

© 2009 Koninklijk Instituut voor Taal-, Land- en Volkenkunde

No part of this publication may be reproduced or transmitted in any form or by any means, electronic or mechanical, including photocopy, recording, or any information storage and retrieval system, without permission from the copyright owner.

Printed in the Netherlands

Contents

Abbreviations

ALS	Algemeen Landbouw Syndicaat
ANRI	Arsip Nasional Republik Indonesia
AVROS	Algemeene Vereeniging van Rubberplanters ter Oostkust van Sumatra
BANAS	Badan Nasional
BIN	Bank Industri Negara
BKR	Badan Keamanan Rakjat
BKSBM	Badan Kerdjasama Buruh dan Militer
BNI	Bank Negara Indonesia
BPM	Bataafsche Petroleum Maatschappij
BPRI	Badan Pemberontak Republik Indonesia
BTC	Banking and Trading Company
BTI	Barisan Tani Indonesia
BTM	Besoeki Tabak Maatschappij
CAO	Collectieve Arbeids Overeenkomst
CMD	Cultuur-Maatschappij Djelboek
CO	Colonial Office
CRO	Commissie voor Rechtsverkeer in Oorlogstijd
CTC	Central Trading Corporation
DJB	De Javasche Bank
DMC	Dasaad Musin Concern
DOAZ	Departement van Oost-Aziatische Zaken
Finec	Financieele en Economische Overeenkomst
FPT	Front Persatuan Tani
GAPPERSU	Gabungan Pengusaha Perkebunan Sumatera Utara
GAPPIS	Gabungan Pemberontak Indonesia Soppeng
GDP	Gross Domestic Product
GMB	Gemeenschappelijke Mijnbouwmaatschappijen Billiton
GTI	Gerakan Tani Indonesia
HVA	Handels Vereeniging 'Amsterdam'
ISK	Ishihara Sangyo Kaisha
KHT	Kwik Hoo Tong
KJCPL	Koninklijke Java-China Paketvaart-Lijnen
KNIP	Komite Nasional Indonesia Pusat
KNILM	Koninklijke Nederlandsch-Indische Luchtvaart-Maatschappij
KPM	Koninklijke Paketvaart Maatschappij
LAAPLN	Lembaga Alat-Alat Pembajaran Luar Negri

LAPRIS	Laskar Pemberontak Republik Indonesia Sulawesi Selatan
LMOD	Landbouw-Maatschappij Oud-Djember
MCA	Malay(si)an Chinese Association
MCP	Malayan Communist Party
MIA	Malay(si)an Indian Association
MITI	Ministry of International Trade and Industry
MoU	Memorandum of Understanding
NDP	Net Domestic Product
NEP	New Economic Policy
NHM	Nederlandsche Handel-Maatschappij
NICA	Netherlands Indies Civil Administration
NISA	Netherlands Indonesian Supply Agency
NDP	Net Domestic Product
OKB	Orang Kaja Baru
ORI	Oeang Republik Indonesia
ORIPS	Oeang Republik Indonesia Propinsi Sumatera
ORNI	Ondernemersraad voor Nederlands-Indië/Indonesië
PAJ	Panitia Agraria Jakarta (Djakarta)
PAY	Panitia Agraria Yogyakarta (Jogjakarta)
PBI	Persatoean Bangsa Indonesia
PELNI	Pelajaran Nasional Indonesia
PERBOEMI	Persatoean Boeroeh Minjak Indonesia
PERMIRI	Perusahaan Minjak Republik Indonesia
PKI	Partai Komunis Indonesia
PNI	Partai Nasional Indonesia
PPKI	Panitia Persiapan Kemerdekaan Indonesia
PPN	Pusat Perkebunan Negara
PSI	Partai Sosialis Indonesia
PP	Peraturan Pemerintah
PSSI	Perserikatan Saudagar-Saudagar Indonesia
PTE	Poesat Tenaga Ekonomi
PTEBI	Persatoean Tenaga Ekonomi Bangsa Indonesia
PTMNRI	Perusahaan Tambang Minjak Negara Republik Indonesia
RI	Republik Indonesia
RCMA	Rubber Cultuur-Maatschappij 'Amsterdam'
RIS	Republik Indonesia Serikat
RTC	Round Table Conference
RTI	Rukun Tani Indonesia
SAKTI	Sarekat Kaum Tani Indonesia
Sarbupri	Sarekat Buruh Perkebunan Republik Indonesia
SBG	Serikat Buruh Gula
SBII	Sarekat Buruh Islam Indonesia
SBTC	Sumatra Banking and Trading Corporation
SCAP	Supreme Command of the Allied Powers
SK	Surat Keputusan
SOB	Staat van Oorlog en Beleg
SOBSI	Sentral Organisasi Buruh Seluruh Indonesia
Socfin	Société Financière

SOEIMEX	Soematera Import and Export
SPA	Sumatra Planters' Association
STII	Sarekat Tani Islam Indonesia
SUMUT	Sumatera Utara
TKR	Tentara Keamanan Rakjat
TMSU	Tambang Minjak Sumatera Utara
TNI	Tentara Nasional Indonesia
TRI	Tentara Rakjat Indonesia
UMNO	United Malays National Organization
VOC	Vereenigde Oost-Indische Compagnie

J. Thomas Lindblad and Peter Post

Indonesian economic decolonization in regional and international perspective
An introduction

The decolonization of Asia and Africa in the mid-twentieth century was a watershed in recent world history. After decades of formal and informal integration in the Western and Japanese empires the subordination of the peoples of both continents came to an end and in a relatively short period, the new nation-states became independent players in the global political arena. Freeing themselves from the yoke of Western imperialism sometimes led to bitter struggles for Independence, as in Algeria, French Indochina and Indonesia. Elsewhere, the process of decolonization went relatively smoothly, for example in India and the Philippines. However, achieving political independence and obtaining administrative and judicial control over one's territory did not automatically mean gaining control over economic institutions and the economic assets of the former colonizing power. Economic decolonization generally lagged behind political decolonization.

In the historiography on decolonization, economic aspects are on occasion mentioned but tend to remain subordinated to politics. Much of the literature assumes a political perspective and is concerned with questions of power and authority and military issues as well as the relationship of decolonization to the Cold War. The lack of interest in the economic side of the process may come as a surprise given the fact that economic exploitation had formed one of the major reasons behind colonial expansion, and that in building up their national economies the newly sovereign nations badly needed the institutions, capital, know-how and management capabilities that in the past had been supplied by the colonizer.

Most former colonies were strikingly ill-prepared to manage a modern banking system, a smooth working industrial and trading sector and an export-oriented estate agriculture. Indonesia is a case in point. When Sukarno and Moh. Hatta declared Indonesia independent in 1945 and when the Netherlands in 1949 formally acknowledged Indonesian sovereignty, hopes ran high. But it soon turned out that the transformation of the colonial economy into a national economy was exceptionally difficult. Economic decolonization thus acquired a momentum and a chronology of its own. This book is about that process. It has a double aim: to identify the unique characteristics of economic decolonization in Indonesia, as opposed to political decolonization, and to find out to what extent economic decolonization in Indonesia differed from similar processes elsewhere in Asia.

There were two types of challenges simultaneously confronting the newly independent nation-state in Indonesia as well as other former colonies. Highest priority was given to the construction of a substantive national economy but precisely at that time, the post-war resurgence of world trade opened up generous opportunities for further integration into the wider global economy. The two trajectories were only partially compatible with one another. Gaining control over economic assets obviously meant a reduction of the role played by private capital from the former colonial power in the domestic economy, but cooperation with such firms was essential in order to reap full benefits from participating in the worldwide boom.

Generally speaking, three preconditions had to be fulfilled for a successful integration into the global economy. First, a well-informed, enterprising and well-connected private business sector was needed. Second, a capable economic administrative apparatus had to be in place. Third, access had to be guaranteed to the capital, know-how and management capabilities which private firms from the former colonial power could most easily provide. Meeting these preconditions was no easy task in the first place, but it became all the more complicated as it coincided with the emancipation from colonialism in economic life.

'The Revolution has yet to begin in the economy.' This saying is attributed to the nationalist leader, later Cabinet Minister Agus Salim at the time of the Indonesian Revolution in the second half of the 1940s (Higgins 1957:102). By the time of the transfer of sovereignty in December 1949, large proportions of the modern sectors of the economy in Indonesia, about one-quarter of the total, were still controlled by private Dutch capital. This included estate agriculture, mining, manufacturing, interisland shipping, international trading and banking. Eight Dutch trading-firms handled 60 per cent of exports, whereas the ubiquitous 'Big Five' (Borsumij, Internatio, Jacobson van den Berg, Lindeteves and Geo. Wehry) predominated in the import trade (Glassburner 1971:79; Dick et al. 2002:174). Economic decolonization in Indonesia arguably only came to a conclusion in 1959 when the Dutch enterprises, which had been taken over in December 1957 and early 1958, were nationalized. In other words, in Indonesia economic decolonization lagged behind political decolonization by at least fourteen years.

The eight contributions to this volume are selected in such a way as to obtain a broad and multi-facetted outlook on the premise that economic decolonization in Indonesia cannot be understood from one single viewpoint alone. The various contributions are arranged according to three perspectives complementing each other: the new nation-state, private business and the international comparison. Each warrants a separate commentary, also incorporating some of the major findings of the individual contributions. The volume as a whole forms a complement to a recent monograph outlining the history of economic decolonization in Indonesia (Lindblad 2008).

The new nation-state

The Indonesian nationalist leaders gave strikingly little attention to economic issues in their writings preceding Independence. Only at the time of the transfer of sovereignty did a slender book appear with the expression 'from a colonial to a national economy' (*dari ekonomi kolonial ke ekonomi nasional*) in its very title (Soejono Hadinoto 1949). Yet this booklet did not contain a precise definition of what was meant by a 'national economy'; rather, it expressed a preference for economic policy-making along the lines of social democracy. For a fuller understanding of this concept, we need to link it to the idea of the new nation-state and economic nationalism developing in its wake.

The concept of a 'national economy' is inextricably bound up with the notion of the nation-state, which in its modern version came to feel the need 'to define the economic space over which it claimed control' (Dick et al. 2002:10). Although it can be argued that a national economy from the point of view of effective control was only substantiated much later, during the New Order government, it is clear that this became a major target for the Indonesian government following the transfer of sovereignty. There is a discussion in the older literature about the changing character of the successive cabinets in the 1950s. The American political scientist John Sutter distinguishes between two periods. The first one is the pragmatic and moderate 'Masjumi period' (after the leading Islamic party), which ran from 1949 to 1953 and covered four cabinets (Hatta, Natsir, Sukiman, Wilopo). The latter period is described as the 'PNI period' (after Partai Nasional Indonesia, Indonesian National Party), containing the three cabinets between 1953 and 1957 (Ali Sastroamidjojo I and II, Harahap) and dominated by 'less tolerant ultranationalist politicians' (Sutter 1959:1190). Benjamin Higgins suggests a different terminology, contrasting the Western-oriented 'economics-minded' cabinets of the period 1949-1953 with the socialist-inspired 'development-minded' cabinets of the years 1953-1957 (Higgins 1957:103). Regardless of the terminology applied, this change in ideological outlook had important repercussions for how economic decolonization took shape in Indonesia, as is documented in Thee Kian Wie's opening account of economic policy-making during the 1950s.

Thee provides an overview of the most important policy measures in the 1950s aiming at the transformation from a colonial into a national economy. The logical point of departure is the Finec (Financieele en Economische Overeenkomst, Financial and Economic Agreement), attached to the Round Table Conference (RTC) Agreement, which in November 1949 laid down the conditions under which the Dutch government was prepared to acknowledge Indonesia's Independence. These provisions severely curtailed the scope for economic policy-making and were deeply resented by the Indonesian delegation attending the conference. Dutch refusal to surrender the western part of New Guinea (later Irian Jaya, now Papua) and the provisions guaranteeing unhindered operations by Dutch firms provoked the most discontent on the Indonesian side. This continued to exert a negative impact on the transfer of Dutch-owned assets into Indonesian hands.

Pragmatic politicians like Vice President Hatta, president of the central bank Sjafruddin Prawiranegara and Cabinet Ministers Sumitro Djojohadikusumo and Djuanda realized that top priority had to be given to economic stabilization and rehabilitation and were willing to make compromises. Nevertheless, various measures were taken to curb Dutch economic control. Early nationalization with financial compensation affected the central bank, the national carrier, public transport (railways) and public utilities (gas and electricity). It can be argued that the moderate cabinets of the so-called 'Masjumi' period achieved more by peaceful means and negotiations than the later, more aggressive cabinets.

Economic nationalism was on the rise in the 1950s, not only in Indonesia but also in other former colonies. It is commonly defined as 'the national aspiration to having property owned by nationals and economic functions performed by nationals' (Johnson 1972:26). This target was to be achieved through the so-called Benteng programme, best described as a policy of positive discrimination favouring Indonesian nationals to counter the predominance of private Dutch firms in trading. As Thee argues, the programme had the auxiliary aim of reducing the role of ethnic Chinese in the Indonesian economy. Chinese dominance of important sectors of the economy had caused much resentment among the indigenous population and in the late 1950s several measures were taken to transfer some of these sectors to the indigenous business class. However, most of these measures caused considerable economic disruption, and although many ethnic Chinese businessmen experienced great difficulties during the 1950s, their economic position was not seriously weakened.

The ultimate act of economic nationalism was the takeover and nationalization of virtually all remaining private Dutch firms in the late 1950s.

Significantly, the concept of a 'national economy' was only shortly afterwards officially linked to Indonesian national identity. In his annual report about 1959, the central bank president wrote: 'An Indonesian economy can only be truly called "national" if based on the Indonesian spiritual and material identity' (Bank Indonesia 1960:2). Such a statement served as legitimization of the nationalization of Dutch firms only one year before, possibly also in defence of the far-reaching discriminatory measures taken against ethnic Chinese merely months earlier.

Nationalist sentiments were increasingly intermingled with the political ideologies of the Cold War. There was traditionally a tendency among leading Indonesian economists to favour co-operatives and active participation by the state in economic life above unrestrained scope for private capital. The populace's trust in private entrepreneurship was severely damaged when the Benteng programme became a public scandal in the mid-1950s. The role of the state as a major player in the economy was greatly enhanced when the Dutch firms were formally nationalized and became the property of the Indonesian nation. This was reinforced by Sukarno's introduction of the doctrines 'Guided Economy' and 'socialism à la Indonesia' in 1958-1960, which met with strikingly little dissent from leading Indonesian economists (Mackie 1971:51). The economic system envisaged in the new nation-state in the late 1950s and early 1960s was one in which the 'people's welfare' was the core principle, an aim which, according to accepted ideology at the time, was not to be achieved by the system of private capitalism that the one-time colonial masters had bequeathed to Indonesia (Robison 1986:37-8).

A uniquely Indonesian feature of the nation-state in an entrepreneurial capacity was the heavy involvement of the military in economic life. Different from previous writers, Bambang Purwanto traces the origins of military-controlled business right to the very beginning of the Indonesian Revolution in 1945. He argues that the link between economic decolonization and increasing military business was established in the late 1940s and successively strengthened in the course of the 1950s. Decolonization placed the military in a key position that was reinforced by the apparent inability of the civilian government to manage the nation's economic resources. This nurtured the interest of soldiers and officers in conducting business, both as a group and as individuals. By the late 1950s, military officers had slotted themselves into a dependence on business activities. They were reaping large profits, not only economically, but also socially and politically. As an institution, the army in particular grew dependent on financial proceeds from its business deals. By the time that economic decolonization was nearing its end, conducting business and being in the military had become two sides of the same coin.

Private business in action

Economic nationalism prescribed private economic activities to be conducted first and foremost by Indonesian nationals, which obviously represented a radical departure from the colonial economy with top positions reserved for Dutchmen. A key analytical tool to further our understanding of economic decolonization in Indonesia, therefore, is the concept of *Indonesianisasi* ('Indonesianization'). This term was introduced into the academic literature by John Sutter in the late 1950s and defined as 'a conscious effort to increase the participation and elevate the role of the Indonesian – and more particularly the "indigenous" Indonesian – in the more complex sectors of the economy' (Sutter 1959:2; Lindblad 2002:52). This effort could assume many shapes, ranging from promotion of Indonesians into supervisory and management positions in private companies, to full-scale appropriation and nationalization of foreign-owned firms. Sutter and other contemporary writers viewed Indonesianisasi as a process of emancipation. Indonesians were to be liberated from Western, in particular Dutch, control of vital sectors of the economy. The Finec Agreement in 1949 included a loose commitment by remaining Dutch enterprises to increase participation of Indonesians in higher staff functions and eventually replace Dutchmen by Indonesian nationals. Throughout the 1950s, Indonesianisasi figured prominently in the public discourse about how to gain control over the nation's economic resources and achieve economic decolonization.

Indonesianisasi had a strong ideological component. It can be argued that it first emerged as an important driving force of Indonesian nationalism with the establishment of the Sarekat Islam in 1912, the first mass organization of the Indonesian nationalist movement. In the late 1920s, it gained momentum with the establishment of the Bandoeng Studieclub (Bandung Study Club) and the Persatoean Bangsa Indonesia, PBI (Indonesian People's Association) of Dr Sutomo. By the second half of the 1930s, Indonesianisasi had evolved as an essential part of the 'nationalist struggle' for Independence. Initially, it was part of a movement aiming at a wider indigenous economic participation in the existing Dutch colonial economy, but later it was increasingly influenced by a more global discussion about the failure of Western capitalism to suit the needs of economic development in Indonesia. Its outlook became more socialist and anti-capitalist.

Indonesianisasi also had an ethnic aspect. To many Indonesians it meant emancipation, not only from Dutch, but also from Chinese control of the economy. In particular this applied to control as exercised by ethnic Chinese (usually *peranakan* groups with roots in Indonesia), who maintained close relations with Dutch capital and were often seen as figureheads of Dutch capitalism. This became a highly complex matter in the 1950s, when officially sanctioned discrimination of non-nationals could be construed as discrimination against those ethnic Chinese who had not unambiguously opted for Indonesian citizenship. The quest for Indonesianisasi offered opportunities for overt expressions of anti-Chinese sentiments, as demonstrated by the Assaat movement in 1956 and the infamous PP 10 (Peraturan Pemerintah, Government Regulation) in 1959, which barred ethnic Chinese from trading in the countryside. Some historians, including Bambang Purwanto in this volume, therefore tend to equate Indonesianisasi with *pribumisasi* (from *pribumi*, 'indigenous').

Indonesianisasi or pribumisasi was not confined to the post-Independence period. In his contribution to this volume, Peter Post points out that economic decolonization started already in the late 1920s, when Japanese investment began to enter the Netherlands Indies. A Japan-oriented niche was created in the colonial economy that brought pribumi business groups in direct contact with Japanese industrial capital. Using the example of one leading pribumi entrepreneur of the time, Agoes Moesin Dasaad, Post demonstrates that private indigenous business interests managed to influence economic policies to a significant degree during the late 1940s and 1950s.

The role of Japan in Indonesia's economic decolonization was twofold. Japanese private capital offered unique opportunities for indigenous entrepreneurship during both the late colonial period and the Japanese occupation (March 1942-August 1945), which went against the very foundations of the Dutch colonial economy. In addition, as Post emphasizes, substantial financial support from the Japanese government to Indonesia materialized in December 1957, precisely at the time when the Dutch enterprises were taken over by local labour unions. There is still disagreement in the international literature whether or not the Sukarno government was involved in, or informed about, the takeovers beforehand (Gardner 1997; A. Kahin and G. Kahin 1995). In any case, the government must have felt so strengthened by the simultaneous agreement on Japanese war reparations and long-tem loans that it retroactively legitimized the actions of labour with great speed.

Indonesianisasi implied competition as well as confrontation. Efforts to promote Indonesian traders at the expense of Dutch (and ethnic Chinese) rivals by means of positive discrimination failed dismally. The Indonesian government's attempt to wrest control over interisland shipping from the fully Dutch-owned KPM (Koninklijke Paketvaart Maatschappij, Royal Packet Company) met with a similar fate, as is shown by Daan Marks in his application of an international comparative perspective. There is, however, evidence to the effect that indigenous Indonesian business did flourish in the 1950s, possibly even despite policies of positive discrimination (Lindblad 2004).

Confrontations in private business became especially intense when the interests of foreign owners clashed with those of labour, locals or the

President Sukarno and Haji Agus Salim, Minister of Foreign Affairs, in Prapat, North Sumatra, during the second Dutch military action in December 1948. At the time of the transfer of sovereignty, one year later, Agus Salim stated that 'the Revolution has yet to begin in the economy'. (KITLV 2642.)

Indonesian government, or all three in combination. We may only learn more about such confrontations by looking at specific case studies. This may be done by reviewing corporate strategies in foreign-owned firms in different former colonies, as is suggested by Jasper van de Kerkhof in his contribution to this volume. Another approach is to focus on regions where vested interests of private Dutch capital were especially strong and where we may expect the transition of management over economic resources to proceed in a dramatic fashion. For this purpose, we selected two regions, both prominent in Indonesian estate agriculture but also widely disparate in terms of location: North Sumatra and East Java.

In his survey of economic performance in North Sumatra before and immediately after the takeover of Dutch estates, Thomas Lindblad distinguishes between external and internal factors. Deteriorating conditions of production barred the estates from reaping full benefit from the positive global market prospects already existent in the mid-1950s. Difficulties due to the transfer of management in 1958 in the wake of the takeovers were aggravated by a short-term price fall in foreign markets. However, production capacity was restored after a relatively brief period of adjustment, as may be demonstrated by highlighting continuities between the situation just before and just after the takeovers. There was even a striking similarity between the periods of Dutch and Indonesian management in terms of clustering of the estates for administrative purposes. Such findings lead Lindblad to conclude that we should be cautious in establishing a direct causal link between the transfer of management in 1957-1959 and the deep economic crisis in which Indonesia found itself in the mid-1960s, an opinion which is not shared by all observers.

Tri Chandra Apriyanto takes a close look at the economic decolonization and nationalization of the sugar and tobacco plantations in the East Java region of Jember (Besuki). He traces the ideological roots of the public debate on estate agriculture during the Indonesian Revolution to nationalist writings preceding Independence. The debate was not only about future social and political developments, but primarily about political substance and its ideological foundation. The contrast between official government-held views and strategies pursued by peasant mass organizations illustrates the dilemmas confronting the Indonesian Republic in the late 1940s and throughout the 1950s. The guarantees given to Dutch estate firms stood in stark contrast to the demands for a full control over land and labour voiced by peasant organizations. The intensity of conflict is illustrated by the dramatic events surrounding the transfer of management of the estates in Jember in late 1957 and early 1958.

There was a relatively long interval between the takeovers and nationalization of Dutch firms such as the estates in North Sumatra and East Java, a time span commencing in December 1957 and reaching far into 1959. Can this time span be construed as an indication that nationalization had not yet become the ultimate aim at the time of the takeovers? The takeovers initially served only to exert pressure on the Netherlands in the rampant conflict over western New Guinea, as was indeed repeatedly asserted in official statements.

It seems that there were two separate but related processes going on at the same time. According to the official explanation, the nationalizations 'served to finish off Dutch economic power' (*dimaksudkan untuk mengachiri kekuasaan ekonomi Belanda*), but 'the process was accelerated by the controversy over West Irian' (*proses dekolonisasi di bidang ekonomi jang dipertjepat djalannja oleh pertikaian mengenai wilajah Irian Barat*) (*Antara*, 8-7-1959). The wider process was economic decolonization, whereas the narrow one was confined to the dispute over the possession of western New Guinea. Initially, the two processes differed in their aims but targets became identical as the Dutch-Indonesian conflict dragged on. This kind of argumentation gives rise to an interesting counterfactual question: would the Dutch firms have been able to escape nationalization if the Netherlands had seceded western New Guinea already in 1958? Perhaps it would not have mattered. The process of economic decolonization had by that time gained such momentum that takeover and nationalization were becoming inevitable.

The international comparison

Economic decolonization in Indonesia should not be studied in a vacuum. After all, the process unfolded itself at a time when numerous other former colonies were confronted with the same tensions between the demands of economic nationalism and fulfilling the preconditions to participate fully in the world trade boom. Also elsewhere ideological choices had to be made in order to position the newly sovereign nation in the spectre of Cold War allegiances. There was a great debate going on among development economists about the degree to which the state should be involved in the achievement of economic growth and structural transformation of the economy. Here an international framework of analysis is proposed with a threefold focus, referring to respectively the legacy of the colonial economy, post-Independence growth performance and strategies pursued by companies controlled by capital in the one-time colonial power.

Anne Booth deals with the colonial legacies by placing Indonesian colonial economic performance in an East Asian perspective. She raises the question whether Japanese colonialism in Korea and Taiwan was more developmental in its aims and achievements in comparison to colonial regimes in other parts of Asia. Drawing upon extensive quantitative data, Booth concludes that if one were to construct a composite index of human development on the basis of per capita GDP (Gross Domestic Product), demographic data and educational enrolment, the Philippines would rank first in 1938 and Taiwan second. Indonesia, despite four decades of efforts by the colonial authorities to 'uplift' the indigenous population, would end up at the bottom of the ranking list.

The verdict on Dutch colonial rule is a harsh one. Indonesia could have been far better prepared for sovereignty in economic life with respect to the reservoir of management capabilities and structural adjustment to sustain economic expansion. By implication, economic decolonization became very difficult, arguably more so than political decolonization. Difficulties were aggravated by the terms under which the Netherlands acknowledged Indonesian Independence in 1949. The Indonesian state took over a huge debt, larger than anywhere else in Asia, from the preceding Dutch colonial administration with the accompanying provision of admitting Dutch interference with Indonesian economic policy as long as the debt had not been repaid. By the time of the unilateral abrogation of the RTC Agreements by

Indonesia in 1956, more than 80 per cent of the debt had in fact been paid off (Dick et al. 2002:170-2).

The point of departure in the contribution by Marks is whether Independence indeed formed a turning point in the long-term economic growth performance of former colonies. He applies a three-layered analysis, considering respectively the relationship in general between decolonization and economic growth, the experiences of selected former colonies in Asia and developments in the interisland shipping industry in Indonesia shortly after Independence. He argues that Independence and decolonization had a direct positive impact on economic growth in India, Malaysia and the Philippines, whereas the first couple of decades immediately following Independence in Indonesia failed to produce a significant break with the growth record of the colonial period. Indonesia remains a 'special case', reaffirming the author's hypothesis, derived from the international literature, that decolonization and rapid economic growth are only positively correlated to one another under specific circumstances.

Economic disruption and political turmoil during the Revolution and the late 1950s up to the establishment of the New Order government in the mid-1960s explain why Indonesia became a 'special case' in the international comparison carried out by Marks. He uses data concerning the shipping concern KPM in the 1950s as evidence of the 'institutional damage' which precluded a positive correlation between decolonization and sustained economic growth. As a corollary, he ascribes the extreme predicament of the Indonesian economy in the mid-1960s to the preceding disruption, including the expulsion of Dutch firms in the late 1950s. In doing so, he presents an alternative view to the one argued by Lindblad in the same volume, which testifies to the scope for debate in historical discourse.

The idea is common that the Dutch companies in Indonesia engineered their own demise by being so ill-prepared to 'indigenize' management and respond adequately to the economic aspirations of the newly independent nation. This issue is taken up by Jasper van de Kerkhof, in his comparison of Dutch and British corporate strategies in Indonesia and Malaysia (British Malaya up to 1957). Neighbouring Malaysia makes an interesting case for comparison, since it is generally acknowledged that economic decolonization there proceeded much more smoothly and less detrimental for post-colonial economic development. Van de Kerkhof's findings show that great care should be taken when making such generalizations. British firms in Malaysia were equally reluctant to vacate their privileged position and 'indigenize' top management.

British and Dutch firms both took active steps to 'indigenize' the lower ranks of their corporation, but they found it equally difficult to appoint well-educated and capable Malay and Indonesian managers into the higher echelons of the companies' hierarchy. This leads Van de Kerkhof to conclude that it was not so much the attitudes and strategies of Dutch and British firms that caused the differences, but rather the institutional surroundings of the countries and the ideological outlook of political leadership. In Malaysia, full economic decolonization was arguably only achieved when the New Economic Policy was put into effect in the 1970s.

A final assessment

This may not be the final word on how economic decolonization took place in Indonesia. It is an account among several, focusing on the unique features of the process as it unfolded. The contributions selected for this volume underscore that it was more difficult to achieve economic as opposed to political decolonization. The process was a highly complex one, extending over a considerable period and involving a variety of sometimes conflicting agents and interest groups, with many regional variations. It was not just a matter of one Indonesian side versus one Dutch side, as has so often been portrayed in the literature on the birth of the Indonesian state. A large number of competing groups (military, pragmatic politicians, indigenous businessmen, economic nationalists, radical socialists, communists, peasant organizations and urban workers' committees) all had a say in the process, and each influenced the legal (and sometimes illegal) transfer of Dutch corporate assets into Indonesian hands in its own way. On the Dutch side, the interests of the large trading corporations on occasion conflicted with the interests of Dutch planters, whereas the political course chosen in the home country increasingly reflected other priorities than those of private Dutch companies remaining in operation in Indonesia. Indonesia's ethnic Chinese, finally, occupied a very special position in the economy, alternately being lumped together with prime targets of emancipation from colonialism and materially benefitting from the transfer of management of economic resources.

Moreover, to complicate matters, economic decolonization was not just a bilateral affair between the Netherlands and Indonesia. Unlike political decolonization, which only involved mother country and former colony, economic decolonization was influenced also by other foreign economic interests in Indonesia, notably American and Japanese investment and trading relations. The international dimension brings us back to the three preconditions that needed to be fulfilled by a newly independent nation in order to fully participate in the worldwide economic boom of the post-war period, that is a well-functioning private business sector, a capable bureaucracy and access to capital and know-how. At first sight, the record appears very disappointing. Capabilities of domestic private business were still insufficient, the state administrative apparatus was not renowned for efficiency and cooperation with private capital from the former colonizing power was brutally cut off. Such a record easily lends support to the idea that Indonesia's long-term economic performance was adversely affected by the way in which economic decolonization was accomplished.

For a fuller understanding of the process and its outcome, we also need to take into consideration some of the complexities highlighted in this volume. The colonial legacy shouldered an extraordinary burden on the new nation-state at a time of rapidly rising expectations. Nevertheless, domestic business thrived to an appreciable extent and Indonesia benefitted, at any rate initially, from the boom in world trade with its favourable market prospects for chief export commodities leaving Indonesia. Economic pragmatism of the early and mid-1950s appeared to strike an acceptable balance between nationalist aspirations and the insistence on what is commonly understood as sound management of economic resources. This balance was lost in the late 1950s, when highest priority was given to the political aspirations of gaining full control over the economy at virtually any cost. Even so, the accelerated transfer of management may not necessarily have had an adverse effect on economic performance in the long run. The overall impression of the Sukarno era (1945-1966), including economic decolonization, remains unduly coloured by the near-collapse of the economy and the regime's cataclysmic conclusion in the mid-1960s.

Historians are fond of speculating about the counterfactual, an exercise that may be aided by looking at comparable situations elsewhere. Could economic decolonization have taken the same peaceful course as in for instance Malaysia, India or the Philippines? The answer is probably no, considering the colonial legacy, the struggle for acknowledgement of political independence and the increasing polarization in politics in Indonesia itself during the 1950s. Could the Dutch government and remaining private Dutch enterprises have done more to smooth the process? It is by no means certain that other policies would have made much of a difference. However, the unresolved conflict about western New Guinea did develop into a formidable obstacle to compromises by either side and may arguably have prematurely caused such radical measures as nationalization. At the same time, the Dutch enterprises lost much goodwill because of the meagre achievements in terms of Indonesianisasi, thus becoming easy scapegoats for everything that was going wrong in the explosive situation of acute crisis that prevailed in Indonesia in the late 1950s (Bondan Kanumoyoso 2001).

Acknowledgements

This volume is one of the results of the *Indonesia Across Orders* (*Van Indië tot Indonesië*) research programme of the Netherlands Institute for War Documentation, NIOD (Nederlands Instituut voor Oorlogsdocumentatie). The programme was commissioned by the Ministry of Welfare, Health and Education in the Netherlands (Ministerie voor Welzijn, Volksgezondheid en Sport) and aimed at producing new insights into the turbulent period of crisis and depression, war, Revolution and decolonization in the Indonesian archipelago during the 1930s-1960s. One of the major challenges of the programme was to integrate the varied experiences of the different population groups in the archipelago and to go beyond the mere political, diplomatic and military perspectives that have thus far dominated this field of enquiry.

This volume forms the proceedings of an international workshop on 'Economic Decolonization in Indonesia in Regional Perspective', which was held on 18-19 November 2005 in Leiden. The workshop was sponsored by the International Institute of Asian Studies, Leiden, and the NIOD. Their support is gratefully acknowledged. We also wish to thank Anthony Reid, Didi Kwartanada, Hersumpana and Dianna van Oosterhout for their contributions to the workshop. The index was diligently prepared by Alexander Tetteroo.[1]

1 The following conventions on spelling are applied. Geographical names are rendered according to current usage except when the name has been altered altogether. Personal names remain unaltered. Indonesian expressions are in modern spelling except when in direct citation.

References

Bank Indonesia
1960 *Report for the year 1959/1960*. Djakarta: Kolff.

Dick, Howard W., Vincent J.H. Houben, J. Thomas Lindblad and Thee Kian Wie
2002 *The emergence of a national economy; An economic history of Indonesia, 1800-2000*. Crows Nest, NSW: Allen and Unwin.

Gardner, Paul F.
1997 *Shared hopes, separate fears; Fifty years of U.S.-Indonesian relations*. Boulder, CO: Westview.

Glassburner, Bruce
1971 'Economic policy-making in Indonesia, 1950-1957', in: Bruce Glassburner (ed.), *The economy of Indonesia*, pp. 70-98. Ithaca, NY: Cornell University Press. [Reprint Jakarta: Equinox, 2007.]

Hadinoto, Soejono
1949 *Ekonomi Indonesia; Dari ekonomi kolonial ke ekonomi nasional.* Djakarta: Jajasan Pembangunan.

Higgins, Benjamin
1957 *Indonesia's economic stabilization and development.* New York: Institute of Pacific Relations.

Johnson, Harry
1972 'The ideology of economic policy in new states', in: David Wall (ed.), *Chicago essays in economic development*, pp. 23-40. Chicago: University of Chicago Press.

Kahin, Audrey R. and George McT. Kahin
1995 *Subversion as foreign policy; The secret Eisenhower and Dulles debacle in Indonesia.* New York: Norton.

Kanumoyoso, Bondan
2001 *Nasionalisasi perusahaan Belanda di Indonesia.* Jakarta: Sinar Harapan.

Lindblad, J. Thomas
2002 'The importance of *Indonesianisasi* during the transition from the 1930s to the 1960s', *Itinerario. European Journal of Overseas History* 26-3/4:51-72.
2004 'Beyond Benteng; Indonesian entrepreneurship in Central Java in the 1950s', *Lembaran Sejarah* 7-1:85-100.
2008 *Bridges to new business; The economic decolonization of Indonesia.* Leiden: KITLV Press. [Verhandelingen 245.]

Mackie, J.A.C.
1971 'The Indonesian economy, 1950-1963', in: Bruce Glassburner (ed.), *The economy of Indonesia*, pp. 16-69. Ithaca, NY: Cornell University Press. [Reprint Jakarta: Equinox, 2007.]

Robison, Richard
1986 *Indonesia; The rise of capital.* Sydney: Allen and Unwin.

Sutter, John O.
1959 *Indonesianisasi; A historical survey of the role of politics in the institutions of a changing economy from the Second World War to the eve of the general election, 1940-1955.* PhD thesis, Cornell University, Ithaca, NY.

The new nation-state

THEE KIAN WIE

Indonesianization
Economic aspects of decolonization in Indonesia in the 1950s

The late professor Harry Johnson at the University of Chicago defined economic nationalism as 'the national aspiration to having property owned by nationals and economic functions performed by nationals' (Johnson 1972:26). Following this definition, the force of economic nationalism in Indonesia, especially during the early Independence period, can be easily understood. Economic nationalism was, and still is, reflected in Indonesian governmental economic policies. To a higher degree than in other Southeast Asian countries, economic nationalism in post-colonial Indonesia has been, and continues to be, an important factor affecting government policy. Economic nationalism during the 1950s was primarily targeted at the continuing economic dominance of Dutch and ethnic Chinese business interests. In the years following the Asian economic crisis in the late 1990s, however, economic nationalism came to be directed primarily at the perceived interference by international organizations, in particular the IMF in the formulation of Indonesia's economic policies. Nevertheless, pragmatic considerations have more often than not overruled popular pressures of economic nationalism, particularly after the advent of the New Order government in 1966. As a result, pragmatic economic policies have often been able to offset adverse economic and political effects of virulent nationalism, except during the final years of President Sukarno's rule.[1]

In the following pages the so-called 'Indonesianization' (*Indonesianisasi*) policies pursued during the 1950s, when economic nationalism was very strong, will be discussed. Using Johnson's definition, Indonesianization is understood here as efforts by the Indonesian government to transfer property,

1 I acknowledge the helpful comments and suggestions of Prof. Anne Booth and Dr Peter Keppy on an earlier draft of this contribution. However, I alone remain responsible for remaining errors and shortcomings.

or more correctly: productive assets owned by foreigners or foreign businesses, to indigenous Indonesians. This especially applied to Dutchmen or residents viewed as foreigners, in particular ethnic Chinese. Indonesianization also implied transferring economic functions performed by foreigners or residents viewed as foreigners to indigenous Indonesians. The drive towards Indonesianization involved various measures taken by the Indonesian government in the 1950s aiming at an 'economic decolonization' considered all the more urgent since the Indonesian government realized in early 1950 that political independence had not been accompanied by economic independence. Indonesianization also formed an official response to the strong appeal by several nationalist leaders, such as Soejono Hadinoto of the Indonesian National Party (Partai Nasional Indonesia, PNI), who wished 'to convert the colonial economy into a national economy' (*merombak ekonomi kolonial mendjadi ekonomi nasional*) (Soejono Hadinoto 1949:1).

Political and economic consequences of the Round Table Conference

With the transfer of sovereignty to Indonesia on 27 December 1949, a new phase began in the often tortuous relationship between Indonesia and the Netherlands. As a sovereign state Indonesia could now deal with the Netherlands on an equal basis. However, during the 1950s Indonesian-Dutch relations were marred by the lingering aftermath of the colonial relationship. While President Sukarno's efforts from the early 1950s onwards were aimed at 'completing the national Revolution', specifically the 'liberation of West Irian' (western New Guinea), which at that time was still under Dutch control, the Netherlands attempted strenuously to hold on to what little was still left of its formerly vast colonial possessions (Houben 1996:160).

The uncomfortable legacy of the colonial past was a direct consequence of agreements reached at the Round Table Conference (RTC) held in The Hague from late August until early November 1949, where the terms of Dutch acknowledgement of Indonesia's Independence were formulated. The Indonesian delegation at the RTC agreed to a number of controversial conditions to facilitate a quick agreement by the Dutch. The expectation of substantial financial assistance from the United States also induced Indonesian leaders to make economic concessions to the Netherlands. However, concessions greatly outweighed the relatively small economic assistance, in the form of a $ 100 million loan from the United States Exim-Bank, which was at long last granted. This loan, which had to be repaid with interest, corresponded to only one-third of post-war credits by the same bank to the Netherlands. This was all Indonesia received after yielding to the insistence of the American observer at the RTC, Merle Cochran, that the United States government would shoulder the overseas debt bequeathed by the Netherlands Indies government to Indonesia (Kahin 1997:26).

Four provisions of the RTC agreement, two political and two economic, were particularly resented by the Indonesians (Dick et al. 2002:170). The first one was that the Netherlands would transfer sovereignty to the Republic of the United States of Indonesia (Republik Indonesia Serikat, RIS), a federation in which the Indonesian Republic (Republik Indonesia, RI), which had waged war with the Dutch, constituted only one state next to the fifteen puppet states created by the Dutch in various regions. The Dutch also insisted on the creation of a Netherlands-Indonesian Union akin to the British Commonwealth. However, within a few months after the transfer of sovereignty the fragile puppet states one by one dissolved themselves and joined the Republic. By 17 August 1950, five years after the proclamation of Indonesia's Independence, RIS was dissolved and replaced by the present unitary Republic of Indonesia.

The second, far more contentious issue concerned the status of western New Guinea (renamed West Irian by the Indonesian nationalists, today's Papua). The Indonesian nationalists considered themselves the rightful inheritors of the Netherlands Indies. At the RTC the Dutch had refused to hand over West Irian to Indonesia, arguing that its Papuan population was racially, culturally and linguistically no part of the Indonesian nation. Since the Dutch adamantly refused to transfer sovereignty over West Irian to Indonesia, Dutch-Indonesian relations were doomed from the start and deteriorated until they were broken off on 17 August 1960 (Houben 1996:173).

One economic matter that disturbed Indonesian nationalists was Dutch insistence that Indonesia would take over the foreign debt incurred by the Netherlands Indies government to the Netherlands to an amount of $ 1,130 million. The debt ran with an interest rate of 3 per cent per year and was due to be repaid in full no later than June 1964 (Kahin 1997:26; Sumitro Djojohadikusumo 2000:95). In addition, Indonesia was obliged to take over rights and liabilities of the colonial government's external floating debt, amounting to another $ 70 million (Kahin 1997:314). The total inherited debt obligation would have been even higher had Sumitro Djojohadikusumo not insisted at the RTC that a large part of it consisted of military expenses by the Netherlands in waging military campaigns against the Republic (Kahin 1997:26; Sumitro Djojohadikusumo 2000:95).

Despite resentment at the huge inherited debt, the Indonesian government faithfully fulfilled its international financial obligations. When the Harahap cabinet on 21 February 1956 unilaterally abrogated the economic and financial agreement of the RTC as a result of the protracted West Irian dispute, only $ 171 million of the original $ 1,130 million, or 15 per cent, remained to be repaid. No other former colony was obliged to take over such a large debt from its former colonial ruler as Indonesia (Kahin 1997:27).

The second, equally contentious economic issue was the guarantee that Dutch business firms would be allowed to continue to operate in Indonesia without any hindrance, just as in colonial times. During the four-year armed struggle against the Dutch (1945-1949), leading Dutch business firms had come to realize that trying to reoccupy Indonesia by military force was futile. Their top priority, therefore, was to rehabilitate and reconstruct their business establishments, estates, mines and factories, which had been severely damaged during the Japanese occupation and the armed struggle against the Dutch (Lindblad 2001:141). Private Dutch business firms exerted heavy pressure on the Dutch government to ensure that the RTC would yield an agreement safeguarding their extensive economic interests in independent Indonesia.

With these guidelines, the Dutch delegation at the RTC refused to make any concessions and insisted on obtaining guarantees for unrestricted operations by Dutch business enterprises in independent Indonesia. Interestingly, on this issue the Indonesian and Dutch delegations quickly reached agreement, as formalized in the Finec (Financieele en Economische Overeenkomst, Financial and Economic Agreement). This agreement secured maximum economic and financial benefits for the Netherlands, in particular private Dutch business in Indonesia. Finec included a clause to the effect that nationalization would only be permitted if it were in Indonesia's national interest and if both parties agreed. A judge would then decide on the amount of compensation to be paid to the owners on the basis of the real value of the nationalized enterprise (Meijer 1994:46-7).

Finec also included an obligation for Indonesia to consult with the Netherlands whenever its fiscal and monetary policies would affect Dutch economic interests in Indonesia (Meijer 1994:46-7). No wonder that the late Professor Henri Baudet, a conservative Dutch economic historian, stated that Finec contained the maximum attainable guarantees for the unhindered continuation of Dutch business (Baudet and Fennema et al. 1983:213).

The achievement of political independence without economic independence posed a serious problem for the Indonesian government. Not being able to exert any control over important segments of the Indonesian economy clearly restricted the scope of action for Indonesia's economic policy-makers. For instance, pursuing an independent monetary policy would be difficult as long as the Java Bank, the bank of circulation serving as the nation's central bank, was still in the hands of the Dutch. It also gave rise to the widely-held notion that the economic phase of decolonization had not even started. Sutan Sjahrir, Indonesia's Prime Minister during the early years of the Revolution and chairman of the Indonesian Socialist Party (Partai Sosialis Indonesia, PSI), expressed widely felt dissatisfaction in 1951 by stating that 'continuing

Dutch economic domination in Indonesia, and not West Irian, was the real fundamental problem adversely affecting Netherlands-Indonesian relations' (Meijer 1994:349).

Dutch domination over the Indonesian economy was, amongst others, reflected by the fact that only 19 per cent of the capital not invested in agriculture was owned by indigenous Indonesians. Economic gains from continued operations of Dutch businesses in Indonesia were substantial: out of the total profits pocketed by foreign private business in Indonesia in 1953, no less than 70 per cent (Rp 449 million) was transferred to the Netherlands. In addition, Rp 464 million or 83 per cent of total overseas transfers for social purposes (pensions, personal savings and the like) also went to the Netherlands in that year (Meijer 1994:349).

Indonesia's economic dependence on the Netherlands was particularly visible in interisland shipping, which was virtually monopolized by the Dutch shipping concern KPM (Koninklijke Paketvaart Maatschappij, Royal Packet Company). Realizing that interisland shipping constituted the vital artery for trade in the Indonesian archipelago, the Indonesian government understandably wished to terminate the domination by the KPM. However, these early plans could not be realized, because the Indonesian government lacked the financial means to take over KPM at a price acceptable to the Dutch shareholders (Meijer 1994:350).

Continuing Dutch economic dominance over the Indonesian economy is evident from an estimate by the late Professor Benjamin Higgins, a United Nations consultant to the Indonesian government in the early 1950s. Higgins calculated that the Dutch-owned segment of the modern sectors in the Indonesian economy accounted for about 25 per cent of GDP (Gross Domestic Product) and about 10 per cent of total employment (Higgins 1990:40). Many senior positions in the fledgling Indonesian public service were occupied by Dutch officials, whose loyalty to a newly-independent Indonesia could not readily be taken for granted. According to one estimate, after the transfer of sovereignty, about 17,000 Dutch public servants entered Indonesia's public service, although many of them were soon relegated to unimportant positions. Their incomes were eroded because of the monetary measures of the Indonesian government to curb inflationary pressures (Houben 1996:171). Eurasians of mixed Dutch and Indonesian descent were also removed from the bureaucracy. They were distrusted by indigenous Indonesians because they had sided with the Dutch during the Revolution (Houben 1996:171).

The president and most directors of the Java Bank were still Dutch (Higgins 1990:40). The head of the Foreign Exchange Control Board was also a Dutchman. The Board was an independent government body that in the colonial period had reported directly to the Governor-General. Sumitro Djojohadikusumo observed that, when he became Minister of Finance in

1952, he entered a department full of Dutch officials who, as he noted caustically, had no clue about economics, but were very good at administrative procedures (Thee 2003:59).

Indonesianization and measures to reduce Dutch economic predominance

Despite unhappiness with the continuing Dutch predominance in the economy, the leading economic policy-makers in the early 1950s, including Vice President Moh. Hatta, Sumitro Djojohadikusumo, Sjafruddin Prawiranegara and Djuanda, were pragmatic men who, while attracted to socialist ideals, did not adhere to any rigid ideological doctrine (Booth 1986:13). They did not constitute a cohesive group and held different views about several economic issues, such as the role of foreign direct investment or the feasibility of rapid industrialization. However, as pragmatic politicians they realized that top priority had to be given to economic stabilization and rehabilitation. Since a large part of the modern export sector, including many estates and mines, were still owned and operated by Dutch private firms, the policy-makers realized that they had to protect the legal rights of the Dutch enterprises, unpalatable as it was. The Dutch enterprises could therefore operate without any official restrictions, although this policy was often criticized by more radical nationalists. Yet, the pragmatic policy-makers also realized that the Dutch export-oriented large estates and mines generated much-needed foreign exchange revenues to import food, raw materials and capital goods.

Despite constraints imposed by Finec, the pragmatic economic policy-makers were determined to match Indonesia's hard-won political independence with meaningful economic sovereignty, although they fully appreciated that it would take a long time and great effort. Since Finec provided the legal basis for nationalization under specified conditions, the Indonesian government soon took steps to nationalize key economic institutions and enterprises of singular economic or strategic importance.

The first important economic institution to be nationalized was the Java Bank, the bank of circulation during the colonial period which had been chosen as the nation's central bank also after 1949. On 30 April 1951, Minister of Finance Jusuf Wibisono announced that the Indonesian government intended to nationalize the Java Bank as soon as possible. He explained to the press that the Masjumi party, of which he was a member, at its national conference in Yogyakarta in December 1949 had already urged for nationalization. He was proud to implement that decision (Thee 2003:71-2).

But Wibisono had made his announcement in the press without consulting the Dutch (Thee 2003:81). Not surprisingly, the Dutch initially attempted to retain control over the Java Bank, but in the end the nationalization of the

Java Bank proceeded relatively smoothly, as the Dutch accepted that control of money and credit was an essential ingredient of sovereignty (Golay et al. 1969:137).

On 3 July 1951, the Sukiman cabinet, dominated by Masjumi, installed a committee for the nationalization of the Java Bank. The committee was authorized to take all necessary preparatory steps towards nationalization, including drafting the required legislation. Members of the committee were Sumitro Djojohadikusumo, Moh. Sediono, Soetikno Slamet, T.R.B. Sabaruddin, A. Oudt and Khouw Bian Tie (Thee 2003:72). Upon advice of the committee, the government decided that nationalization would be implemented through the purchase of shares from both domestic and overseas shareholders. To speed up the purchase of shares, the government sent two officials to the Netherlands, Moh. Saubari, Secretary-General at the Department of Finance, and Khouw Bian Tie, advisor of the Java Bank. Their talks with Pieter Lieftinck, the Dutch Minister of Finance, and the Dutch association for trade in securities (Vereeniging voor de Effectenhandel) in Amsterdam went smoothly, resulting in a decision to suspend trading of Java Bank shares on the Amsterdam Stock Exchange. The announcement was signed by Moh. Saubari and published in *Het Financieel Dagblad* (Financial Daily) on 3 August 1951 (Thee 2003:72).

In Indonesia, Wibisono issued a statement on the same day about the government's offer to purchase privately held shares at 120 per cent of the nominal value as expressed in Dutch guilders, or 360 per cent as expressed in Indonesian rupiah. The purchase of the shares proceeded well and within a couple of months, 97 per cent of all shares had already been acquired by the government. On 6 December 1951, the law on the nationalization of the Java Bank was enacted (Thee 2003:72-3).

A. Houwink, the last Dutch president of the Java Bank, had resigned and been succeeded by Sjafruddin Prawiranegara already prior to the nationalization. Sjafruddin Prawiranegara, Minister of Finance in the cabinets headed by Hatta and Natsir, was at first reluctant to take up the position at the Java Bank, as he wanted to retire from public life. Sjafruddin wanted to earn enough money for the education of his children, but was only in a position to do so in a private capacity as he, possibly as a result of his Dutch-styled education, did not want to abuse his power as a public servant to make money (Thee 2003:80). Sjafruddin therefore put forward as a condition that his salary, and that of all Indonesian staff, should not be changed to an Indonesian level and that privileges enjoyed by the Dutch staff should also be made available to the Indonesian staff. The government agreed and Sjafruddin became the first Indonesian president of the Java Bank. His candidacy was also supported by the staff at the Java Bank, including his predecessor Houwink (Thee 2003:80). On 1 July 1953, the Java Bank was transformed into Bank Indonesia with Sjafruddin Prawiranegara as its first Governor.

Nationalization also affected other Dutch-owned enterprises occupying key positions in the Indonesian economy, for instance the railways in Java and public utilities such as electric and gas companies (Burger 1975:170). Domestic air transport was transferred from the Koninklijke Nederlandsch-Indische Luchtvaart-Maatschappij (KNILM, Royal Netherlands Indies Airlines) to Garuda Indonesian Airways, Indonesia's national carrier. This airline was initially established as a joint venture between the Royal Dutch Airlines KLM and the Indonesian government. However, in 1954 Garuda was transformed into a fully state-owned airline with the role of KLM limited to providing technical assistance and advice (Burger 1975:170).

However, efforts to nationalize the Dutch-controlled KPM, which in 1956 still dominated interisland shipping, did not succeed. In the end, the newly established PELNI (Pelajaran Nasional Indonesia, Indonesian National Shipping), a state-owned company which received financial assistance from the government, was able to make steady inroads into the market dominated by KPM. Whereas in 1956 PELNI carried 25 per cent of the cargo, in 1957 it increased its share to 29 per cent. Although KPM was more successful in retaining its dominance in passenger traffic, with 94 per cent of the total, introduction of six new passenger ships by PELNI in 1956 enabled the Indonesian rival to double the number of passengers carried by 1957 (Dick 1987:18).

The nationalization of the Java Bank and other enterprises deemed to be of crucial importance to the Indonesian economy, proceeded relatively smoothly. Both the Dutch government and the owners of the enterprises in question realized that no sovereign government could leave its central bank, public utilities and vital modes of transport in the hands of foreigners.

Other efforts to counter Dutch economic control included Vice President Hatta's instruction to the executive board of the Central Trading Corporation (CTC), Indonesia's first government-owned trading company established in Bukittinggi in 1948, to challenge the monopoly of the five leading Dutch trading firms, the famous 'Big Five' (Thee 2003:256). The establishment of the CTC had been urged by Hatta as he did not approve of the involvement by Indonesian revolutionary army units in smuggling. This trade mainly consisted of shipping agricultural commodities to Singapore and British Malaya, in order to acquire military equipment and arms for the struggle against the Dutch. Therefore, Hatta wished to legalize the trade by separating smuggling from military operations through the establishment of a formal trading house (Thee 2003:255).

Heeding Hatta's instruction to challenge Dutch control over Indonesia's export and import trade, yet lacking much business experience themselves, the two Acehnese directors of the CTC, Teuku Moh. Daud and Teuku Hamid

Azwar, realized they had to look for people who possessed the required experience and skills, especially in international business. At the time, the only people who had such business experience and skills were ethnic Chinese. Daud and Azwar therefore approached some Sino-Indonesian managers employed in the few large companies owned by Sino-Indonesians such as the Liem Goan Seng and Kian Gwan firms (Thee 2003:257).

At first, the CTC directors experienced some difficulty persuading the company's board of trustees to recruit mainly Sino-Indonesian managers. They eventually succeeded because it was obvious that Daud and Azwar were not playing politics and were only concerned with making CTC an efficient and viable corporation. This would be imperative to achieve the first task of CTC of reducing the domination by the Dutch companies over the Indonesian economy (Thee 2003:257).

Daud and Azwar were successful in recruiting a senior manager from the Liem Goan Seng company, Koo Liong Bing, who was willing to join CTC. Through Koo, CTC was able to recruit several other Sino-Indonesian managers, mainly from the Kian Gwan company. Later Koo himself became one of the directors of CTC (Thee 2003:257).

Another measure to try to counter the 'Big Five' was the so-called Benteng programme launched in 1950 (Thee 2003:59). This programme was also the first major official strategy to further the development of a strong indigenous Indonesian business class. The Benteng ('Fortress') programme focused on securing national control over the import trade by reserving import licenses in certain restricted categories of easy-to-sell goods exclusively for indigenous Indonesian importers. The provisions of the programme did not specifically exclude ethnic Chinese businessmen who possessed Indonesian citizenship (Mackie 1971:47-8). In practice, however, the Benteng programme was primarily aimed at countering both Dutch and Chinese economic domination.

To promote the development of an indigenous Indonesian business class, the government established new financial institutions to provide credit for eligible businessmen. Such institutions included the Bank Industri Negara (BIN, State Industrial Bank), which extended credit to large-scale agricultural enterprises and manufacturing and mining enterprises; the Bank Negara Indonesia (BNI, State Bank of Indonesia), which extended loans to exporters and importers; and the Jajasan Kredit (Credit Foundation), which provided guarantees for loans for which the customary business collateral was not available (Burger 1975:171).

Another important measure to 'Indonesianize' the Dutch companies was a 'gentlemen's agreement' between the Indonesian government and the Dutch firms, which stipulated that 70 per cent of the companies' personnel had to be (indigenous) Indonesians. However, this Indonesianization programme turned out to be limited to the lower functions in the companies. In fact,

Vice President Moh. Hatta was arguably the most prominent representative of the pragmatic economic policy-makers in Indonesia in the early 1950s. The picture is from 1950 when Hatta was also serving as Prime Minister. (KITLV 105660.)

the Dutch companies were only mildly motivated to train their Indonesian personnel in order to enable them to occupy higher functions, as stipulated in provision 12 of Finec. The Dutch companies refrained from including the most competent among their Indonesian staff in their board of directors, as laid down in that same provision. At the estates, the top function occupied by Indonesian personnel was usually that of *mandur* (supervisor) (Meijer 1994:352).

Aware of the fact that the Dutch companies were reluctant to promote their Indonesian staff to higher and managerial positions, the Wilopo cabinet (March 1952-June 1953) resorted to drastically reducing work permits for Dutch citizens in Indonesia. While in 1950 Dutch citizens could still freely enter Indonesia, after 1951 strict entry quotas were introduced. The number of Dutch citizens given work permits was gradually reduced and in 1953, only 1,000 work permits were issued (Meijer 1994:353).

The Dutch companies soon experienced great difficulties because of the restrictive visa quotas. Despite offering higher salaries and other favourable incentives, the firms were unable to slow down, let alone stop the steady outflow of Dutch employees. While the remaining Dutch staff was initially able to take over the tasks of those who had repatriated, over time this proved no longer possible as more and more Dutch employees were leaving (Meijer 1994:352-3).

The outflow of Dutch employees seriously threatened continuity in the operations of Dutch businesses in Indonesia. The companies therefore reluctantly started to train Indonesian staff in greater numbers to occupy the higher functions left vacant by departing Dutch employees. To this end, Dutch import and export companies established a trading school for their Indonesian staff. In general, however, numbers of participants in the training programmes remained small, as the directors of most Dutch companies were concerned that to elevate their Indonesian staff to senior managerial positions or allow participation of Indonesian capital might pave the way to nationalization of their enterprises (Meijer 1994:353).

The curtain falls: nationalization of all Dutch enterprises

Relations between Indonesia and the Netherlands deteriorated rapidly from the mid-1950s due to the Dutch government's adamant refusal to discuss the status of West Irian (Papua). When the Indonesian government in November 1957 failed to persuade the United Nations General Assembly to adopt a resolution calling on the Netherlands to negotiate a settlement with Indonesia on the West Irian dispute, anti-Dutch demonstrations broke out in Jakarta. On 3 December 1957, workers of local labour unions, federated in the Sentral

Organisasi Buruh Seluruh Indonesia (SOBSI, Central Organization of Workers in All Indonesia) and often affiliated with the Indonesian Communist Party, PKI (Partai Komunis Indonesia) began seizing control of Dutch enterprises and business offices (Meijer 1994:584).

The head office of the Dutch interisland shipping company KPM in Jakarta, a prime symbol for Dutch economic dominance, was the first to be taken over by the workers. Another symbol of Anglo-Dutch economic power, Royal Dutch Shell, was not taken over as it was partly British-owned.

On 5 December 1957, the Department of Foreign Affairs contacted the Dutch chargé d'affaires and presented him with a note announcing that all Dutch citizens had to leave the country within the shortest time possible. The subsequent Dutch exodus proceeded relatively smoothly. By March 1959, some 30,000 of the last remaining Dutch had repatriated, leaving only about 6,000 Dutch citizens behind. These people stayed because they were either working under contract with non-Dutch foreign enterprises (about 3,500), or serving as missionaries (about 1,600) (Meijer 1994:585, 592).

During the following two weeks the action at KPM was followed by similar takeovers of other Dutch firms throughout Indonesia. Although the Indonesian government had not directly initiated the takeovers, it did not attempt to resist the actions (Glassburner 1971:92). Some senior government officials, notably Sjafruddin Prawiranegara at Bank Indonesia, openly spoke out against the takeovers (Thee 2003:81). Sjafruddin felt that Indonesians through education and training first had to acquire the required skills to manage and run the modern Dutch enterprises.

Concerned about the economic and political chaos caused by unauthorized takeovers, General A.H. Nasution, Army Chief of Staff, took control of events on 13 December 1957 by issuing an instruction to the army to manage the seized enterprises. PKI and SOBSI, anxious to avoid an open confrontation with the army, promised to support the military forces by keeping the seized enterprises operational (Ricklefs 1993:261).

In December 1958, the legal foundation was laid down for the nationalization of seized Dutch enterprises. The nationalization was effectuated for various categories of enterprises during the first half of 1959. All nationalized companies became state property (Dick et al. 2002:184). With one drastic action, the powerful Dutch business firms that had operated in Indonesia since the second half of the nineteenth century were eliminated. Unlike the nationalization of the Java Bank and the public utilities at an earlier stage in the 1950s, which had been achieved by mutual consent, the nationalization of Dutch enterprises in 1959 was a unilateral measure taken by the Indonesian government in response to the collapse of Dutch-Indonesian relations due to the acrimonious dispute about West Irian.

Dealing with the 'Chinese problem'

The nationalization of Dutch enterprises went a long way towards satisfying the national aspiration 'to convert the colonial economy into a national economy' (Soejono Hadinoto 1949:1). The nation's important productive assets, formerly owned by the Dutch, were now Indonesian-owned, and important economic functions, formerly performed by the Dutch, were now fulfilled by Indonesian nationals. However, this conversion was still not felt to be complete. The large indigenous Indonesian population was still facing the economic dominance of ethnic Chinese businessmen, including both Indonesian and Chinese nationals, who since colonial times had played a major role in the economy, particularly in intermediate trade, rice milling and money lending. Their economic predominance and the perceived usurious activities of Chinese money lenders (*Cina mindering*) caused much resentment, if not outright hatred, among indigenous Indonesians. For this reason the late Professor Everett Hawkins, an American economist who worked in Indonesia in the 1950s and early 1960s, once referred to the 'double colonialism' that prevailed in Indonesia.[2]

Next to efforts to limit Dutch economic dominance, the Indonesian government took steps in the early 1950s to reduce the economic role of ethnic Chinese. However, measures to limit Chinese economic activities proved far more difficult than eliminating Dutch economic interests. For one thing, the number of ethnic Chinese was much larger than the Dutch. Through intermediate trade and money lending, their economic activities in the rural areas were also far more intertwined with the economic activities of the indigenous population than the Dutch activities had ever been. Moreover, the large ethnic Chinese group included Indonesian citizens as well as citizens of the People's Republic of China and a small group of pro-Taiwan 'stateless' citizens. It was difficult for the Indonesian government to take measures that were directed at all ethnic Chinese, as this category included a relatively large group of Indonesian citizens. Having fought against Dutch colonialism and its implied racism, many Indonesian leaders found that overly discriminatory policies against its citizens of Chinese descent did not accord well with the ideals of the Indonesian Revolution. Nevertheless, given strong political pressure, the Indonesian government did initiate measures in the early 1950s in order to reduce the economic role of the ethnic Chinese and promote the development of indigenous Indonesian (*Indonesia asli*) entrepreneurs.

2 Personal communication from Professor Everett Hawkins.

The Benteng programme

Pressure to promote the development of indigenous Indonesian business grew stronger, but by and large economic activities of indigenous Indonesians were confined to small-scale agriculture, small retail stores and small-scale industries, such as batik, handicrafts and clove cigarettes. To promote the development of indigenous entrepreneurs, Minister of Prosperity Djuanda in April 1950 issued a regulation which gave priority to indigenous businessmen to import goods from abroad. To facilitate their import trade, indigenous businessmen were given priority access to cheap credit (Bisuk Siahaan 1996:168). The Benteng programme was primarily aimed at countering the dominance of the Dutch 'Big Five' trading companies in imports and exports.

Protection to the indigenous importers was provided by reserving imports of specified categories of goods, referred to as *benteng* goods, solely for indigenous importers, and by channeling credits to these importers through the state-owned BNI (Sutter 1959:1017-8). The required qualifications for receiving preferential treatment through the Benteng programme were, at least on paper, quite stringent.

Choosing import trading as the first major economic activity to promote indigenous entrepreneurship was understandable, as at the time almost all export and import trade was handled by Dutch and ethnic Chinese firms (Suhadi Mangkusuwondo 1967:218). Focusing on the import trade to secure indigenous Indonesian dominance appeared to be the most feasible option since this line of business was considered the most responsive to state direction through controls over the allocation of import licenses (Robison 1986:44). The import trade was also the most accessible business for indigenous entrepreneurs. They could easily set up a business with a minimum of overhead investment and concentrate on products sufficiently standardized to require a minimum of business experience. In addition, they could specialize in goods that were protected by import restrictions (Golay et al. 1969:168).

The Benteng programme attracted a great deal of interest. While in 1951 some 250 businessmen had registered with this programme, in 1952 their numbers had increased to 741. Numbers climbed to 1,500 in 1953 and 2,211 in 1954 (Bisuk Siahaan 1996:68). As a result, the percentage of total foreign exchange credit allocated to the Benteng importers increased from 37 per cent in 1952/3 to 76 per cent in late 1954 (Robison 1986:45). By the early 1950s, around 70 per cent of the import trade was reportedly done by indigenous Indonesian businessmen (Burger 1975:171).

Many of the new indigenous Indonesian importers who received preferential treatment under the Benteng programme lacked capital and/or business experience. They engaged in business practices which, although not in violation of the letter of the law, did offend ethical standards. There were of course new, capable indigenous importers whose trading enterprises grew into viable companies. However, there were many more cases which could hardly be labelled bonafide enterprises; these were the so-called 'Ali-Baba' enterprises, involving indigenous importers and ethnic Chinese businessmen (whether Indonesian citizens or foreign nationals). Such enterprises proliferated under various guises, including the use of fronts and strawmen and the selling of import licenses to genuine, mostly ethnic Chinese importers (Sutter 1959:1027).

The Benteng programme failed to foster a strong, self-reliant indigenous merchant class, but rather furthered a group of licensed brokers and political fixers, unproductive 'rent-seekers' or 'rent-harvesters'. These importers were often referred to as 'briefcase importers' (*importir aktentas*), whose sole qualification as an importer was that they carried a briefcase containing their license (Bisuk Siahaan 1998:168).

As the Benteng programme progressed, it became increasingly apparent that it was not effective in nurturing a viable group of indigenous entrepreneurs. To eliminate abuses, Roosseno, Minister of Economic Affairs from November 1954, introduced a foreign exchange auction system in the textile sector. He also banned discrimination on ethnic grounds, and thus allowed Sino-Indonesian businessmen to openly participate in the import trade. The auction system, however, turned out to be unsuccessful, as it did not give indigenous importers with inadequate financial resources access to the auctioned foreign exchange quota. Hence, such indigenous importers continued to serve as agents for ethnic Chinese businessmen (Golay et al. 1969:174-5). Indonesia's experience with its first affirmative programme, which aimed to promote a strong and self-reliant indigenous business class, proved a failure. In the second half of the 1950s, when the Indonesian government realized that its aim of fostering a strong indigenous Indonesian class of entrepreneurs had not been achieved, it came to an inglorious end. However, the Benteng programme was never officially abolished.

Limitations on ethnic Chinese activities

In 1954 the Indonesian government issued a regulation that foreign entrepreneurs (*pengusaha golongan asing*) were not allowed to expand the capacity of their weaving-mills beyond pre-war capacity. To circumvent this restriction, Chinese mill-owners turned to subcontracting and recruited indigenous (*asli*) weavers. This practice enhanced the bargaining position of indigenous weavers vis-à-vis their contractors, namely the Chinese weavers (Keppy 2001:156).

Subcontracting in the weaving industry was in a sense illegal as it involved unlicensed weaving capacity and production based on materials that had been purchased on the black market. Because of its nature as a 'hidden business', subcontracting was vulnerable to punitive action by the government. Moreover, several of the ethnic Chinese weavers were small businessmen lacking the political protection and patronage which the big Chinese businessmen, notably the textile king Thee Tjie Tjhoen, were able to enjoy (Keppy 2001:156-7).

Since the Dutch colonial period, Chinese businessmen had owned and operated most of the rice mills in Indonesia. In 1952, no less than 138 out of 154 rice mills in East Java were owned by ethnic Chinese (Golay et al. 1969:182). In view of the great economic importance of these rice mills, the Indonesian government in 1954 issued a regulation that Chinese-owned rice mills had to be transferred to indigenous Indonesians by March 1955. The regulation decreed that no new licenses for operating rice mills would be issued to foreign nationals, while existing mills had to be transferred to indigenous Indonesians, specifically persons having only Indonesian citizenship. Since Indonesian citizens of Chinese descent still had, at the time of the regulation, dual citizenship, the 1954 regulation also affected them. However, because of the difficulties in implementing this regulation, the government still granted licenses to Chinese citizens on an annual basis (Suryadinata 1992:32).

Although until late 1957 most enterprises handling stevedoring, harbour transport and warehouses were owned and operated by the Dutch, other enterprises were owned and operated by the Chinese. For this reason the government issued a decree in 1954 that these Chinese-owned enterprises had to be transferred to indigenous Indonesians by 1956. Because of the difficulties in implementing the decree, this date was continuously extended, with the last extension running to June 1959 (Golay et al. 1969:184).

Angered by the support of the Taiwan government and 'stateless' Taiwan-oriented local Chinese to regional rebellions in West Sumatra and Sulawesi, the Indonesian government in 1958 closed down all Chinese organizations, schools, newspapers and enterprises officially and unofficially associated with Taiwan. Taiwan-oriented community leaders who were pro-Kuomintang were also arrested (Suryadinata 1992:175). Yet this measure did not seriously affect economic activities of the ethnic Chinese in Indonesia because of the relatively small number of pro-Taiwan Chinese. The government of the People's Republic of China predictably applauded these measures, but its satisfaction did not last long. In 1959, the Indonesian government took a far more drastic measure to curtail economic activities by 'foreign' Chinese, especially citizens of the People's Republic.

With the nationalization of Dutch enterprises in 1959, the Chinese community emerged as the strongest element in the economy, aside from the government itself. Since the Dutch colonial period, the Chinese in rural areas had built up a position of dominance in retail trade, rice milling and rural finance (Mackie 1971:9). Given Chinese economic dominance, deteriorating economic conditions and general distrust of the political loyalty of the ethnic Chinese, it was only a matter of time before the Chinese, particularly those who were nationals of the People's Republic, would be the next target of government action.

A major step was an attempt in 1959 to break the Chinese hold on intermediate trade throughout the country by eliminating all 'foreign' Chinese from retail trade in rural areas. In May 1959, Rachmat Muljomiseno, then Minister of Trade and a strong supporter of the strongly anti-Chinese Assaat Movement,[3] announced a regulation banning foreign nationals from rural trade requiring them to transfer their businesses to Indonesian citizens by 30 September 1959 (Suryadinata 1992:135). Rachmat's regulation adversely affected the traditional Chinese economic role as middlemen in collecting agricultural produce for the towns or for export and in the distribution of city-produced or imported goods in rural areas (Somers Heidhues 1964:24). Before this regulation could be implemented, a new cabinet headed by President Sukarno himself was installed on 5 July 1959 following the launch of Sukarno's 'Guided Democracy and Guided Economy' (Demokrasi Terpimpin dan Ekonomi Terpimpin).

The new cabinet was equally committed to Rachmat's plan and on 16 November 1959, Government Regulation no. 10 of 1959 (Peraturan Pemerintah, PP 10/1959) was issued. It decreed that from 1 January 1960 foreign nationals would be banned from rural trade and would have to transfer their business to Indonesian nationals (Suryadinata 1992:135). Although Indonesian nationals benefitting from this decree could in principle also include Indonesian citizens of Chinese descent, the government hoped that much of the rural trade run by the 'foreign' Chinese would be taken over by co-operatives and businesses owned and run by indigenous Indonesians.

Although PP 10/1959 applied to all foreign nationals, it was mainly an army-instigated move to hurt the foreign Chinese who, as the fiercely anti-communist army suspected, could be a fifth column for China. Another purpose of the regulation was to weaken Jakarta's (that is, Sukarno's) growing friendship with China, and to embarrass the PKI. Although the Chinese government put heavy pressure on the Indonesian government not to carry out, if not revoke, this decree, the army in late 1959 began forcibly removing 'foreign' Chinese from rural areas below the district (*kabupaten*) levels,

3 In 1956 Assaat, president of the short-lived Republik Indonesia when it was a constituent part of the Republic of the United States of Indonesia (Republik Indonesia Serikat) from January to August 1950, launched a popular movement of businessmen (*Gerakan Assaat*), which aimed at ending Chinese domination over the Indonesian economy. The Assaat movement was discredited when Assaat joined the anti-Sukarno rebellion in West Sumatra in 1958.

to the towns and cities of Java. As a result of the expulsion, in the course of 1960/61 about 119,000 Chinese nationals were repatriated to China (Ricklefs 1993:267). The ban also caused a serious rupture in the political relations between Indonesia and China.

Since most co-operatives and/or indigenous businessmen were not able to replace the Chinese traders, or to engage in rural trade with equal efficiency, the ban caused considerable economic disruption. At least in the short run, the ban above all caused hardship to the villagers it was supposed to help (Somers Heidhues 1964:28). In order not to weaken the position of Sukarno, who was viewed as a strong ally of China, and since it had difficulty accommodating the large number of repatriated Chinese, China soon tuned down its anti-Indonesia rhetoric. Sukarno himself, realizing the danger to both the country's economy and his own position if the anti-Chinese campaign were to be continued, eventually succeeded in curbing the anti-Chinese actions. Although PP 10/1959 was never officially repealed, its further implementation was suspended temporarily (Suryadinata 1992:137).

As economic conditions continued to deteriorate in the early 1960s and Sukarno's and the army's attention increasingly focused on reclaiming West Irian from the Dutch, the implementation of PP 10/1959 was not resumed. With the emphasis on 'Indonesian-style socialism', pursuing new affirmative programmes to promote indigenous private businessmen was no longer a priority.

Conclusion

While the nationalization of the Dutch enterprises in 1959 was considered a crucial step in satisfying aspirations of economic nationalism, in the short run this measure caused serious economic disruption. The nationalized Dutch enterprises were turned into state enterprises, mostly managed and run by military officers not familiar with running commercial enterprises efficiently. Not surprisingly, the performance of the nationalized enterprises declined rapidly, at any rate in the short run. As the ethnic Chinese minority had owned and run important economic activities since colonial times, measures against the Dutch were sometimes accompanied by measures to curtail the economic activities of the ethnic Chinese. Although many ethnic Chinese businessmen experienced great difficulties during the 1950s, the anti-Chinese measures during the period 1950-1965 did not significantly reduce their economic importance. In view of the shortage of experienced indigenous businessmen, the niches created through the nationalization of Dutch enterprises paved the way for the entry of ethnic Chinese businessmen into wholesale trade and other activities formerly dominated by Dutch enterprises.

References

Baudet, H. and M. Fennema et al.
1983 *Het Nederlands belang bij Indië*. Utrecht: Aula.

Booth, Anne
1986 'The colonial legacy and its impact on post-independence planning in India and Indonesia', *Itinerario. European Journal of Overseas History* 10-1:1-30.

Burger, D.H.
1975 *Sociologisch-economische geschiedenis van Indonesia*. Amsterdam: Royal Tropical Institute, Leiden: KITLV Press.

Dick, Howard W.
1987 *The Indonesian interisland shipping industry; An analysis of competition and regulation*. Singapore: Institute of Southeast Asian Studies.

Dick, Howard W., Vincent J.H. Houben, J. Thomas Lindblad and Thee Kian Wie
2002 *The emergence of a national economy; An economic history of Indonesia, 1800-2000*. Crows Nest, NSW: Allen and Unwin.

Glassburner, Bruce
1971 'Economic policy-making in Indonesia, 1950-57', in: Bruce Glassburner (ed.), *The economy of Indonesia*, pp. 70-98. Ithaca, NY: Cornell University Press. [Reprint Jakarta: Equinox, 2007.]

Golay, Frank H., Ralph Anspach, M. Ruth Pfanner and Eliezer B. Ayal
1969 *Underdevelopment and economic nationalism in Southeast Asia*. Ithaca, NY: Cornell University Press.

Hadinoto, Soejono
1949 *Ekonomi Indonesia; Dari ekonomi kolonial ke ekonomi nasional*. Djakarta: Jajasan Pembangunan.

Higgins, Benjamin
1990 'Thought and action; Indonesian economic studies and policies in the 1950s', *Bulletin of Indonesian Economic Studies* 26-1:37-47.

Houben, Vincent
1996 *Van kolonie tot eenheidsstaat; Indonesië in de negentiende en twintigste eeuw*. Leiden: Vakgroep Talen en Culturen van Zuidoost-Azië en Oceanië, Rijksuniversiteit Leiden. [Semaian 16.]

Johnson, Harry
1972 'The ideology of economic policy in new states', in: David Wall (ed.), *Chicago essays in economic development*, pp. 23-40. Chicago: University of Chicago Press.

Kahin, George McT.
1997 'Some recollections from and reflections on the Indonesian Revolution', in: Taufik Abdullah (ed.), *The heartbeat of Indonesian Revolution*, pp. 10-27. Jakarta: Gramedia.

Keppy, Peter
2001 *Hidden business; Indigenous and ethnic Chinese entrepreneurs in the Majalaya textile industry, West Java, 1928-1974*. PhD thesis, Free University of Amsterdam.

Lindblad, Thomas
2001 'Politieke economie en de dekolonisatie in Indonesië', in: Thomas Lindblad and Willem van der Molen (eds), *Macht en majesteit; Opstellen voor Cees Fasseur,* pp. 132-46. Leiden: Opleiding Talen en Culturen van Zuidoost-Azië en Oceanië, Universiteit Leiden. [Semaian 22.]

Mackie, J.A.C.
1971 'The Indonesian economy, 1950-63', in: Bruce Glassburner (ed.), *The economy of Indonesia,* pp. 16-69. Ithaca, NY: Cornell University Press. [Reprint Jakarta: Equinox, 2007.]

Mangkusuwondo, Suhadi
1967 *Industrialization efforts in Indonesia; The role of agriculture and foreign trade in the development of the industrial sector.* PhD thesis, University of California, Berkeley.

Meijer, Hans
1994 *Den Haag–Djakarta; De Nederlands-Indonesische betrekkingen 1950-1962.* Utrecht: Aula

Ricklefs, M.C.
1993 *A history of modern Indonesia since c. 1300.* Second edition. London: Macmillan. [First published in 1981.]

Robison, Richard
1986 *Indonesia; The rise of capital.* Sydney: Allen and Unwin.

Siahaan, Bisuk
1996 *Industrialisasi di Indonesia; Sejak hutang kehormatan sampai banting stir.* Jakarta: Pustaka Data.

Somers Heidhues, Mary
1964 'Peranakan Chinese politics in Indonesia'. Interim Report, Modern Indonesia Project, Cornell University, Ithaca, NY.

Sumitro Djojohadikusumo
2000 *Jejak perlawanan begawan pejuang.* Jakarta: Sinar Harapan.

Suryadinata, Leo
1992 *Pribumi Indonesians, the Chinese minority and China.* Third edition. Singapore: Heinemann Asia. [First published in 1978.]

Sutter, John O.
1959 *Indonesianisasi; A historical survey of the role of politics in the institutions of a changing economy from the Second World War to the eve of the general election, 1940-1955.* PhD thesis, Cornell University, Ithaca, NY.

Thee Kian Wie
2003 *Recollections; The Indonesian economy, 1950s-1990s.* Singapore: Institute of Southeast Asian Studies.

BAMBANG PURWANTO

Economic decolonization and the rise of Indonesian military business

Even the layman can sense the pull of military business in Indonesia. Like any military in a developing country, it disseminates power. It is here that important things occurred in Indonesian history. We also gain a feeling of Indonesian economic history as it unfolded throughout the process of decolonization following the declaration of Independence on 17 August 1945. The rise of business among soldiers in Indonesia from early Independence on was a key event, remarkable for its juxtaposition of three parallel sub-functions: those of national freedom fighters, economic brokers and illicit treasurers. It is difficult to imagine a more striking contrast in Indonesia's economic history than that between the three roles - military, economic and socio-political - of Indonesian generals and military groups during the process of decolonization. Next to local politics and international diplomacy, the Indonesian military actively participated in institutional as well as individual construction of economic capacity.

Military activities have so far not been considered systematically as an integral part of the process of decolonization, although military business has proved an attractive theme for both foreign and domestic researchers. Much emphasis has been put on Indonesian politics and Indonesian political economy during the New Order period. Those studies generally suggest that military business was formed and operated solely during the New Order period when there was military predominance in the country's socio-political institutions (Robison 1986; Yahya Muhaimin 1990; Iswandi 1998; Indria Samego et al. 1998; Bilveer Singh 2001; Danang Widoyoko et al. 2003). Most historians discussing pre-New Order military business argue that the formation of Indonesian military business dates from 1950 at the earliest, and that the process only gained momentum as the Dutch companies were nationalized in the late 1950s. One exception to the rule is Twang's description of export trading and military finance during the Indonesian Revolution (Twang 1998).

One of the earliest studies on this topic, conducted by Harold Crouch, reflects the general opinion among scholars that the 1950s were the starting-point for the formation of military business in Indonesia (Crouch 1975/76). Richard Robison's oft-quoted synthesis explicitly avoids discussing the economic realities of the years 1945-1949. To Robison, capital formation and military involvement in Indonesian economic and political history began with the collapse of colonial capitalism and the failure of domestic private capitalism in the period 1949-1957. He considers the Japanese occupation and the Indonesian Revolution to be of no significance in terms of economic history (Robison 1986:36). Even in the two chapters about the years 1949-1965, Robison remains largely silent on the topic of military business. This is all the more surprising as he himself argues that the emergence of the military as the most powerful 'politico-bureaucratic' force in Indonesia was probably the single most significant development between 1957 and 1965 (Robison 1986:36-101). Instead, Robison focuses on business activities of political parties, indigenous entrepreneurs and economic policies.

A similar approach is found in two Indonesian works which both acknowledge the importance of the period 1945-1949 in the formation of Indonesian military business. Unfortunately, not much information on military business can be gleaned from these two books (Indria Samego et al. 1998; Danang Widoyoko et al. 2003). Yet, on the basis of fragmentary information, it has been shown that the military was involved in economic life and capital formation at an early stage and remained so throughout the entire process of decolonization.

This study traces the emergence and development of military business in Indonesia between 1945 and the early 1960s. Despite the fact that the Dutch at long last acknowledged Indonesian Independence officially in December 1949, and despite differences of opinion among historians as to the status of Indonesian Independence prior to the Round Table Conference (RTC), it remains an undeniable fact that the process of decolonization, whether political, social or economic, began immediately after Sukarno and Hatta had proclaimed Independence on 17 August 1945. Several fundamental questions arise. When exactly did the Indonesian military get involved in the economy and participate in capital formation? To what extent did the process of decolonization shape military business in Indonesia? Why did the Indonesian military conduct business outside its core task as an institution for defence? Who, or which military groups, conducted these businesses? Were there different strategies adopted by different military groups in their response to opportunities to do business?

The period of declining colonial influence and increasing assertion of Indonesian identity and authority between 1945 and the early 1960s can be divided into five phases:

1 from the proclamation of Independence on 17 August 1945 until the arrival of Allied and Dutch troops in late 1945 and early 1946;
2 from the arrival of Allied and Dutch troops until the transfer of sovereignty on 27 December 1949;
3 from the establishment of the Republic of the United States of Indonesia (Republik Indonesia Serikat, RIS) in December 1949 until the proclamation of martial law, SOB (Staat van Oorlog en Beleg, ' State of War and Occupation') in March 1957;
4 the phase of takeover of Dutch economic assets from December 1957 onwards;
5 the period of nationalization of Dutch-owned business in late 1958 and 1959.

Earlier studies tended to view the development of Indonesian military business only through the lens of the principle of *dwifungsi* (dual function) (Bilveer Singh 2001). By contrast, this contribution addresses the significance of decolonization to the formation of an Indonesian military business complex. The words 'military' or 'soldier' do not only refer to men belonging to official military organizations such as the various security forces preceding the formation of the TNI (Tentara Nasional Indonesia, National Armed Forces of Indonesia). These early military organizations were the Badan Keamanan Rakjat (BKR, Body for People's Security), the Tentara Keamanan Rakjat (TKR, People's Security Forces) and the Tentara Rakjat Indonesia (TRI, Indonesian People's Army). The terms 'military' and 'soldier' need to be applied also to other armed groups such as youth militias taking an active part in the process of decolonization.

The origins of military business

The nationalism fuelling the Indonesian struggle against returning Dutch colonial power after the Pacific War reflected the emergence of the military as a separate category in Indonesian society. Decolonization resulted in the creation of a historical institution that was unique in comparison to the military in most other former colonies in Asia. The establishment of BKR on 22 August 1945 and TKR on 5 October 1945 was not done by military men who had been fighting for Independence during the colonial period. It was also not a continuation of the previous colonial army, whether in terms of personnel or as an institution. Although members of BKR and TKR had received military training during the colonial period and the Japanese occupation, these soldiers had never themselves fought against the colonial rulers. Suddenly they now faced new challenges, forcing them to work together with newly armed civilian groups to fight against their former masters.

In the context of the Indonesian nationalist movement, the war for Independence transformed the armed forces from non-existence into one of the dominant elements in the formation of the image and identity of Indonesian nationhood. Civilian politicians, who had shaped Indonesian nationalism forty years before, now faced the fact that their role had been marginalized or even vanished because of the war. The military became the new symbol of Indonesian nationalism and was positioned as the nation's new dominant elite . This state of affairs could only emerge because Indonesia's early decolonization met with such a strong military opposition, bent on restoring Dutch colonial rule. This development was furthered by both sociological conditions during the Japanese occupation producing a new elite and the subsequent socio-cultural adaptation to the conditions of war for Independence.

During the war period, a consolidation of personnel and institutions occurred in the Indonesian military. Differences inherited from diverse social and ideological backgrounds, as well as the unique role played by the army in protecting Independence, resulted in political conflict and competition both within the armed forces itself and between the armed forces and other parties, including the government. On the other hand, the military had grown to become a corporation functioning as an institution conducting matters of practical politics, bureaucracy and economy. Since its very inception, the Indonesian military under the leadership of General Sudirman identified itself as the representation of the people while at the same time serving as an apparatus of the state responsible for the freedom of the newly proclaimed Indonesian state and as an institution intent on giving substance to Independence (Salim Said 1991). This idea was mirrored in military involvement with civilian policies and expressed in the creation of an all-encompassing people's defence and security system (*sistem pertahanan dan keamanan rakjat semesta)*.

There is general agreement that the combination of civilian and military roles of the soldier and freedom fighter began as early as during the BKR period and not after TKR had been set up (Bambang Purwanto 2000). It is often stated that BKR did not yet have a military organizational structure or a clear recruitment policy and therefore cannot be labelled a military organization in its own right. Nevertheless, considering the development of BKR at the regional level, for instance as set up by Sudirman in Banyumas, A.K. Gani in South Sumatra or Dahlan Jambek in West Sumatra, it is difficult to maintain that BKR was an unstructured armed organization without a command line. In many areas, BKR did not function merely as a peacekeeper, but also engaged in active self-defence against foreign enemies thought to be arriving at any minute. In many places BKR membership was dominated by young people who had received their military training during the Japanese occupation. Elsewhere, however, it is difficult to tell who belonged to BKR and who was part of a youth militia or a member of the provisional parliament, the Komite Nasional Indonesia Pusat (KNIP, Central Indonesian National Committee), then in charge of civilian administration.

Next to acting as soldiers, members of BKR and the militias were routinely involved in political, social and economic activities. Most members of the KNIP were also members of BKR or militias. On the other hand, the Hizbullah and Barisan Pelopor (Frontier Pioneers), trained by the Japanese military, also had participants with a dual membership of both BKR and KNIP. The evidence shows that TKR was merely a superficial transformation of BKR, given the ranks and the fixed structure in accordance to the professional military organization. Almost all regional units of TKR formed after 5 October 1945 came from BKR. Many TKR commanders, for instance Sudirman in Banyumas, were former BKR officers. Moreover, the formation of TKR as an official army did not as such imply the disappearance of armed youth groups or affiliated militias with certain political or ideological powers (Bambang Purwanto 2000).

Because of the lack of separation between military and civilian functions, the process of decolonization placed the army in a dominant position in society. This combination of responsibilities became a defining characteristic of the Indonesian military and played a key role in determining later involvement by the military in economic life. It was reinforced by the fact that military confrontations with the Dutch forces weakened the civilian government and its ability to fulfill its functions and take responsibility for the economy from September 1945 onwards. The Republican government even had to be moved from Jakarta to Yogyakarta in January 1946. As the war dragged on, massive logistic support was needed to maintain the government, the people and especially the army, both formal forces and militias.

The general assumption is that the logistics relied exclusively on community support once the Dutch naval blockade had been imposed. Such an assertion is not altogether wrong but it does not do full justice to the situation. This assertion consciously or inadvertently overlooks other realities such as the presence of other sources of logistic support, to run the government and continue the armed struggle. One supplementary source was the army and its own economic activities, whether large or small, legal or illegal. The emergence of warlords in many places where civilian government was weak provided a strong basis for military business activities during the process of decolonization.

The involvement of the army, formal forces or militias, in the control and management of economic resources began when BKR and subsequent TKR members took over strategic economic sources such as factories, telephone offices, estates, power generators and installations, transport firms, mines and the distribution of daily needs previously managed by the Japanese army. In Wonosobo, Central Java, for example, the military took over Dutch-owned tea estates and factories that had been used by the Japanese to meet economic needs during the occupation. In Yogyakarta, the military gained control of metal tool factories or workshops of Dutch-owned companies and even seized several Chinese-owned companies, factories and warehouses. Similar takeovers were reported from other cities, such as Surabaya, Semarang, Surakarta (Solo), Cirebon, Jakarta, Palembang, Padang, Medan and Makassar. Military groups on occasion even acted as if they were officially representing Indonesian civilian authority as consolidated in the Poesat Tenaga Ekonomi (PTE, Centre for Economic Efforts), an institution dating from the Japanese occupation. In reality, these business activities often focused on personal or group gains.

The important role of the military in the economy can also be seen in the regulation of currency circulation from October 1946. The Republic's national currency, ORI (Oeang Republik Indonesia) and similar currencies issued by regional authorities were intended to replace Japanese money and compete with the currency issued by the Netherlands Indies Civil Administration (NICA). The chaos and confusion brought about by the wish of each region to print and circulate its own currency furthered military involvement in economic activities. When the currency for the province of Sumatra, ORIPS (Oeang Republik Indonesia Propinsi Sumatera) was to be printed in Bukittinggi (West Sumatra) after the printing press had been moved from Pematang Siantar (North Sumatra), the printing fell under direct responsibility of local military leaders (Mestika Zed 1997). Although formally supervised by the civilian government and local banking authorities, the printing of currencies during the Indonesian Revolution in reality occurred without any explicit control. On several locations, army groups or warlords purposely produced low-quality currency that could be washed away easily. This resulted in rapid inflation as too much money was brought into circulation (Mestika Zed 2003; Kahin 1997).

Examples from other areas also show how military involvement in the economy became an important facet of decolonization, notably in Sumatra and Sulawesi. Although Resident A.K. Gani of Palembang was a civilian, he also enjoyed the rank of General-Major and from November 1945 served as military coordinator for all of Sumatra (Mestika Zed 2003). His dual function resulted in the absence of a clear division between civilian and military involvement in economic activities in Palembang and other parts of Sumatra under Gani's jurisdiction. In reality, the military played an important role not just in the battlefield against Dutch military action, but also in fund-raising to support the activities of the civilian government and the military struggle. This is shown in the 'oil diplomacy'-policy and the presence of 'oil militias' and 'oil battalions', which made a considerable contribution to the finances of both local governments and the central authority. Yet another example was the acquisition of funds through tax and tariffs, known as *iuran perang* (war contribution). The war contribution was collected by the local authorities in West Sumatra, which in turn reported to the local military command.

One important measure taken by Gani in support of military business in Palembang was the creation in January 1947 of a separate agency to serve as a liaison for oil and coal sales and procurement of vital needs for the Indonesian government and military (Mestika Zed 2003). Gani also offered opportunities for young TRI officers to conduct trading through the Usaha Muda (Young Effort), an organization in Bukittinggi that was fully controlled by the military. The policies of Gani offered an incentive for military-controlled groups to handle much of Sumatra's trading. Trading organizations, such as the Soematera Import and Export (SOEIMEX) company, an important player in the economy of Palembang, were also part of the military network. The same holds true for the Central Trading Corporation (CTC) and the Sumatra Banking and Trading Corporation (SBTC) that were set up in Bukittinggi in 1948. The trading organizations were under control of army traders serving as military commanders in West Sumatra. This can be demonstrated by simply looking at the military domination of the boards of trading companies with members originating from both army and navy ranks (Mestika Zed 2003).

Militias, such as the Laskar Pemberontak Republik Indonesia Sulawesi Selatan (LAPRIS, South Sulawesi Rebel Militia) and the Badan Pemberontak Republik Indonesia (BPRI, Rebel Body of the Republic of Indonesia) in Pare Pare (Central Sulawesi), were involved in interisland trade, especially with Kalimantan and Surabaya. Copra was a major commodity traded by the army groups. Many army groups associated with BPRI also ran other businesses, such as land and sea transport facilities, daily goods stores and even barber shops. Other groups of soldiers, brought together in the Gabungan Pemberontak Indonesia Soppeng (GAPPIS, Soppeng [town] Association of Indonesian Rebels), did the same. Apart from copra, the military also shipped coffee and rice to Kalimantan to be sold or exchanged against other necessities, including firearms. Although the military groups were formally integrated into the TRI in January 1947, the business activities of these groups continued (Daud Limbugau 2000). Evidence suggests that the business activities of the military widened as a result of organizational consolidation and the emergence of young officers capable of taking advantage of the circumstances, whether for their men or for own personal gain. As warlords, the military groups could easily consolidate their power and run their business enterprises without much intervention by the civilian government.

The presence of oil diplomacy, oil militia and oil battalion is important to keep in mind when we reconstruct the role of the military in large-scale economic processes during the decolonization. As explained by Mestika Zed, since 1946 'the role of the militias and the TRI is no longer warfare, but actually trading and other productive activities for logistical support and supplies for civilian and the military of all the areas of Sumatra' (Mestika Zed 2003). The military controlled all productive oilfields and oil refineries in the hinterland of South Sumatra as well as the distribution network. They did not only meet the oil needs of all of South Sumatra, but also the needs of supporters of the Republic of Indonesia in West Sumatra and Java. Although the Plaju and Sungai Gerong oil refineries (South Sumatra) had been handed over to the Allied forces in August 1946, the military's oil business continued unabatedly in other oil-producing regions. It therefore comes as no surprise that this period was characterized by the appearance of 'oil barons' in South Sumatra, who also happened to be military rulers or warlords. In 1947, the town Prabumulih (South Sumatra), where the command headquarters of the Second TRI Division were located, became the main centre of Indonesian oil production in the Palembang region. Production and distribution stood under management of the military-controlled PERMIRI (Perusahaan Minjak Republik Indonesia, Petroleum Company of the Republic of Indonesia).

A similar situation evolved in Aceh and North Sumatra. The Indonesian army controlled oil production and distribution in the northern part of Sumatra through various companies, in particular the Perusahaan Tambang Minjak Negara Republik Indonesia (PTMNRI, State Petroleum Mining Company of the Republic of Indonesia). Consequently, most individuals involved in the oil business were of military origin. Men like Hasymi A. Taher and Ibnu Sutowo became directors in the state oil company Permina, predecessor of present-day Pertamina.

Elsewhere, the military played an important part in barter trading, especially the trade between Sumatra and the Malay Peninsula and Singapore (Kustiniyati Mochtar 1992; Yong 1997, 2003). Audrey Kahin wrote that barter trade between West Sumatra and the Malay Peninsula shortly after the proclamation of Independence was effectively dominated by the Ninth Army Division in Bukittinggi (Kahin 1997). Apart from daily provisions, soldiers also traded firearms which were distributed to Republican struggle groups. This was also done in Riau through Pekan Baru. In Palembang, these trader-soldiers succeeded in making rubber, coffee and quinine into lucrative economic resources next to the traditional oil and coal. These resources contributed considerable sums of money to the Republic.

Opium was another important commodity traded across the Straits of Malacca. Not only was Sumatran opium traded by the army, but according to Dutch intelligence, Javanese opium was brought in as well. Dutch military intelligence reported that many of the regular and militia army units in Java, including those under the command of Soeharto, the later President, regularly traded opium from Yogyakarta, the Republic's capital, to occupied territories in close cooperation with Chinese middlemen (Cribb 1988; Elson 2001:21). It is worth noting that some military groups and individuals were also active in trading goods which had been confiscated from smugglers or suspected traders, as depicted in imaginative language in short stories and novels written during or shortly after the war (Trisno Yuwono 1962).

We may conclude that military business activity conducted during this period not only provided a strong economic basis for local military rulers, but also had a huge political impact that would greatly affect developments during the following period. Military involvement in economic activities cannot be simply explained away as a mere manifestation of war economy. Instead, it prospered and became an important business category in the period after the transition of sovereignty, representing a new phase in Indonesia's decolonization.

Enlarging the economic stakes

To what extent did the end of warfare provide a fertile ground for the expansion of military business in Indonesia? Together with the cessation of hostilities, Dutch acknowledgement of Indonesian Independence on 27 December 1949 and the unilateral dissolution of the Republic of the United States of Indonesia on 17 August 1950 marked the beginning of a new period of Indonesian decolonization. Economically speaking, there was much determination on the part of the Indonesian government and society to transform the colonial economy into a national economy as increasingly advocated by economic nationalists. Yet in a relatively short time, as a result of weaknesses in the capacity of the state and local businessmen to run the local economy, the predominance of foreign corporations in the economy was again cemented. Two major patterns therefore characterize the macroeconomic decolonization after 1950. One refers to the takeover of corporations formerly owned by the colonial government, with or without compensation. Aside from Bank Indonesia, successor to the Java Bank, most seized corporations were public utilities such as railways, port facilities, bus transport, waterworks, post offices, telephone companies, pawn shops, gas and electricity companies and hospitals. The second pattern includes support of the development of indigenous Indonesian businessmen, resulting in indigenization or *pribumisasi* (Sutter 1959; Robison 1986:40-2; Yahya Muhaimin 1990).

After 1950 the policy of takeovers and pribumisasi offered good opportunities for the military to get involved in business. This was reinforced by the fact that the government had not been able to provide sufficient funds for the costs of military operations. The pribumisasi under the banner of the Benteng

Soldiers from the Indonesian national armed forces, TNI (Tentara Nasional Indonesia), disembarking in Ambon in 1950 from a vessel of the Dutch-owned shipping company KPM (Koninklijke Paketvaart Maatschappij). Scant attention has so far been given to the considerable involvement by the TNI in business, especially in regions outside Java (KITLV 16466)

policy, although attempting to limit opportunities for Chinese businessmen, in fact did little damage, allowing them to retain their dominant role in the Indonesian economy. Those policies had a greater impact in terms of producing dependent groups or individuals of military or indigenous civilian businessmen as opposed to independent indigenous merchant capitalists. The military not only functioned as a patron, but also as a player directly involved in economic activities. The practice of giving preferential licenses to indigenous copra traders to compete with their Chinese rivals in Sulawesi, for instance, inadvertently prompted a trading alliance between the military and Chinese traders which merely enhanced the strength of local individual military leaders in business. Such joint ventures paved the way for an expanding copra trade between Sulawesi and Singapore. Later, similar business combinations involving the military and Chinese middlemen appeared also elsewhere. Under the excuse of routine and military operations and raising funds for soldiers' welfare, the military business activities, which involved most of the local elite military rulers, became a neat and profitable commercial enterprise. This is why the decolonization process, at least to an extent, served as an important justification for military business.

Opportunities for soldiers to conduct business widened as a result of political strife and labour conflicts. Such difficulties in the sphere of production caused severe security problems in the early 1950s in several areas such as West Java, Central Java, the Moluccas, most of Sulawesi, Aceh and North Sumatra. Because of armed political conflict involving Andi Aziz and Kahar Muzakar in South Sulawesi, one of the battalions of the Seventh Territory Army gained control of the trade of copra, rice and other daily necessities. The army then forced the growers of copra, rice and other export commodities to sell their produce cheaply to companies designated by the military or directly to the military. The military also prohibited sale to third parties and did not hesitate to use violence against farmers who got in touch with other buyers or refused to sell their produce in the prescribed way. There is evidence that the army or its henchmen harvested coconuts from growers' fields that were left unattended because of unsafe conditions. Aside from that, the military also maintained trading companies in Majene (South Sulawesi) and controlled the import and export trade between Sulawesi and Singapore. Not surprisingly, this battalion became known as the 'dollar battalion' (Daud Limbugau 2000).

Involvement of the military in business increased as the government declared martial law, SOB (Staat van Oorlog en Beleg, 'State of War and Occupation') in March 1957. This extraordinary measure was motivated by armed rebellions in Sumatra and Sulawesi, increasingly uncontrollable labour and land conflicts, and the collapse of the (second) cabinet led by Ali Sastroamidjojo. These business ventures gained even stronger legitimacy after the diplomatic failure of Indonesia on the issue of West Irian in the United Nations, the issuing of the 5 July 1959 Presidential Decree and the launch of the confrontation with Malaysia in 1963. Just as with the hostile conditions after the proclamation of Independence and the arrival of Allied-Dutch troops in 1945-1946, the declaration of martial law in 1957 gave the military a very important position. The serious situation was aggravated by incessant conflicts among civilian politicians and general political instability. The explosive situation as such equipped the military with political as well as social and economic authority.

In Semarang, the late President Soeharto founded an institution to run the businesses of the Diponegoro Division. This measure was defended as a means for raising funds needed both for the troops and for safeguarding the security of the country, thus sustaining Indonesia's sovereignty. In a fairly short time, several types of business activity - trading of agricultural goods, fisheries, shipping, sugar factories, all involving Chinese businessmen – began generating substantial profits for the Diponegoro Division. By the beginning of 1959, the capital owned by the Division's corporation reached Rp 35 million rupiah or the equivalent of almost $ 800,000 (Elson 2001:62-3). The development of the Diponegoro Division's military arm was supported by its ability to conduct illegal barter trade between Semarang and Singapore, in particular sugar exchanged for rice.

Not all business activities of the Diponegoro Division were conducted openly or officially. Military businessmen elsewhere in Indonesia consciously created conditions under which civilian traders, especially Chinese traders, had to pay a certain tax or levy for each economic activity in addition to the official tax they paid to the government. Aside from that, civilian traders also faced conditions forcing them to forge alliances with military businessmen. Manipulation and corruption have always been the hallmarks of military business and have never been considered unusual.

In his biography of the late President Soeharto, Elson states that the business development of the Diponegoro Division was not largely determined by the personal relationship between Soeharto and Liem Sioe Liong, as has often been suggested, but rather by links with other Chinese trading groups, such as Bob Hasan and Sukatia. Liem Sioe Liong had in fact moved from Kudus to Jakarta at the time when Soeharto started to develop his military business. Nevertheless, a business relationship between the Diponegoro Division and Liem Sioe Liong was established through Sudjono (Elson 2001:64). In addition, Bob Hasan (The Kian Seng) a businessman deeply involved in the business ventures of the Diponegoro Division, was the adopted son of the influential General Gatot Subroto in Central Java.

Military business developed in a similar way in Sumatra and Sulawesi, although based on a different set of conditions compared to the situation in Java. Trading activities by army groups in defiance of the policy of economic centralization resulted in armed conflicts with the central government or with other army groups loyal to the central government. Long before an open political and military conflict erupted with the central government the army leaders of Sulawesi, supported by the local civilian government, routinely conducted trade or condoned smuggling, especially shipping copra from Sulawesi to Singapore. This trade was permitted under the guise of raising revenues for the regional government and the military budget, a matter never attended to by the central government. A similar procedure was pursued by military leaders in Sumatra trading in rubber and oil with the outside world in order to obtain cash money or exchange commodities in barter trade (Danang Widoyoko et al. 2003).

The army kept trying to monopolize the copra trade of Sulawesi. The formation of the Jajasan Kopra (Copra Foundation) created opportunities for businessmen outside the army but met with little response from local traders.

This resulted in instructions of the military authorities to monopolize purchases of copra. The instructions were signed by the commander of *Teritorium VII* and the Copra Regulating Board (Badan Urusan Kopra), an organization under direct command of the military governor. The signing took place in March 1957, just after the Permesta rebellion of 2 March 1957. Meanwhile, several individual soldiers from the 710th Battalion of South Sulawesi, which supported the central government in Jakarta, became influential businessmen in the late 1950s and early 1960s (Daud Limbugau 2000). These soldiers-cum-businessmen from South Sulawesi became an important main element in the formation of a new social group in each locality and at the national level. The new social class emerged in the 1950s and became known as the Orang Kaja Baru (OKB, 'New Rich'). These facts facilitate our understanding of the political revolts in Sulawesi in the late 1950s. The armed revolts were more than just conflicts between local civilian and military authorities and the central government; they were caused by competition for economic resources among soldiers or other interest groups involving soldiers as well.

The expansion of military business at the local level was also expressed in charity-like activities. Most military groups regularly organized fancy fairs. Although the military tended to consider such activities as a social service, in fact they generated tremendous amounts of money. These funds were subsequently used to finance their official activities, including an improvement in living standards of soldiers and their families (Soengkowo Sunjoto 1961).

From December 1957, the escalating conflict between Indonesia and the Netherlands about western New Guinea caused a massive takeover of Dutch-owned companies. The climax was reached with the formal nationalization of Dutch-owned enterprises in 1959. Local labour unions, in particular those with ties to political parties, notably the Indonesian Communist Party (Partai Komunis Indonesia, PKI), took the original initiative to these actions. But in various regions, the process of takeovers had begun earlier, at a time when talks between Indonesia and the Netherlands were still going on. Anti-Dutch sentiments had been expressed by President Sukarno in many speeches. Sukarno demanded the repatriation of western New Guinea back into the folds of the Republic. His speeches also helped boosting the confidence of workers to demand an accelerated *Indonesianisasi* in the foreign corporations where they were employed. In December 1957, the actions of especially leftist labourers increased in scope and intensity. This aroused the interest of the army, which became increasingly involved on account of issues of safety and the increasing rivalry between the armed forces and PKI. The army did not merely get involved to keep peace during the takeovers; its involvement also served to deny economic resources to its most important political rival. In an effort to gain control over labour unions, the military formed joint organizations such as the Badan Kerdjasama Buruh dan Militer (BKSBM, Cooperation Body for Military and Labour) (*Pikiran Rakjat*, 11-12-1957).

Widespread involvement of the military, especially the army, in connection with the takeovers can be demonstrated by the many regulations and actions conducted not just by the central military leaders, but also at a regional level. On 9 December 1957, the Second Territory Army commander in West Java, where there were many seized Dutch-owned plantations, issued a regulation specifying that all transfers of rights of foreign corporations in the region had to be conducted through the military. On the next day, the same military leaders announced that all Dutch-owned companies in West Java would be under military supervision in order to avoid uncontrollable takeovers (*Keng Po*, 9-12-1957 and 11-12-1957; *Pikiran Rakjat*, 11-12-1957). Prior to that, the Bandung military commander of the Executive Military Command Bandung (Pelaksana Kuasa Militer Bandung) had taken over the Fateru company, the firm Vorkink and De Kleyne publishers, which had already been seized by labourers (*Pikiran Rakjat*, 7-12-1957).

Similar actions were conducted by the Fifth Territory Army in Malang, East Java, and the Greater Jakarta military command. Both issued proclamations stating that all Dutch-owned companies were under direct supervision of the military (*Keng Po*, 10-12-1957 and 12-12-1957). Already in September 1957, the military leaders of East Java had taken over the distribution of Gresik cement (*Keng Po*, 17-9-1957). In South Sulawesi, the 710th Battalion, which had developed its business since 1945, took over Dutch-owned coconut and coffee plantations in Polewali, Mamasa, Majene and Mamuju. In December 1957, the West Java military commander of the Chief Executive Military Aide (Pembantu Utama Pelaksana Militer) similarly ordered the takeover of a tea estate in Ciawi, Bogor (*Keng Po*, 5-12-1957). The takeovers were not limited to business firms, but included also company-owned housing. Up to February 1958, the military commander of Jakarta expropriated no less than 321 houses; the houses were subsequently distributed among the civil service and military personnel (*Keng Po*, 20-2-1958). The position of the military in the takeover process was strengthened after the decree issued by Sukarno in July 1959, which, according to Douglas Paauw, 'opened the opportunity for real takeovers of important economic and political function by the military elite' (Paauw 1960:146).

The takeover of foreign oil companies and the formation of a national oil company strengthened military business participation in the process of economic decolonization (Yahya Muhaimin 1990; Bondan Kanumoyoso 2001). Although the government had started paying more attention to the oil industry since at least 1954, it did not take much action prior to 1957. At the time, the decolonization or Indonesianisasi of the oil companies was mostly influenced by activities related to oil labour unions. But a shift favouring the military occurred when labour activism in the oil companies became more militant, including calls to take over the foreign corporations to aid the construction of a national economy. The Department of Industry, ultimately responsible for the oil sector, allowed the Eksploitasi Tambang Minjak Sumatera Utara (North Sumatra Petroleum Exploitation Company) to be controlled by the army under General A.H. Nasution. In October 1957, it was consolidated as Permina with Colonel Ibnu Sutowo as president-director and Major S.M. Geudong as director (Humas Unit I PN. Permina 1966). Ibnu Sutowo then appointed Major Harijono, Major Pattiasina and Captain Affan to run the newly created national oil company. The first office of the company was even located within the army headquarters (Bartlett III 1972).

The activities of the national oil company, starting with production facilities at Pangkalan Brandan (North Sumatra), developed fast after the company had gained working capital from a Japanese consortium and in 1968, the military-controlled Permina merged with Pertamin into Pertamina ((Mara Karma 2001). The further Indonesianisasi of the Indonesian oil business from 1957 onwards had been accompanied by an increasingly strong position of the military. Military involvement in the oil sector was enhanced by the nationalization of the government's joint venture with Royal Dutch Shell, the NIAM (Nederlandsch-Indische Aardolie-Maatchappij, Netherlands-Indies Petroleum Company), and its transformation into the Indonesian Oil Mining company, Permindo (Pertambangan Minjak Indonesia) in 1958. The nationalization of the Sorong Petroleum-Maatschappij (Sorong Petroleum Company) and Nederlandsche Nieuw-Guinea Petroleum-Maatschappij (Netherlands New Guinea Petroleum Company) in the early 1960s similarly resulted in a greater military participation in Indonesia's oil sector, both at an individual and at an institutional level.

In Java, Dutch-owned sugar and tobacco companies, once among the chief earners of foreign exchange, were taken over by the military as the nationalization policies were executed. On 10 December 1957, the Diponegoro Fourth Territory Army, which held the highest command in Central Java during the SOB, issued a notification about the takeover of Dutch-owned companies. The Gondangwinangun sugar factory in Klaten, for instance, was immediately placed under command of the Klaten Regency Supervision Officer (Perwira Pengawas Perusahaan Kabupaten Klaten) and Surakarta's 15th Infantry Regiment (Heru Suyitno 1996). The Tjipiring sugar factory in Kendal, taken over by farmers and labourers on 15 December 1957, was put under control of the Kendal military commander (Zaenuri Afandi 2004). It was from these factories that the Diponegoro Division got its sugar to be bartered as described above. The takeover of those sugar factories preceded the takeover by the Diponegoro Division of 31 plantations and 13 sugar factories owned by six Dutch companies on 26 December 1957. Similar takeovers occurred in Cirebon, the sugar-producing centre of West Java. All sugar and *spiritus* factories in the Paliaman area were seized by the local military just before Christmas 1957 (*Pikiran Rakjat*, 24-12-1957).

Conclusion

Several facts compel us to infer a close correlation between decolonization and the rise of military business in Indonesian economic development. The appointment of Colonel Soeprajogi as Minister for Economic Stability and Colonel Soehardiman as Head of the Nationalization Board in the cabinet of Prime Minister Djuanda in 1958, shows that the military had indeed taken over a substantial part of economic life in Indonesia as economic decolonization was nearing its end. The commercial banks, which had once been politically controlled by various parties, started to change hands as a result of the shift to the Guided Economy, whereas military businessmen gained control over Dutch-owned banks pending nationalization. At the same time, the military expanded its business activities to embrace rice monopolies, trading companies, shipping lines, plantations, sugar factories, oil fields, foreign exchange dealings and many other economic activities previously controlled by Dutch and Chinese companies.

The process of decolonization had placed the military in a central position that was reinforced by the inability of the civilian government to guarantee political stability and manage the economic resources of the nation. This nurtured the interest of soldiers and officers for conducting business, as a group or at an individual level. After the takeover of Dutch firms, this did not only imply military involvement for the execution of martial law, but also included the appointment of military personnel as board members of civilian companies and the expansion of control of military organizations into every line of business. It positioned the military as the main power in the business world of Indonesia, whether through the private sector or the government bureaucracy.

When General A.H. Nasution realized that major violations were being conducted by the army and called for an investigation of fraudulent and misbehaving soldiers in mid-1959, it was already too late. The military officers had by then slotted themselves into a dependence on their business activities. They were reaping large profits socially, economically and politically. The army as an institution had become dependent on financial benefits gained from military business. As decolonization was nearing its end, business and the military had become two sides of the same coin.

The army was not the only group to venture into business activities. Every other part of the military, including the police force, was directly or indirectly involved. The navy, for instance, had its business ventures with the official support from a cabinet meeting held in 1958, which authorized it to own companies and to militarize trade shipping lines (*Kedaulatan Rakjat*, 6-6-1958). Decolonization provided a firm basis for military business in Indonesia underpinning the creation of a new and more sophisticated military business format from the 1960s, a format that was to flourish in particular during the New Order period. The emergence of co-operatives in all armed groups, from the central level down to local officers, reinforced the role of military business. These co-operatives were able to expand their activities in various economic sectors, from daily groceries, shipping companies and cinemas to circus, real estate, airlines and the oil business. Neither the nation nor low-ranking officers enjoyed the benefits from the military economic activities, as has often been asserted. It was the medium- and high-ranking officers and the generals who profited the most. It is therefore necessary to add the term *militerisasi* to the concepts of *nasionalisasi*, Indonesianisasi and pribumisasi in order to adequately write the economic history of Indonesia at the time of economic decolonization.

Finally, there is reason to elaborate on the rise of military business and its competition with communist groups in the 1960s. The military, in particular the army, took over and controlled enterprises which employed large numbers of workers at the time of economic decolonization. The central issue can be understood not only in terms of ideological differences between the army and communism, as is usually done, but also by incorporating the power struggle and economic rationality. The army tried to protect its economic interests by controlling labour, while the communist group used labour to justify its political existence and gain political support. Therefore, it is not surprising that, when the military supported the New Order regime after the September 1965 event, the labour movement was effectively subdued by the new government, politically as well as economically. Any labour activist was easily labelled a communist.

References

Afandi, Zaenuri

2004 'Perkembangan pabrik gula dan perubahan ekonomi pedesaan Cepiring, Kendal, tahun 1948–1966'. MA thesis, Department of History, Gadjah Mada University, Yogyakarta.

Bartlett III, A.G.

1972 *Pertamina; Indonesian national oil*. Jakarta: Amerasian.

Cribb, Robert

1988 'Opium and the Indonesian revolution', *Modern Asian Studies* 22:701-22.

Crouch, Harold
1975/76 'Generals and business in Indonesia', *Pacific Affairs* 48:519-40.

Elson, R.E.
2001 *Suharto; A political biography*. Cambridge: Cambridge University Press.

Humas Unit I PN Permina
1966 *Permina; Dulu, sekarang dan dimasa datang*. Medan: Humas Pusat PN Permina.

Iswandi
1998 *Bisnis militer Orde Baru; Keterlibatan ABRI dalam bidang ekonomi dan pengaruhnya terhadap pembentukan rezim otoriter*. Bandung: Remaja Rosdakarya.

Kahin, Audrey R.
1997 'Trade and taxes; Aspects of the West Sumatra economy during the Revolution', in: Taufik Abdullah (ed.), *The heartbeat of Indonesian Revolution*, pp. 199-210. Jakarta: Gramedia.

Kanumoyoso, Bondan
2001 *Nasionalisasi perusahaan Belanda di Indonesia*. Jakarta: Sinar Harapan.

Karma, Mara
2001 *Ibnu Sutowo mengabdi misi Revolusi sebagai dokter, tentara, pejuang minyak bumi*. Jakarta: Sinar Harapan.

Limbugau, Daud
2000 'Keterlibatan TNI dalam perdagangan di Sulawesi Selatan dari masa revolusi sampai tahun 1970-an', in: Edward L. Poelinggomang and Suriadi Mappangara (eds), *Dunia militer di Indonesia; Keberadaan dan peran militer di Sulawesi*, pp. 321-44. Yogyakarta: Gadjah Mada University Press.

Mochtar, Kustiniyati (ed.)
1992 *Memoar pejuang Republik Indonesia seputar 'zaman Singapura' 1945-1950*. Jakarta: Gramedia.

Muhaimin, Yahya. A.
1990 *Bisnis dan politik; Kebijaksanaan ekonomi Indonesia 1950-1980*. Jakarta: LP3ES.

Paauw, Douglas S.
1960 *Financing economic development; The Indonesian case*. Glencoe, IL: Free Press.

Purwanto, Bambang
2000 'Historiografi dan legitimasi peran sosial politik militer di Indonesia', in: Edward L. Poelinggomang and Suriadi Mappangara (eds), *Dunia militer di Indonesia; Keberadaan dan peran militer di Sulawesi*, pp. 135-58. Yogyakarta: Gadjah Mada University Press.

Robison, Richard
1986 *Indonesia; The rise of capital*. Sydney: Allen and Unwin.

Said, Salim
1991 *Genesis of power; General Sudirman and Indonesian military in politics, 1945-1949*. Singapore: Institute of Southeast Asian Studies.

Samego, Indria
1998 *Bila ABRI berbisbis*. Bandung: Mizan.

Singh, Bilveer
2001 'The Indonesian military business complex origins; Course and future'. Canberra: Australian National University. [SDSC Working Paper 354.]

Sunjoto, R. Soengkowo Imam
1961 *Pradjurit Jon H N 008-Lapris Kodam XIV 'Hasanuddin'*. Macassar: Bataljon Inf. 008 ROI-II/Lapris.

Sutter, John O.
1959 *Indonesianisasi; A historical survey of the role of politics in the institutions of a changing economy from the Second World War to the eve of the general election, 1940-1955*. PhD thesis, Cornell University, Ithaca, NY.

Suyitno, Heru
1996 'Pabrik gula Gondangwinangun sebelum dan sesudah nasionalisasi tahun 1950-1963'. MA thesis, Department of History, Gadjah Mada University, Yogyakarta.

Twang Peck Yang
1998 *The Chinese business elite in Indonesia and the transition to independence, 1940-1950*. Kuala Lumpur: Oxford University Press.

Widoyoko, Danang, Irfan Muktiono, Adrian Topan Husodo, Barley Haliem N, Agung Wijaya
2003 *Bisnis militer mencari legitimasi*. Jakarta: Indonesia Corruption Watch.

Yong Mun Cheong
1997 'Indonesia's Singapore connection, 1945-1948', in: Taufik Abdullah (ed.), *The heartbeat of Indonesian Revolution*, pp. 232-50. Jakarta: Gramedia.
2003 *The Indonesian Revolution and the Singapore connection, 1945-1949*. Leiden: KITLV Press. [Verhandelingen 208.]

Yuwono, Trisno
1962 *Di medan perang dan tjerita-tjerita lain*. Bukittinggi: Nusantara.

Zed, Mestika
1997 'Indonesian economy in the revolutionary era; The struggle to find financial resources to fund the Revolution (1945-1950), in: Taufik Abdullah (ed.), *The heartbeat of Indonesian Revolution*, pp. 181-98. Jakarta: Gramedia.
2003 *Kepialangan politik dan Revolusi; Palembang 1900-1950*. Jakarta: LP3ES.

Private business in action

PETER POST

Indonesianisasi and Japanization
The Japanese and the shifting fortunes of *pribumi* entrepreneurship

Since Sutter's introduction of the term in 1959, *Indonesianisasi* is defined as 'a conscious effort to increase the participation and elevate the role of the Indonesian – and more particularly the "indigenous" Indonesian – in the more complex sectors of the economy' (Sutter 1959:2; Lindblad 2002:52). Indonesianisasi has so far largely been discussed as part of the economic decolonization process and conceived as a predominantly bilateral Dutch-Indonesian affair. However, it can be argued that the economic decolonization of Indonesia and the process of Indonesianisasi were part of a wider global process of economic change and restructuring of international trading and finance, in which the Japanization of the Western-controlled colonial economies of Southeast Asia played a decisive role. This process began already around 1900, after Japan's acquisition of Taiwan in 1895 and Japan's victory over Russia in 1905, and gained prominence after the First World War, especially during the 1930s, with the creation of Japan's formal and informal empires in Asia (Duus, Myers and Peattie 1989; Narangoa and Cribb 2003).

Japanization, defined as the increasing predominance of Japanese capital, trade and industry in Southeast Asian economies, took place on informal and formal levels. Informally, it operated through personal networks within the established pre-war international colonial order and rested upon private initiative and the creation of Japan-oriented local economic networks and intra-Asian business alliances. On a formal level, usually through state initiatives, Japanization confronted and challenged the colonial system. In colonial Indonesia, the formal challenge emerged in the mid-1930s with Japan's diplomatic offensive and official trade and shipping negotiations in 1934, 1936 and, the most 'notorious' ones, in 1940/1941. The Kobayashi and Yoshizawa missions of 1940/1941 were meant to secure Indonesian oil and to negotiate the integration of the Netherlands Indies into a Japan-centred economic co-prosperity sphere (Dick 1989; Post 1991; De Jong 2002).

Although processes with very different dynamics, Japanization and Indonesianisasi reinforced each other in the pre-war and wartime economy of the Netherlands Indies. Especially since the late 1920s, when direct communications between Japan and the Netherlands Indies were well established, Japanese trade and investment expanded, and Japanese and Indonesians increasingly encountered each other in various social-cultural platforms and in the marketplace. It was around this time that among influential segments of both communities the notions of a shared 'Asian' identity and a common destiny intensified. This Japanese-Indonesian encounter was increasingly seen as an opportunity for building a new independent Indonesia which might be liberated from the legacies of Dutch imperialism and its wealthy allies, the ethnic Chinese business community. Disillusioned with Western liberal society and colonial capitalism, these groups were opposed to the free reign of market forces and the unlimited pursuit of private gain. To many Indonesians, the Japanese economic system – in which the state exercised strong control and an organic view of society prevailed – offered a promising alternative to Western capitalism (Nakamura 1999; Goto 1997; Post 1997).

In this contribution I take a closer look at the Japanese role in the Indonesianisasi process by paying specific attention to the shifting fortunes of *pribumi* entrepreneurship. The first section concentrates on the informal role of private Japanese businessmen in this process, the significance of the Nanshin-ron ideology and the rise of large pribumi trading firms during the 1930s. In the second section I deal with the Japanese occupation period, pointing out that the three and a half years of Japanese military rule had differential impacts on pribumi entrepreneurship. The third section covers the post-war period and analyses the role of large pribumi business groups in the development of Indonesian's post-war economic relations with the United States and Japan.

Prewar Japanese business and pribumi entrepreneurs: the Nanshin-ron factor

In an earlier publication, I analysed the formation of the pribumi business elite in Indonesia in relation to Japan's inroads into the Dutch colonial economy (Post 1997). The major argument was that the political economy of the Dutch colonial state in Java and the economic ideology of Dutch colonial officials in general had a negative impact on the formation of an indigenous business elite in Java. In other areas of the Netherlands Indies, where effective colonial control was lacking and Dutch welfare policies were not strictly enforced, indigenous business groups proved far more successful and capable of controlling large sections of the local and regional economy, despite severe competition from ethnic Chinese and other Asian business networks.

In addition, I argued that precisely these business groups, most of whom came from Sumatra and were of Minangkabau origin, had linked up with Japanese capital by the early 1930s, and succeeded in taking part in the direct import trade of Japanese textiles and other manufactured goods during the late colonial period.

To this institutional approach should be added the ideology of Nanshin-ron (Southern Advance). This theory was a powerful tool in bringing individual Japanese businessmen closer to pribumi entrepreneurs and the indigenous population. The theory itself is rather vague and in its original conception did not point to an aggressive or military advance into colonial Southeast Asia (Shimizu 1987). On the contrary, Nanshin-ron, as it developed from the late nineteenth century until the late 1920s, stressed the peaceful and gradual Japanese economic advance into the region. In essence, it states that the Japanese (especially the young and spirited) should build up a living in the Southern Areas and bring the positive radiation of the Imperial Household to the colonized indigenous peoples, who lived wretched and miserable lives under the brutal exploitative colonial systems created by Western imperial powers. Through their hard work and dedication, these loyal Japanese subjects should dedicate themselves to uplifting the welfare of the indigenous subjects, both spiritually and materially, thus enabling them to share in the splendour of the Japanese empire. Nanshin-ron terminology reflected critical discussions in Japan itself about capitalist society and the ruthless exploitation of Asian people by the West, stressing harmony and public spirit, solidarity and consensus, and national achievement over private gain.[1]

Many Japanese traders and businessmen who built up successful enterprises in pre-war Indonesia were caught by the Nanshin-ron ideals and most of them played a major part in 'elevating the role of indigenous Indonesians in the colonial economy'. Tsutsumibayashi Kazue, the founder of the trading firm Nanyo Shokai, may serve as an example. He was born in Yamagate prefecture (northern Honshu) in 1873 and moved to Taiwan at the age of 22. There he entered the employment of Kwik Djoeng Eng, one of the founders of the famous trading firm Kwik Hoo Tong (KHT) in Solo, Java (Post 2002). After having worked for KHT for five years, Tsutsumibayashi opened his own kimono- and pawn shop in Taipei in 1902. In the next few years Tsutsumibayashi regularly made trips to Japan, South China and Java as a KHT employee. These ventures helped him acquire some knowledge about Japanese medicines and its demand in Java. In 1909 he settled in Semarang

1 One of the most influential Japanese Nanshin-ron ideologists, Takekoshi Yosaburo, in many writings compares Japanese colonial rule in Taiwan to Western colonial rule in Southeast Asia. He never tires of pointing out how favourable Japanese colonialism was compared to Western colonial rule.

and opened his own firm, Nanyo Shokai (Oba 1988).

In due time, the firm of Tsutsumibashi became a major enterprise specializing first in Japanese-patent medicine and after the First World War in textiles. Unlike Dutch trading firms at the time, he established his own integrated distributive networks, bypassing Chinese intermediary traders. He brought in young Japanese salesmen who were given a short in-house training and then directed to open their own shops in Java's interior and other large cities. At the same time, he trained young indigenous Indonesians, who came to work in the company´s branch offices. Nanyo Shokai's business network operated in the southern part of Central Java and East Java with branches in Solo, Yogyakarta, Magelang and Kediri. In 1918 the firm employed 91 sales agents.[2] Tsutsumibayashi ran his business like a 'typical' Meiji entrepreneur, always having Japan's national economic interest in his mind. He imposed strict rules upon Indonesian employees and Japanese staff and expected sobriety, loyalty and filial piety, hard work and thrift, honesty and sincerity (Yano 1977).

During the First World War, Japanese southward economic advance became more coordinated and the Netherlands Indies archipelago, in particular Java, emerged as a key target for Japan's export industries (textiles) and a major supplier of agricultural products (mainly sugar from Java and rubber from Sumatra and Kalimantan). Japanese banks, business conglomerates (*zaibatsu*), trading companies, and shipping lines opened branch offices in the major port cities, and all over Java Japanese retail shops (Toko Jepang) were set up. In creating links with indigenous social networks in Java, the Japanese banks and trading companies began recruiting indigenous personnel. These staff members were usually employed in the lower ranks of the companies (servants, cleaners, porters), but occasionally some of them became employed as clerks and sales assistants. Besides making use of ethnic Chinese to create distributive outlets, the trading companies also used Japanese staff to contact local wholesalers and retailers.

The Japanese trading firms and banks in the three major cities in Java depended mainly upon ethnic Chinese networks, but the situation was quite different in other parts of the archipelago. In Sumatra, Japanese trading firms, with some exceptions, only employed indigenous staff. Also in Java's interior, the Toko Jepang hardly employed local Chinese but rather indigenous youngsters. Many of these Japanese, like Tsutsumibayashi, held idealistic views on uplifting the indigenous people from their purely agricultural status into the world of trade and commerce. To train the indigenous population for modern commerce became part of their 'calling' regarding their working life in the

2 Information from two Japanese-language sources, Gaimusho Tsusho Kyoku, *Gaigai Nihon Jijutsugyosha no chosha* (Tokyo: Ministry of Foreign Affairs 1915:100) and Gaimusho Tsusho Kyoku, *Zaikai Hompo Jijutsugyosha shirabe* (Tokyo: Ministry of Foreign Affairs 1918:165).

'South'. Typical examples are Sawabe Masao and Kaneko Kenji (Kwartanada 1998; Kaneko 1988).

Sawabe Masao, the batik king of Yogyakarta, was one of the most famous Japanese entrepreneurs in pre-war Java. He arrived in the Netherlands Indies in 1908 and in 1914 he was already known as a successful businessman. Later on, his shop Fuji Yoko (Toko Fuji) would become the largest department store in Central Java. In 1926, he employed 14 Japanese staff members and 118 Javanese. He maintained close relations with the Sultan's family and the Susuhunan of Solo, and his batik factory was to give the local batik industry a new impetus in the 1930s.

Kaneko Kenji arrived in Java in 1914 and started working for Fuji Yoko of Sawabe. He married a niece of Sawabe in 1921 and after that opened his own shop, Toko Kaneko, near Yogyakarta. He learned Javanese in order to be able to communicate directly with the local Javanese people and ordered goods directly from Japan. He too became a visitor to the Sultan's palace and soon the Sultan's relatives and associates became regular customers. He was able to read classical Chinese and was invited to become a member of the local Chinese trading society. This affiliation rescued him from becoming a victim of Chinese boycotts. By inviting his younger brothers and other relatives, he was able to set up a chain of some ten retail shops in Java and Sulawesi, all of which imported Japanese goods directly from Japanese manufacturers. In all shops he employed indigenous clerks and salesmen. In the mid-1930s, he opened two branches that were headed by young Javanese. By the late 1930s, he was planning to expand his business to Banjarmasin and Balikpapan, but in January 1941, he received an order by the Japanese military to return to his native prefecture Gunma.

Sawabe and Kaneko and others like them prided themselves on the fact that their efforts to raise the commercial consciousness and entrepreneurial spirit among the indigenous inhabitants of Yogyakarta ultimately met with success.

After the outbreak of the worldwide economic depression and the devaluation of the Japanese yen in 1931, the Japanese textile industry intensified its efforts to conquer the Netherlands Indies markets. In 1933, Japan's share of total imports of cotton piece goods had risen to 90 per cent for unbleached goods, 70 per cent for bleached goods and 85 per cent for printed and dyed goods. In the same year, Japanese shipping, banks, wholesale traders and retailers constructed a unified system of import and distribution, seemingly creating 'one Japanese chain that ran from Yokohama to the native village', as one Dutch delegate at the Dutch-Japanese trade negotiations was heard to say (Sugiyama 1994:64-5). The different positions in this 'chain' were partly Japanese, but for the larger part in the hands of ethnic Chinese trading networks.

The Japanese contribution consisted of efforts by the Japanese trading corporations to set up their own shops and distributive outlets, and to intensify relations with pribumi networks. Mitsui Bussan had taken the lead in the late 1920s. After 1932, partly due to the anti-Japanese boycott by the Chinese community, such trading companies as Marushin Yoko, Kuga and Co. and Takenokoshi Trading Co. followed suit. One of the most successful undertakings in this respect was initiated by the manager of Daishin and Co., Okano Shigezo, who set up a chain of large modern department stores under the name of Toko Tjijoda in Bandung, Surabaya, Yogyakarta and Batavia. He became known as the 'grocery king of the Nanyo'. During the 1930s, he was one of the most influential Japanese businessmen in Java. Okano has been portrayed as a typical hard-working Japanese entrepreneur, who in the true Nanshin-ron spirit single-handedly built up his business empire from nothing.

After working in a Toko Jepang in Padang and Surabaya since 1914, Okano Shigezo returned to Japan in 1918 and was able to raise funds to start his own firm. He was 27 years old when he returned to Surabaya and founded Daishin and Co. The firm at first engaged in the lucrative sugar trade. Okano signed a contract with a Chinese sugar merchant. Having little knowledge of the ins and outs of the highly risky sugar market, he speculated far too heavily, acquiring a huge debt with the Chinese businessman. However, Okano was able to reach an agreement and signed a contract specifying that he would pay back his debt within 15 years. He was subsequently approached by Suzuki Shoten, one of the major Japanese sugar traders at the time, who was willing to buy Daishin Yoko. With this money and an additional loan from the Taiwan Bank, he now entered the ceramics trade. This proved highly successful and he opened a new store in Surabaya's Chinese business quarters, where he came to work closely with Chinese wholesale dealers. Due to his Chinese connections, his business was hardly touched by anti-Japanese boycotts in the 1920s and early 1930s. In contrast to many other Japanese shops, Daishin Yoko prospered greatly. Okano had always deliberately employed Chinese and Javanese staff and in 1933 he decided to open a large and modern department store, Toko Tjijoda, in Surabaya to be able to sell large Japanese items like furniture and piano's, which until that time had not reached the Netherlands Indies market. His many Chinese and Indonesian staff were specifically trained in modern sales techniques, language and customer service. In 1937, the department store in Surabaya employed a staff of 40 Japanese, 60 Javanese and over 50 Chinese. The department stores in Bandung, Yogyakarta and Batavia were significantly smaller, but also in these stores large numbers of Chinese and Javanese were employed (Okuyama 1988).

The examples of Okano, Sawabe, Kaneko and Tsutsumibayashi show that large and successful Japanese shopowners in pre-war Java deliberately employed and trained young Javanese, partly for economic reasons (to tackle

Chinese competition in the retail and distributive trade), partly for ideological reasons. Their Nanshin-ron ideals were an important denominator in fostering these linkages. This local economic dynamic of Nanshin-ron in late colonial Java closely overlapped with indigenous efforts to 'increase the participation and elevate the role of (indigenous) Indonesians in the more complex sectors of the economy', in Sutter's formulation. On a local commercial level the result was that Nanshin-ron ideals and Indonesianisasi were closely intertwined, albeit centred on Japan's trade expansion.

Crossing colonial borders

The Japanese owners of Toko Jepang and modern department stores, particularly those adhering to the Nanshin-ron ideology, devoted much energy to training young Javanese staff for modern commerce. Other, more powerful Japanese enterprises, with similar ideologies and partial connections to Japanese governmental and military circles, supported the larger pribumi trading businesses by increasing their participation in the foreign trade of the Dutch colony. This move was the result of a series of anti-Japanese boycotts by ethnic Chinese traders, starting in 1928 and continuing through the following years and erupting again after the Manchurian incident of 1931. Efforts were intensified in December 1931, when the Kongres Koperasi Indonesia, in which most large pribumi businesses participated, decided that it would establish direct links with Japanese business houses and manufacturers in order to eliminate foreign (meaning: Chinese) control of the intermediate trade. The most famous of these powerful Japanese businessmen were Ishihara Shinsaburo of Ishihara Sangyo Kaisha (ISK) one of the largest pre-war Japanese conglomerates in Southeast Asia, and Handa Yisaburo of Nanyo Veem. These persons established close relations with pribumi business groups, who were linked to Ayoeb Rais (uncle of Moh. Hatta), Agoes Moesin Dasaad, Abdul Ghany Aziz and Rahman Tamin, which enabled them to take direct part in the trade between Japan and the Netherlands Indies. Following Ayoeb Rais' and Hatta's trip to Japan early 1933, Djohan and Djohor as well as Dasaad opened agencies in Tokyo and Osaka and began importing Japanese textiles (Post 1997:96-9). In 1937, Dasaad, Rais and Aziz founded the Malay Import Company, which opened a branch office in Japan, called the Malaya-Nippon Trading Co. Rahman Tamin also joined forces with Dasaad to engage in the Japan-Indonesia trade.

The outbreak of the European war in 1939 sent shockwaves around the world immediately affecting international trading patterns and Indonesia's export industries. The Dutch colonial government reacted swiftly and instituted a semi-war-economy. After the German invasion of the Netherlands in

May 1940, all financial, monetary and economic ties between the Netherlands and the Netherlands Indies were broken off. The colonial government issued an Ordinance on Wartime Legal Traffic and established a Commissie voor Rechtsverkeer in Oorlogstijd (CRO, Committee for Wartime Legal Proceedings). The committee was originally set up to take control over enemy (German) assets, but within a few months its range of operations was extended to cover all matters concerning the foreign economic relations of the Netherlands Indies. On 27 May 1940, a foreign exchange ordinance was issued in order to counter capital flight from the colony. International transactions of banks, shipping companies, trading firms and insurance companies came under tight government control and were strictly regulated. The Netherlands Indies Foreign Exchange Institute became the administrative office of the foreign exchange ordinance. On 8 December 1941, with Japan's attack on Pearl Harbor and its declaration of war, the Netherlands Indies Foreign Exchange Institute started to manage Japanese assets in the Netherlands Indies. The Institute then made use of the services of the Java Bank, the colony's central bank, and the major Dutch trading companies.

From the scarce sources available on the period between May 1940 and March 1942, it appears that Agoes Moesin Dasaad, Rachman Tamin and other prominent pribumi traders expanded their connections with Japan. They also began importing Japanese textiles through a number of Japanese firms in Kobe and Osaka. Dasaad acquired goods from S. Tagaki Shoten, Nishimatsu and Co. and Gomei Kaisha Takeda Co. in Kobe, whereas Rachman Tamin and Dafaar Tamin and a large number of other pribumi trading firms in Padang and Batavia received their textiles directly from Japanese textile firms such as Toyo Menka and Mataiti Kabushiki Kaisha in Osaka. Yet, the value of their imports was rather small compared to Japanese, Chinese and Dutch businesses.[3]

Early in 1941, Dasaad bought the textile factory Kantjil Mas at Bangil, East Java, which had been confiscated by the colonial authorities from its previous owner, a German national. Dasaad ran the factory jointly with Abdul Ghany Aziz, using credit provided by the Java Bank. With the acquisition of Kantjil Mas, the Dasaad Musin Concern (DMC) became by far the largest pribumi firm with an annual turnover of about 10 million guilders (Wolf 1948:3).

On the eve of Japan's military occupation of the Netherlands Indies, we find that the Japanization of the pre-war Indonesian economy contributed positively to the process of Indonesianisasi. It supported the emancipation of the pribumi business class and helped elevating the role of indigenous Indonesians in the more complex sectors of the economy. The key to under-

3 Bank Indonesia, Jakarta: De Javasche Bank (DJB), 2971.

standing how Japanese and pribumi entrepreneurial strategies linked up with each other in the pre-war period should be sought in the dominant position of ethnic Chinese networks in the distributive trade and the import and wholesale trade of East Asia with the Dutch colony (Post 2001). In the pre-1942 period, both Japanese and pribumi businesses were less concerned with the control of large Dutch trading firms or the foreign trade of the Netherlands Indies since this trade was mostly directed towards Europe and the United States. In addition, the imports handled by these firms were not destined for the indigenous mass population, but rather catered to the wealthy upper layers of Dutch colonial society.

Pribumi business in Japan's war economy

Under Japan's military rule things changed significantly. The war economy created by the Japanese in the Indonesian archipelago had various impacts on the development of pribumi entrepreneurship. On the one hand, it offered opportunities and chances for a large number of small pribumi businesses and local entrepreneurs (Post 1997:103-7; Sutter 1959: 135-6, 173-6). On the other hand, however, it hindered the expansion of the large pre-war pribumi trading companies.

Immediately upon the establishment of Japanese military rule, interregional trade within the Greater East Asian Co-Prosperity Sphere came to be controlled by military agencies, of which the Koeki Eidan was the most important. Merchandise had to be exported or imported under special war accounts and special licenses had to be obtained in order to engage in trade or in industrial activities in the occupied areas. There was fierce competition among the large companies and the *zaibatsu* about the most profitable concessions and trading licenses. The successful companies usually had close connections within the higher ranks of the military bureaucracy and were able to pay large sums, often including bribes.

In the commercial links between Japan and Indonesia, 63 companies became engaged in exports from Indonesia and 241 in imports. These 304 companies comprised 44 per cent of the total number of Japanese trading firms in the Southern Areas (Hikita 1997:143). Among the importers, there were only nine local Japanese firms that had been engaged in Japan's pre-war trade with the Netherlands Indies and built up extensive branch networks in Java and elsewhere. Among these was Daishin Yoko of Okano Shigezo. But trade volumes remained small compared to pre-war performance. Throughout the wartime period, Daishin Yoko only received 41 import orders from the wartime control agency (Hikita 1997:143).

During the years 1942-1945, trading connections between Japan and

A group of prominent Indonesians gathering in Jakarta at the time of the Japanese occupation, including the later President Sukarno (third from right). The Japanese military authority encouraged Indonesian leaders to set up committees preparing for decolonization. (KITLV 25245.)

the Southern Areas were largely conducted by zaibatsu such as Mitsui and Mitsubishi, while the remaining sectors of the economy, in particular food production and manufacturing industries, were left to pribumi, Chinese, Arab and Indian merchant-entrepreneurs. Just like in the 1930s, Mitsui Bussan developed its own distributive and purchasing networks in which Japanese occupied managerial positions. The company only reluctantly allowed Javanese to rise to higher positions. From the pribumi point of view, the zaibatsu did very little to enhance their position in the wartime economy.

The only major company that had been closely involved in supporting pribumi entrepreneurs before the war and now gained a prominent position was ISK. This firm, led by Ishihara Hiroichiro, obtained mining rights in the Solo area (copper), Rembang and Tasikmalaya (coal). It was engaged in shipbuilding at Surabaya, and started factories for electric wires in Surakarta. Also Nanyo Shoko, the warehousing subsidiary of ISK, was given a license to operate in Java (Hikita 1995:704-5). Little is known about how relations developed between Ayoeb Rais and Agoes Moesin Dasaad with Ishihara, Handa Yisaburo, Ando Seiichi and other Japanese private businessmen under Japan's military rule.

During the Japanese occupation, the DMC, Djohan and Djohor, the Tamin Brothers and other pre-war pribumi trading firms were cut off from the import and export trade of Indonesia with Japan, and relegated to an economic intermediary position, which the Dutch colonial office had also envisioned for these indigenous business groups. Rather than taking part in Indonesian foreign trade, they were expected to help restructuring the colonial economy into a war economy and to assist the Japanese bureaucracy in developing a local textile industry based on regional self-sufficiency. Agoes Moesin Dasaad was appointed a seat in the Kigyo Tosei Kai (Textiles Control Board) in June 1942 and in September of the same year he became an advisor to the Persatoean Perniagaan Indonesia (Association for Indonesian Commerce). In September 1943 he was made a member of the Sangikai (Advisory Council) of Batavia, and within a month he became vice-chairman of this council. In April 1945 he became a member of the newly established Investigative Committee for the People's Economy. These official appointments during the Japanese occupation gained him a great deal of influence and a strong power-base in Indonesia, which was undoubtedly of great help during his post-war career. Under Japanese military rule, however, Dasaad's major concern was how to meet his financial obligations and how to run his private businesses under the strains of a war economy.

Liquidation of enemy banks and its effects on large pribumi business firms

After an initial plan to continue the Dutch banking system had been abandoned, the Japanese military decided to liquidate all enemy banks.[4] The liquidation of the nine enemy banks took place in two phases, between 20 October 1942 and 31 March 1944 and between 1 April 1944 and 10 October 1945 respectively. During the first phase, the liquidation was supervised by Yamamoto Hiroshi, employee of the Bank of Japan.

Given the wartime situation the liquidation of the banks was actually a failure from the start; in practice liquidation was impossible. First of all, the banking interests were not confined solely to Java. A considerable part of the banks' capital was spread all over the world and impossible to convert into working funds. The same held true for negotiable papers, which also represented a sizeable proportion of the banks' capital. Second, most debtors were enemy firms or nationals, whose fortunes were being controlled by the Tekisan Kanribu Kanrika (Enemy Control Board) and hence could not be used for liquidating the banks' liabilities. Third, due to economic circumstances non-enemy debtors (Chinese, Arabs, Indonesians and others) were hardly able to repay their debts. Finally, much of the merchandise held as collateral for advances by the banks was under control of the military, and its disposal was in fact very difficult (Keppy 2006:123). These factors combined to make the liquidation a very awkward process.

Despite institutional and practical restraints, the liquidation of the banks was undertaken as planned. The Japanese staff of Yamamoto Hiroshi was dispatched all over Java, and together with the European employees of the banks' branches, they drew up balances and put administrations in order. As stipulated in the rules for liquidation, the first and major task was recovery of outstanding debts. Since most Dutch and other enemy debtors were interned or abroad, their debts could not be retrieved. Yamamoto Hiroshi and his staff, including the Dutch senior and local staff, therefore concentrated on non-enemy debtors such as Chinese, Arab and pribumi businesses. These were called upon to appear at the local branch offices and to negotiate a repayment scheme.

Agoes Moesin Dasaad was one of those pribumi entrepreneurs who had a large debt and a highly complicated relationship with a major enemy bank, the Java Bank. A closer look into his negotiations with Yamamoto Hiroshi as

4 These banks were: De Javasche Bank (DJB, Java Bank), Nederlandsche Handel-Maatschappij (NHM, Netherlands Trading Society), Nederlandsch-Indische Handelsbank (Netherlands Indies Commercial Bank), Nederlandsch-Indische Escompto-Maatschappij (Netherlands Indies Escompto Bank), Chartered Bank, Hongkong and Shanghai Banking Corporation, Bank of China, Overseas Chinese Banking Corporation. and the Bank of Batavia.

well as the complications surrounding the outbreak of the war reveals the difficulties under which leading pribumi entrepreneurs had to manoeuvre under Japan's military rule.[5]

The Textielfabriek en Handel-Maatschappij 'Kantjil Mas' was originally German property and had been expropriated in May 1940, immediately after the German occupation of the Netherlands, by the CRO. Initially business was continued as usual, but in 1941 the CRO decided to dispose of the factory. Intended buyer was Agoes Moesin Dasaad, managing-director of the Malaya Import Company. The reason to offer Kantjil Mas to Dasaad was that the Department of Economic Affairs wanted the factory to be brought into the 'native sphere'. Dasaad was considered extremely wealthy (he belonged to a very well-to-do family) and he had knowledge of the textile trade. On 25 August 1941 the deed of sale was signed. The selling price of Kantjil Mas – excluding stocks of weaving yarn, chemicals, dyes and fabrics – was 255,000 guilders. An amount of 105,000 guilders was paid in cash immediately, while the remaining 150,000 guilders would be paid as soon as the factory was transferred to N.V. Textielfabriek en Handel-Maatschappij Kantjil Mas, a limited liability company established specifically for this purpose by Dasaad. Pending final payment, the N.V. Kantjil Mas handed over shares worth 225,000 guilders to the CRO. These shares were to be returned after payment of the remaining 150,000 guilders.

To enable Dasaad to effectuate his final payment upon transfer of the factory to N.V. Kantjil Mas, the Java Bank declared itself willing to grant Kantjil Mas a credit to the same amount secured by a lien on promissory notes and a mortgage on the grounds, buildings and machinery of the company. The Malang branch of the Java Bank was instructed to proceed with the necessary paperwork as soon as possible. Due to the outbreak of the war with Japan on 8 December 1941 and the fact that the factory was located within the 10 kilometre coastline range, special lengthy formalities with the Dutch military authorities were required. In addition, Agoes Moesin Dasaad himself was interned as he had been working intensively with the Japanese and was considered a dangerous person. The transfer of the property to Kantjil Mas could therefore not be effectuated and, as a consequence, no final payment to the CRO took place. Therefore, the CRO still held 225,000 guilders' worth of shares in N.V. Kantjil Mas, while Kantijl Mas still had to pay 150,000 guilders to the CRO.

Prior to internment, Dasaad had concluded consignment agreements with Guntzel and Schumacher and in November 1941 he had ordered machinery from Lindeteves for the extension of his weaving department. When he was

5 Bank Indonesia, Jakarta: DJB, 2975.

released, in March 1942, and the Japanese liquidators started investigating the books of the Java Bank, they found that Kantjil Mas owed the Java Bank 287,835 guilders and called upon Dasaad to appear at the liquidator's office in Bandung. After the first meeting, probably in July 1942, Dasaad was ordered to hand over the balances of Kantjil Mas so that the liquidator could properly asses his financial position and see what kind of repayment scheme could be negotiated. In October 1942, based on the information given, the liquidator's office drew up a balance sheet for Kantjil Mas (Table 1). From this balance sheet it becomes clear under what difficult conditions Agoes Moesin Dasaad and other non-enemy businessmen (pribumi, Arabs, Chinese, Indian and Eurasian) were operating during the Japanese occupation. They would only have been able to fulfil the liquidator's demands if their factories could operate at full capacity and under 'normal' circumstances. But now things were quite different.

Table 1. Balance sheet of the N.V. Textielfabriek en Handel-Maatschappij 'Kantjil Mas' as of 31 October 1942 (in guilders)

Buildings and machinery	254,538	Capital stock issued	245,000
Inventory, automobiles, etc.	19,075	Reserve funds	71,777
Machine parts, weaving equipment	20,678	Depreciation account	38,943
Weaving yarn	137,178	De Javasche Bank	287,835
Dyes and chemicals	23,776	Guntzel and Schumacher	
Fabrics	147,965	- account I	78,000
Fabrics in consignment with Guntzel and Schumacher	203,059	- account II	238,202
		A.M. Dasaad	46,018
Cash	10,430	Creditors	30,306
Japanese banks	102,322	Bonus	2,992
Debtors	130.759	Balance	42,665
Foundation expenses	6,743		
Sundry assets	2,789		
Bonds	5,000		
CRO	10,800		
Differences	6,626		
	1,081,738		1,081,738

Note: This balance sheet was drawn up by the liquidator's office and based upon the balance sheets of the head office in Batavia, the Surabaya branch office and the factory at Bangil. Source: Bank Indonesia, Jakarta: DJB, 2975.

Dasaad's stock of weaving yarn was destroyed as a consequence of the war; the fabrics in consignment with Guntzel and Schumacher had been partly destroyed and the remainder was under the control of the Tekisan Kanribu. The debtors were all Dutch firms, which were under control of the Tekisan Kanribu. The Tekisan Kanribu demanded the settlement of the debts to Guntzel and Schumacher, an amount of 316,202 guilders in total. Also the creditors were under control of this board. The only good fortune for Dasaad was that his machinery was still intact. Still, it was difficult to start business again and make the profits necessary to fulfil his financial obligations to the bank.

During the initial negotiations Dasaad seemed quite optimistic about the outlook of the economy under the Japanese. He agreed to a monthly repayment of 5,000 guilders to settle his debt with the bank; this amount was raised to 15,000 guilders in February 1943. But in June 1943 he apparently had some difficulty in raising the necessary sum and only paid 10,000 guilders. Since business was bad, he requested a reduction of his payment and to convince his Japanese counterparts he presented a draft balance of his firm. The liquidator discussed this balance sheet with officials of the Department of Economics and Statistics, in order to find out more about the future prospects of the Javanese economy. Because it was increasingly difficult to get weaving yarns for Kantjil Mas, a reduction from 15,000 to 5,000 guilders was agreed upon in September 1943. In the second half of 1944 a further reduction to the amount of 2,500 guilders was necessary. In the final months of the Japanese occupation, Dasaad, despite his prominent role in all kinds of economic organizations and committees, was hardly able to come up with even this amount. In his report over March 1945, the liquidator remarked disappointedly that 'Kantjil Mas have paid nothing in this month, so they now have an arrearage of 2 monthly instalments amounting to *f* 5,000'. Later, however, the report noted that this amount had been paid in on 6 March 2605.

Djohan and Djohor, the other major pribumi trading firm with close Japanese contacts in the pre-war era, also encountered great problems, albeit of a slightly different kind. Their total stock of weaving yarn had been requisitioned by the Japanese army in March 1942 and the army refused to return it to its rightful owners. This stock of yarn was pledged to the Java Bank. Ayoeb Rais, manager of Djohan and Djohor, uncle and confidant of Hatta, regularly went to the liquidator's office to negotiate. In his monthly report of January 1943, Yamamoto Hiroshi wrote: 'As Djohan and Djohor still remain responsible for the debt with the Bank, this firm was advised to communicate with the authorities concerned in order to try to get at least a compensation in cash.' Two months later he reported with obvious satisfaction: 'Mr Djohor from Djohan Djohor informed us that after some discussion with the authorities concerned at least part of the yarn pledged to the Bank and requisitioned by the Nippon Army will be released before long, as a consequence of which this debt still seems collectable.'[6]

Despite the difficulties the large pribumi firms and other non-enemy businesses faced during the wartime period, they somehow managed to repay the largest part of their pre-war debts to the Java Bank. In his final monthly report over July 1945, the liquidator stated: 'In total the debtors of the Produce Department of the Bank paid as from the beginning of the Liquidation-activities until ult. of June 2605 an amount of *f* 434,121.59 or about 72 per cent of the total remaining collectable debts of these clients.'

In April 1944, the military administration in Java announced plans for a new economic order (Sutter 1959:200-11). Rejecting Western capitalism, it decreed that the economic order in Indonesia should be based upon a so-called 'Oriental Morality', of which loyalty, cooperation and public service comprised the essential elements (Sato 1994:14-7). By that time, most pribumi entrepreneurs were convinced that the Japanese administration would not deliver the economic opportunities which they had expected. But they also shared a common feeling that the pre-war colonial economic system, in which the Dutch and Chinese predominated, should not be restored. Agoes Moesin Dasaad, Abdul Ghany Aziz and Achmad Bakrie were all members of the Investigative Committee for the People's Economy set up in April 1945. Making the most of their opportunities, the Indonesians stepped up business activities. Various associations of Indonesian manufacturers were established. Dasaad met with several other leading business and political figures in Bandung in June 1945 to discuss the necessity of a Java-wide Indonesian business organization. This meeting gave rise to the major business event of the year: the All-Java Conference of Indonesian Economists (Permoesjawaratan Kaoem Ekonomi Indonesia seloeroeh Djawa). The conference was held in Bandung on 20-24 July 1945. Principal speaker was Moh. Hatta, who called for a socialist-type of economy based on the spirit of *gotong royong*. All businessmen present were conscious of an atmosphere of unity, service and brotherhood. One of the resolutions passed at the conference led to the establishment of the Persatoean Tenaga Ekonomi Bangsa Indonesia (PTEBI, Association of the Indonesian People's Economic Efforts). Members of the board included major Indonesian businessmen such as Abdul Ghany Aziz and B.R. Motik. On 1 August 1945, two weeks before the Japanese sur-

6 Bank Indonesia, Jakarta: DJB, 2975. This is the second to last reference to Djohan Djohor (as the company was called by the liquidator's office) in the monthly liquidation reports, which run up to July 1945. In the report over June 1943, it is noted that a balance sheet of the firm as of 31 May 1943 had been drawn up. Regrettably, I have not been able to trace this balance sheet, but apparently Djohan and Djohor came up with a satisfactory repayment scheme and were able to fulfil its financial obligations to the liquidator.

render, the PTEBI opened an office under the name Poesat Tenaga Ekonomi (PTE, Centre of Economic Efforts).

By the end of Japan's military rule, after three and a half years of exposure to an overwhelming Japanization effort, pribumi businessmen, despite the limits set by the war economy, had developed into a self-conscious, spirited group of entrepreneurs, eager to put their talents at work to build an independent Indonesian Republic. They had taken on high positions in the more complex sectors of the economy, and were running important enterprises in competition with the Chinese business class.

The post-war period

After Japan's surrender and the proclamation of Independence, the young Indonesian Republic stood for the tremendous task of building up a national economy from the ruins left by the Japanese military. Unlike Sukarno, Hatta looked to the West for economic cooperation: first the United States, later the Netherlands. For the future economic development of Indonesia, compromises should be made with the former colonial mother-country. Hatta was supported by other influential economists and Republican leaders surrounding him. Sukarno, however, from the very early years of Indonesian Independence favoured closer alliances with non-Western countries, especially China, Russia and Japan (Nishihara 1976:9-14).

In establishing economic connections with the foreign countries, influential pribumi entrepreneurs with differing political backgrounds played an important part. Agoes Moesin Dasaad was one of them. Through his close alliance with Djohan and Djohor, Dasaad belonged to the inner circle of Hatta's Sumatran business networks. At the same time, Dasaad was a close personal friend of Sukarno (both men shared similar passions) and had aided him on several occasions.

Dasaad, the Republic and the United States

In the revolutionary period Dasaad had been heavily involved in economic transactions between the United States and the Republican territory, acting at times as an intermediary for Hatta and A.K. Gani, but most of the time working to expand his own business empire. He became a major supplier of medicines, car tyres, weapons and ammunition for the Republican forces. Through his vast Lampung business networks, Dasaad also had a part in the so-called 'Singapore connection' and by 1947 the DMC had become an important factor in Indonesian power politics. The years 1946-1949 witnessed a protracted Dutch naval blockade and two Dutch military inventions. The central and regional Republican leaders, local army commanders and private pribumi entrepreneurs each tried hard to develop and expand their own business interests and to reduce Indonesia's dependence on Dutch-controlled foreign trade. Large stakes were involved and the different parties competed heavily, forming short-lived alliances for one particular deal but fighting with the same partners over another lucrative transaction.

In December 1946, upon instigation of Sumitro Djojohadikusumo at the Department of Finance, the Republican government set up the first and largest of these trading corporations, the Banking and Trading Company (BTC) with headquarters in Jakarta, Sumitro as president-director and Ong Eng Die as vice-director. On behalf of the BTC, Dasaad, A.K. Gani, A.A. Maramis and Laoh went to New York to set up an office there and establish contacts with American corporations. Dasaad found the American Isbrandtsen Corporation prepared to sign an agreement for the shipment of rubber, sugar, cinchona bark and sisal from Java and the import of textiles from the United States. In the event, the chartered ship, the 'Martin Behrman', was seized by a Dutch destroyer in early March 1947 (Twang 1998:278). Although the BTC did not seek a monopoly in trading, many considered the firm a monopolistic institution, and it received criticism from various sides. During the first Dutch military action (July-August 1947), the BTC headquarters in Jakarta became moribund when losing its administrative offices and valuable cargo (Yong 2003:50). The Jakarta BTC office was then liquidated and the company continued operations from Yogyakarta.

In late 1946, A.K. Gani, fearing that Sumitro and Ong Eng Die wished to monopolize the Republic's foreign trade, started furthering his own business interest. As Minister of Economic Affairs in the Sjahrir cabinet, he offered full support to a fugitive businessman from Yogyakarta, T. Oesman bin Abdoellah Rahman, in setting up the Namsoco (Nusantara Malaya-Singapore Company). In October 1946, Gani established the Namsoco headquarters in Palembang as well as an import-export agency in Singapore. Namsoco was in fact controlled by Gani with the intention of linking up with Chinese business networks and serving as a major business conglomerate in the region with connections between Singapore, Sumatra and the Republican territories of Java (Yong 2003:49).

In Bukittinggi military commanders had started their own trading business and here it was Hatta who intervened, urging them to operate their business under the banner of the Republican government. In August 1948, the Central Trading Corporation (CTC) was inaugurated. It became the single most powerful Sumatra-wide corporation (Twang 1998:261; Thee 2003:251-64).

The BTC (Sumitro), CTC (Hatta), Namsoco (Gani) and the SBTC (the

Sumatra Banking and Trading Corporation, sister-company of BTC) can all be considered state enterprises, although they were not fully owned by the state. Private shareholding (many of it Chinese) kept these corporations running and private pribumi entrepreneurs, like Dasaad, held shares as well. In fact, many pribumi entrepreneurs, such as Herling Laoh, Koesmoeljono, Hasjim Ning, Djohan and Djohor, Soetan Sjahsam (brother of Sutan Sjahrir), Sidi Tando as well as some Arab businessmen, were actively involved in developing both state-run corporations and their own private business firms. This makes it difficult to draw a clear distinction between a government and a private enterprise during the Indonesian Revolution.

In the case of the agreement with Isbrandtsen in New York, for example, a formal contract was drawn up between Isbrandtsen and DMC for import of textiles and delivery of agricultural produce from Java. DMC had made an agreement with the trading firm Dahlan Sapi-Ie for the textile imports and with the trading company 'Intraport' for trans-shipment to Banten and Tuban, whereas it was given a guarantee for delivery of agricultural products by BTC.[7] The financial risks of the agreement with the American corporation were carried solely by DMC.

Hatta and partners wanted to establish a central banking and trading organization in New York, an 'American-Indonesian Corporation', which would be exclusively oriented towards the Republic. To that aim the Republican leaders sought participation (capital, know-how and networks) from large pribumi trading firms. Upon advice from Margono Djojohadikusumo, president-director of Bank Negara Indonesia (BNI, State Bank of Indonesia), Hatta in early 1948 contacted F.M. Martak, president-director of the well-respected trading firm 'Marba'. At the same time, Martak was also negotiating with Dasaad to combine forces and establish one single large pribumi trading corporation.

The result of all this was that in March 1948 a Republican delegation signed a contract with an American businessman, Matthew Fox, on behalf of eight American corporations. The Indonesian side would establish one large, privately owned pribumi trading corporation, consisting of the DMC, 'Intraport' (partly owned by Dasaad) and the Marba concern. The Perserikatan Saudagar-Saudagar Indonesia (PSSI, Indonesian Commercial Union) in Yogyakarta, of which Dasaad was a director since November 1947, would execute the contract with Fox. Dasaad, fearing that his own personal business relations in the United States might suffer from this, opposed the proposal and wanted the Fox contract for himself. For this he was fiercely attacked by other members of the PSSI and by such long-time friends as Maramis and Herling Laoh. As a

7 Nationaal Archief, The Hague: Koloniën. Algemene Secretarie, 2586.

result, Maramis resigned from the board of directors of DMC.[8]

In 1947 and 1948 Dasaad, together with his elder brother Baki Musin and Soetan Sjahsam also opened an office in Amsterdam, at first under the name Netherlands Indonesian Supply Agency (NISA), from May 1948 as a branch of the Malaya Import Co. Soetan Sjahsam had accompanied Dasaad to the United States and also established his own private firm there, the Soetan Sjahsam Corporation.

In December 1949, with the Dutch acknowledgement of Indonesian sovereignty, the DMC operated thirteen branches of the Kantjil Mas Trading Company and seven branches of the Malaya Import Co. in Indonesia, and also maintained offices in the United States and Europe. Agoes Moesin Dasaad was by far the most important pribumi entrepreneur at the time.

Japan-Indonesia relations

Dasaad's close association with Sukarno secured him a sound footing in the internal power politics of the time, and it was on Sukarno's request that he also became involved in the post-war negotiations with Japan over repayment issues.

In the immediate post-war period both the Republic and the Dutch wanted to re-establish trade relations with Japan. Yet, such relations were strictly regulated by the SCAP (Supreme Command of the Allied Powers), which did not allow private firms to establish themselves in Japan and decreed that all trade should be handled by government-appointed commercial organizations.

For both the Dutch and the Republic, the most important item was the import of Japanese textiles; almost 90 per cent of Indonesian purchases in Japan consisted of textiles. However, the SCAP (Supreme Command of Allied Powers) refused to buy any raw materials from Indonesia. The MacArthur administration looked to the Middle East for oil, to British Malaya for rubber and to the United States for other raw materials (Van Poelgeest 1999:134-5). This policy resulted in a structural deficit on the balance of trade between Indonesia and Japan. Sound agreements were necessary for regular commercial contacts. In 1947, it was initially decided that an 'open account' under SCAP would offer the necessary credit facilities and that the Dutch colonial office in Jakarta would exercise formal control over all trade relations between Japan and Indonesia.

Negotiations continued during the following several years whereby the Dutch mission in Tokyo and a trade delegation from Jakarta declared that

8 Nationaal Archief, The Hague: Koloniën. Algemene Secretarie, 2586.

they also represented Republican Indonesia and that the open account would be open to the Republic. SCAP did not inquire any further into this delicate matter, and it was agreed in 1949 that Indonesia would import textiles worth $ 63 million and that Japan would import Indonesian products worth $ 24 million (Van Poelgeest 1999:137). The textile imports from Japan were financially backed by the Marshall Aid to the Netherlands. But when the Netherlands in December 1948 launched the second military action against the Republic, the Americans immediately halted the channelling of Marshall Aid to Indonesia. The financing of textile imports from Japan vanished. In 1949 trade negotiations with SCAP continued, but due to the uncertainty about the situation after the transfer of sovereignty and the risk that the Netherlands would be held responsible for losses caused by orders from the Indonesian Republic in Japan, the Netherlands in December 1949 decided to postpone negotiations with SCAP.

After December 1949, the Netherlands and the Republic of Indonesia started negotiating with SCAP separately. During these negotiations, the Dutch were eager to have a say in the negotiations between the Republic and Japan as well. Negotiations were scheduled for May 1950. In early May, the Indonesian government informed the Dutch that they were not welcome to participate, but that the Indonesian party was willing to represent Dutch interests. The Dutch High Commissioner in Jakarta, J. de Beus, was very disappointed, since officially the Netherlands and the Republic were Union partners (Goto 2003:258). He requested that the Indonesian delegation in Tokyo, headed by Sudjono, Indonesia's first Ambassador to Japan, contact H. Mouw, head of the Dutch mission in Tokyo. The talks between Sudjono and Mouw were only perfunctory and the Dutch official was deeply hurt. Mouw, a long-serving and distinguished member of the colonial administration who had headed the DOAZ (Departement van Oost-Aziatische Zaken, East Asia Office), a prewar intelligence office that scrutinized Japanese activities in the Netherlands Indies, was very annoyed that Sukarno appointed Sudjono as head of the Indonesian delegation. Sudjono had accompanied the Japanese forces during their invasion in 1942 and had rendered them much service during the occupation. Mouw became very angry when he learned that Sudjono had contacted the famous propagandist Shimizu Hitoshi and that during the reception hosted by MITI, the Japanese Ministry of International Trade and Industry, the Indonesian delegation was welcomed with popular wartime songs (Van Poelgeest 1999:281). Having thus lost the possibility of a tripartite Dutch-Indonesian-Japanese commercial agreement, SCAP pressed the Netherlands for a separate Dutch-Japanese agreement, regulating trade between the Netherlands proper and Japan. This treaty was officially signed on 13 April 1951 (Van Poelgeest 1999:141).

Japan's post-war role in the economic decolonization of Indonesia can be divided into two phases: 1945-1951 and 1952-1958. During the first phase, when Indonesian sovereignty was still not recognized by the Dutch and Japan fell under SCAP, the role of Japan was informal and clandestine resting largely on individual initiatives, business interests and lobby groups. Important players during this period were the so-called *Nisei*, Japanese who had been born in the Netherlands Indies before the Pacific War and who found it difficult to find a job in Japan after the war. These people soon started to engage themselves as intermediaries, agents and consultants of Indonesian and Japanese firms and shipping lines interested in developing economic ties between the two countries. Another important group of Japanese consisted of soldiers and civilians who had stayed behind in Indonesia after Japan's surrender. These people too were instrumental in bringing pribumi business enterprise back to Japan. In 1951, when SCAP relaxed its economic control, allowing foreign firms to establish themselves in Japan, DMC, Bakrie Bros., CTC and other leading Indonesian firms such as the Oei Tiong Ham Concern opened offices in Tokyo and Osaka (Nishihara 1978:153; Thee 2003:258).

The establishment of branch offices in Japan probably coincided with the Djuanda Mission of December 1951, which was Indonesia's first official mission to discuss the wartime reparations issue. Japan's influence on Indonesia's economic decolonization became visible after 1952, in particular due to the rising power of Kishi Nobusuke. Unlike his predecessor Yoshida Shigeru, Kishi favoured a close economic integration with Southeast Asia, especially Indonesia. In May 1957, Kishi was the first Japanese Prime Minister after the war to visit Southeast Asia. Kishi had also served as Minister of Commerce and Industry in Tojo's first cabinet. In the words of Goto, 'Kishi's interest in Southeast Asia lay in establishing Japan's position in the region, namely to make it unmistakenly clear that Japan was the center of Asia' (Goto 2003:299). Kishi's policies towards Southeast Asia were designed to make Japan a more equal partner in relations between Japan and the United States.

At the same time, the San Francisco peace negotiations were proceeding. The Dutch and Indonesian sides shared common burdens and different points of view also in this international forum. In 1951 the Dutch side reluctantly accepted the peace treaty and it was decided that the Indonesian Republic would negotiate a war reparations scheme with Japan separately, without interference by the Dutch. During these negotiations the Japanese government was much pressed by Japanese Indonesia lobbyists, among whom the famous pre-war and wartime businessman Ishihara Hiroichiro. For many years the negotiations dragged on without reaching a satisfactory agreement. But in late 1956 or early 1957, when tensions in Indonesia about the future role of Dutch companies in the economy intensified, a satisfactory solution offered itself. If the Dutch enterprises and technical staff were to leave Indonesia, their place could be taken by the Japanese. Subsequent official missions of Kishi probably accelerated this plan.

On 28 November 1957, Kishi and Sukarno reached an agreement. The Japanese would give $ 400 million in developmental aid and another $ 400 million in war reparations. On 8 December 1957, the Indonesian-Japanese agreement was publicly announced (Nishihara 1976:51-2). Now Sukarno had the backing of the Japanese and his position vis-à-vis the Dutch was considerably strengthened. In the very same week, he ordered diplomatic relations with the Dutch to be broken, the Royal Dutch Airlines (KLM) lost its landing rights and the Dutch were ordered to leave the country. Starting on 3 December 1957, Dutch enterprises were seized all over the country. In early 1959, following legislation in December 1958, the seized Dutch firms were formally nationalized (Van Poelgeest 1999:189-91).

Conclusion

This contribution demonstrates that the process of Indonesianisasi and the economic decolonization of Indonesia were closely related to Japanese inroads into the Indonesian economy. In the pre-war period, Japanese trade and industry offered various opportunities for pribumi trading firms to take part in the intra-Asian economy, and for elevating the role of Indonesians in local commerce. During the wartime period, many enterprising Indonesians were able to move into economic positions, which had been closed to them under Dutch colonial rule. But that same period denied the large pribumi trading firms a role in Indonesian foreign trade, which was largely reserved for Japanese *zaibatsu* such as Mitsui and Mitsubishi. In this respect, Japanese military rule resembled Dutch colonial economic policy, which also aimed at keeping pribumi enterprise in a subordinate position. It was only after the Japanese surrender and the Indonesian proclamation of Independence that pribumi entrepreneurs could truly hope to acquire a larger stake in the more complex sectors of the Indonesian economy and the nation's foreign trade.

A proper account of the Japanese role in the shifting fortunes of pribumi entrepreneurship requires making an analytical distinction between personal Japanese-pribumi networks and formal governmental policies. Many Japanese private entrepreneurs and adherents of the Nanshin-ron doctrine in the pre-war, wartime and post-war periods entertained close personal relations with pribumi businessmen and had a sincere wish to develop a strong private entrepreneurial business class in Indonesia. These personal networks, some of which created during Japan's military administration, proved instrumental during the negotiations over war reparations and in terms of bringing Japanese firms back into Indonesia after 1957.

References

Dick, Howard W.
1989 'Japan's economic expansion in the Netherlands Indies between the First and Second World Wars', *Journal of Southeast Asian Studies* 20-2:244-72.

Dick, Howard W., Vincent J.H. Houben, J. Thomas Lindblad and Thee Kian Wie
2002 *The emergence of a national economy; An economic history of Indonesia, 1800-2000*. Crows Nest, NSW: Allen and Unwin.

Duus, Peter, Ramon H. Myers, and Mark Peattie (eds)
1989 *The Japanese informal empire in China, 1895-1937*. Princeton, NJ: Princeton University Press.

Goto, Ken'ichi
1997 *'Returning to Asia'; Japan-Indonesia relations 1930s-1942*. Tokyo: Ryukei Shyosha.
2003 *Tensions of empire; Japan and Southeast Asia in the colonial and postcolonial world*. Athens, OH: Ohio University Press.

Hikita, Yasuyuki
1995 *Nampo Kyo-eiken. Senji Nihon-no-Tonanajia Keizai Shihai*. Tokyo: Taga Shuppan.
1997 'Japanese company inroads into Indonesia', in: Peter Post and Elly Touwen-Bouwsma (eds), *Japan, Indonesia and the war; Myths and realities*, pp. 87-110. Leiden: KITLV Press. [Verhandelingen 173.]

Jong, L. de
2002 *The collapse of a colonial society; The Dutch in Indonesia during the Second World War*. Leiden: KITLV Press. [Verhandelingen 206.]

Kaneko, Kenji
1988 'Chubu Jawa zairyu sanju-nen no omoide', in: Jagatara Tomonokai (ed.), *Jagatara Kanwa*, pp. 131-6. Tokyo: Jagatara Tomonokai.

Keppy, Peter
2006 *Sporen van vernieling; Oorlogsschade, roof en rechtsherstel in Indonesië, 1940-1957*. Amsterdam: Boom.

Kwartanada, Didi
1998 'The Chinese trading minority in a changing order; A preliminary study of Yogyakarta, 1930s-1945'. Paper presented at the international conference 'The Economic (Dis)Integration of East and Southeast Asia, 1920s-1960s. Policies and Practices'. Tokyo, Rikkyo University.

Lindblad, J. Thomas
2002 'The importance of *Indonesianisasi* during the transition from the 1930s to the 1960s', *Itinerario. European Journal of Overseas History* 26-3/4:51-72.

Nakamura, Takafusa
1999 'The Japanese war economy as a "planned economy"', in: Erich Pauer (ed.), *Japan's war economy*, pp. 9-23. London/New York: Routledge.

Narangoa, Li and Robert Cribb (eds)
2003 *Imperial and national identities in Asia, 1895-1945*. New York/London: RoutledgeCurzon

Nishihara, Masashi
1976 *The Japanese and Sukarno's Indonesia; Tokyo-Jakarta relations, 1951-1966.* Honolulu: Hawaii University Press.
Oba, Jotaro
1988 'Nampo Senkusha Tsutsumibayashi Kazue shi to Nanyo Shokai', in: Jagatara Tomonokai (ed.), *Jagatara Kanwa*, pp. 64-8. Tokyo: Jagatara Tomonokai.
Okuyama, Kimihei
1988 'Okano Shigezo to Daishin Yoko', in Jagatara Tomonokai (ed.), *Jagatara Kanwa*, pp. 244-9. Tokyo: Jagatara Tomonokai.
Poelgeest, L. van
1999 *Japanse besognes; Nederland en Japan 1945-1975.* Den Haag: Sdu.
Post, Peter
1991 *Japanse bedrijvigheid in Indonesië, 1868-1942; Structurele elementen van Japan's economische expansie in Zuidoost-Azië.* PhD thesis, Free University of Amsterdam.
1997 'The formation of the *pribumi* business elite in Indonesia, 1930s-1940s', in Peter Post and Elly Touwen-Bouwsma (eds), *Japan, Indonesia and the war; Myths and realities*, pp. 87-110. Leiden: KITLV Press. [Verhandelingen 173.]
2001 'Trust and status in a dual regional economy; Dutch trading firms in Japan's prewar trade with Southeast Asia', in: Shinya Sugiyama and Linda Grove (eds), *Commercial networks in modern Asia*, pp. 182-99. Richmond, Surrey: Curzon.
2002 'The Kwik Hoo Tong Trading Society of Semarang, Java; A Chinese business network in late colonial Asia', *Journal of Southeast Asian Studies* 33:279-96.
Sato, Shigeru
1994 *War, nationalism and peasants; Java under the Japanese occupation, 1942-1945.* Sydney: Allen and Unwin.
Shimizu, Hajime
1987 'Nanshinron; Its turning point in World War I', *Developing Economies* 25-4:386-402.
Sugiyama, Shinya
1994 'The expansion of Japan's cotton textile exports into Southeast Asia', in: Shinya Sugiyama and Milagros C. Guerrero (eds), *International commercial rivalry in Southeast Asia in the interwar period*, pp. 40-73. New Haven, CT: Yale Southeast Asian Studies.
Sutter, John O.
1959 *Indonesianisasi; A historical survey of the role of politics in the institutions of a changing economy from the Second World War to the eve of the general election, 1940-1955.* PhD thesis, Cornell University, Ithaca, NY.
Thee Kian Wie
2003 *Recollections; The Indonesian economy, 1950s-1990s.* Singapore: Institute of Southeast Asian Studies.
Twang Peck Yang
1998 *The Chinese business elite in Indonesia and the transition to independence*

1940-1950. Kuala Lumpur: Oxford University Press.

Wolf Jr., Charles
1948 *The Indonesian story; The birth, growth and structure of the Indonesian Republic.* New York: John Day.

Yano, Toru
1977 'Tsutsumibayashi Kazue no seishinteki 'Kaiki', 'Nampo kanyo' no kindaite kiruikei', *Tonan Ajia Kenkyu* 15-3:307-33.

Yong Mun Cheong
2003 *The Indonesian Revolution and the Singapore connection.* Leiden: KITLV Press. [Verhandelingen 208.]

J. THOMAS LINDBLAD

The economy of decolonization in North Sumatra

Language sometimes defines trends in historical writing. In the historiography of economic decolonization in Sumatra, we encounter three different strands of thought suggested by the language used. There is an internationally oriented literature in English focusing on conflicts between foreign enterprises on the one hand and labour or local occupants of estate land on the other (Pelzer 1982). Politics here take the back seat to tensions between owners of factors of production. A second tradition is represented by the Dutch-language literature often siding unequivocally with the losers in the Dutch-Indonesian conflict, which easily results in a rather one-sided account of circumstances and events (Van der Zwaag 1991; Goedhart 1999). Negative rather than positive impacts of economic decolonization are stressed here. A third strand of thought is offered by Indonesian-language publications emphasizing accomplishments of leading indigenous businessmen, for instance T.D. Pardede in Medan and Achmad Bakrie from Lampung (Tridah Bangun 1987; Syafruddin Pohan et al. 1992). Such linguistic demarcations mirror different biases and use of different types of sources. This contribution offers a more balanced view by presenting a wider spectre of outlooks based on a greater variety of sources compared to either one of the three literatures listed.[1]

Language may determine outlook and sources but answers depend on the questions asked. It is all too tempting to recount the dramatic chain of events culminating in the takeover and nationalization of Dutch enterprises in the late 1950s without paying sufficient attention to the wider context of regional economic development in North Sumatra. We need to know which external and internal factors determined economic development in the region at the

1 This article was written during the preparation of a book-length monograph on the economic decolonization of Indonesia (Lindblad 2008). Versions of this contribution were presented at an international workshop on the decolonization of Sumatra, held at Padang, West Sumatra, on 1-2 August 2005, and an international conference on the history of Southeast Asia, held at Auckland, New Zealand, on 1-3 February 2006.

time. An additional and rarely addressed question concerns the immediate consequences of the sudden transfer of management of the region's economic resources from private Dutch capital to the Indonesian state following the takeovers (in Indonesian *pengambilalihan*). In conceptual terms, the appropriation and subsequent nationalization of Dutch corporate property are perceived as the ultimate manifestation of *Indonesianisasi*, a useful analytical tool to further our understanding of the transition from a colonial to a national economy (Soejono Hadinoto 1949; Sutter 1959; Lindblad 2002).

Sources used here include annual reports of the Indonesian central bank (Java Bank/Bank Indonesia), contemporary news agency reports (*Berita Antara*), articles in newspapers (*Waspada, Merdeka*) and unpublished documents traced in the Arsip Nasional Republik Indonesia (ANRI, National Archives of Indonesia) and at the local branch of the employers' organization Algemeene Vereeniging van Rubberplanters ter Oostkust van Sumatra (AVROS, General Association of Rubber Planters in East Sumatra) and its successor, the Sumatra Planters' Association (SPA) or, in Indonesian, Gabungan Pengusaha Perkebunan Sumatera Utara (GAPPERSU).[2] The argument is arranged in a straightforward fashion with two separate sections focusing on the situation respectively before and after the takeovers. Answers to the questions addressed are given in a separate conclusion, while summary statistics are presented in the Appendix.

Before pengambilalihan

In the 1950s, the province of North Sumatra embraced most of the pre-Independence residency East Sumatra (Sumatra's Oostkust) as well as the former residencies Aceh and Tapanuli.[3] Estate agriculture dominated the economic structure of the region to an extraordinary degree. This sector served as one of the prime earners of foreign exchange for Indonesia in both colonial times and afterwards. It is instructive to start with an overview of the sector. The total planted area amounted to 400,000 hectares, with as much as 94 per cent (375,000 hectares) located in what used to be the residency of Sumatra's Oostkust. Rubber was by far the most important crop accounting for 70 per cent of the total planted area, whereas palm oil and tobacco occupied the

2 The archival collections of AVROS and GAPPERSU/SPA are kept in the office of Bank Agro in Medan. I gratefully acknowledge the assistance given by Undri, then student of history at Andalas University in Padang, in consulting these sources.

3 Aceh later became a separate province whereas Tapanuli has remained part of North Sumatra (Sumatera Utara). Some districts in the southern part of Sumatra's Oostkust were incorporated into the province of Central Sumatra, but this did not affect the main estate area.

remaining majority. In the early 1950s, the entire island of Sumatra counted some 240,000 estate workers of whom 85 per cent were found in North Sumatra alone. Large estates in Sumatra were 96 per cent foreign-owned (*Antara*, 8-7-1954; AVROS 1956: Tables I, VIII).

Dutch firms owned and operated more than two-fifths of the estates in North Sumatra, whether measured in numbers or planted area (Table 1).[4] Nevertheless, non-Dutch foreign ownership was stronger in North Sumatra than in most other regions in Indonesia. British and American estates accounted for almost one-third of the total, the latter larger than the former. These estates focused primarily on rubber whereas Belgian enterprises were above all found in palm oil. Indonesian estates, occupying a smaller proportion than any of the four nationalities already mentioned, were almost all state-owned.

For administrative convenience, the employers' organizations arranged the estates into two categories. One category comprised single large owners of estates. Among the top six, we come across four Dutch corporations: the Deli Maatschappij (Deli Company) and Senembah, the region's leading tobacco producers, as well as the Handels Vereeniging 'Amsterdam' (HVA, Trading Association 'Amsterdam') and the Rubber Cultuur-Maatschappij Amsterdam (RCMA, Rubber Cultivation Company 'Amsterdam'), market leaders in rubber. The other two were subsidiaries of the American giants US Rubber and Goodyear of which the latter ran the huge Wingfoot plantation, which measured 14,000 hectares on its own.

The second category of estates was made up of clusters under authority of a management agency entrusted with operating a whole range of estates. The largest two clusters were administered by respectively Harrisons & Crosfield, the leading British managing agency in Malaya's rubber industry, and the Belgian Socfin concern (Société Financière des Caoutchoucs), which specialized in palm oil. The top six also included the prestigious Nederlandsche Handel-Maatschappij (NHM, Netherlands Trading Society) and another three British managing agencies: Gruemitt, Reid & Co., Sandilands Buttery and Guthrie. Between them, the 12 largest estate operators (the six large estate owners identified above and the top six management agency clusters) accounted for 75 per cent of total planted area. This testifies to a considerable degree of oligopolization in North Sumatra's estate agriculture.

Estate production was almost exclusively geared towards exports, and volumes recorded for the three major commodities – rubber, palm oil, tobacco – above all reflect responses to market prospects abroad (Table 2). The rubber

4 Calculations are based on a list of all estates in North Sumatra compiled in 1958, after the seizure of Dutch property but prior to nationalization.

sector offers the best illustration of the highly favourable situation in world markets for major Indonesian export commodities during most of the 1950s. Indonesia supplied slightly more than one-third of world exports of natural rubber, which then still exceeded exports of synthetic rubber by at least 50 per cent. The 700 estates operating in Indonesia at the time were responsible for approximately one-third of Indonesia's total rubber exports. Among them, the 230 or so estates in Deli delivered approximately one-half of Indonesia's estate rubber produce (Bank Indonesia 1958:154-62; Mackie 1971:29, 31). Simple arithmetic tells us that the Deli rubber estates alone accounted for more than 5 per cent (one-eighteenth) of total world supplies of natural rubber.

Exports from the Deli rubber estates surpassed pre-war levels already in 1951 and continued to expand during the Korean War boom. Although prospects in overseas markets remained favourable, production was stabilized in the mid-1950s at about four-fifths of the level that had been reached in 1953. In 1956 Bank Indonesia stated in its annual report that 'the improvement of export markets was not sufficient to halt the process of decreasing production, actually a process of dis-investment or de-capitalization' (Bank Indonesia 1956:17). In 1956 and 1957, prices began to fall following a tendency towards recession in the United States and Western Europe. The overall price index for Indonesian exports commodities, which to a considerable extent reflected the price of rubber, fell by almost 9 per cent in 1956 and 1957 (Bank of Indonesia 1956:17, 1958:12).

North Sumatra had a near-monopoly in supplying Indonesia's large-scale exports of palm oil, a branch of export agriculture which had expanded exceptionally fast during the immediate pre-war decade. Rehabilitation of the sector in the early 1950s in response to a vigorous external demand restored production and exports to about three-quarters of the level which had been achieved in the late 1930s. Physical constraints such as the ageing of trees dating from the 1930s effectively precluded a further enlargement of output, although market prospects remained favourable at least up to 1956. In 1957, two-thirds of total exports were destined for the Netherlands (Bank Indonesia 1958:164-5, 1960:163-4).

In the colonial past, the Deli estate area had gained an international reputation because of the Deli tobacco leaves used worldwide in cigar-making. By the 1950s, however, Deli tobacco had been surpassed by rubber and palm oil in the Deli estate area itself and dwarfed by tobacco exports originating elsewhere in Indonesia. Almost all tobacco estates were owned and operated by four large Dutch producers, including the Deli Maatschappij and Senembah. The restoration of Dutch colonial authority by military means in the late 1940s had facilitated a speedy recovery of production to a level approaching one-half of the pre-war level but in the 1950s, the pattern of production became highly erratic with sudden peaks alternating with sharp drops in output, for instance in 1952 and 1956. Foreign demand remained strong and an extension of acreage and higher yields should have made it possible to raise output again. Nevertheless, by 1957, total production of Deli tobacco amounted to only one-quarter of its pre-war level and Deli accounted for a mere 20 per cent of total exports of tobacco from Indonesia. Almost the entire harvest was auctioned in Amsterdam (Bank Indonesia 1958:181-2, 1960:177-9).

The response to external market signals differed significantly by export crop and it is tempting to explain differences in export performance by looking at differences in nationality of owners. Did tobacco fare worse than rubber because of more adverse conditions of production on Dutch estates compared to plantations with British or American owners? Why did physical constraints cause stagnation also at the Belgian-owned palm oil estates? Did the exceptionally strong demand for rubber in the world market turn the scale? Such questions can only be addressed by combining incentives from the world market with internal factors affecting estate production at the time.

Changing conditions of production at foreign-owned estates in North Sumatra during the 1950s included a dramatic increase in labour unrest as a result of trade union militancy and rising expectations. Measured by numbers of working-days lost due to strikes, labour unrest increased steadily in the region between 1952 and 1956 (Table 3). In April 1956, virtually all estate workers in North Sumatra went on strike for two days as negotiations between unions and AVROS broke down (*Antara*, 13-4-1956 and 14-4-1956). But in December 1956, martial law was imposed in the region in response to the failed coup attempt by Colonel Simbolon. Emergency conditions were prolonged by the nationwide martial law imposed in March 1957 under the Dutch-language label SOB (Staat van Oorlog en Beleg, 'State of War and Occupation'). Labour unrest did decline steeply, but this obviously did not imply that tensions between management and labour had vanished.

The most common source of disturbances in labour relations concerned wages and there is abundant evidence of complaints by employers about 'exorbitant' wage demands made by militant labour unions. In 1953, to cite but one example, the rubber companies reported to the Minister of Agriculture, Moh. Sardjan, that workers were demanding an increase from Rp 2.50 to Rp 4.80 per kilogram, since costs of living corresponded to Rp 4.50 per kilogram. The higher wage rate, however, would be very close to the international unit price for rubber, which oscillated between Rp 4.80 and Rp 5.20 depending on the quality of the product.[5] Low wage rates in combination with rising costs of living caused an exodus from the estate labour force into smallholder pro-

5 Arsip Nasional Republik Indonesia (ANRI), Jakarta: Kabinet Presiden RI 1950-1959, 1586.

duction when international prices were rising. The acute shortage of labour at the estates was aggravated by such problems as widespread theft, lack of spare parts and loss of equipment (Pelzer 1971:153-4).

Another source of conflict at the estates in North Sumatra was the so-called 'agrarian question'. This concerned occupations of estate land by local dwellers claiming that their traditional (*adat*) rights superseded those based on concessions granted by the colonial authorities, especially if no planting had taken place. The Indonesian government was in a very difficult position, sympathizing with locals but also obliged to protect property rights of foreign investors. The Wilopo cabinet (March 1952-June 1953), even had to step down after a violent confrontation on this issue. Negotiations with AVROS dragged on for years without tangible result. In 1953, no less than 130,000 hectares of tobacco land had been claimed of which at least one-quarter was used on a permanent basis by villagers (*Antara*, 1-1-1953 and 13-4-1953). On 1 October 1956, the second Ali Sastroamidjojo cabinet introduced emergency legislation to forestall new occupations but the law was repealed already on 13 December after vehement protest from the North Sumatra chapter of the ruling Partai Nasional Indonesia (PNI, Indonesian National Party). Needless to say, this did little to inspire confidence among foreign estate owners (*Waspada*, 2-10-1956 and 13-10-1956).

Estate area in permanent use by local peasants continued to increase in 1955 and 1956 and also after the imposition of military rule in the region in December 1956 (Table 4).[6] Only in September 1957 was an agreement reached by which the estate owners conceded to release land that was not considered essential for continued profitable operations. However, implementation was held up by the takeovers shortly afterwards. But the 'agrarian question' did not disappear after the seizure of Dutch estates. The area under permanent settlement by squatters continued to increase even though local police authorities in Medan were attempting to prevent this from happening (Pelzer 1982:165-6). It was more an issue of use of land than wresting control from Dutch owners of land.

Whether or not the Deli estates were plagued by difficulties in production, this was clearly a time of substantial profits. Annual dividend payments by Dutch estate companies in the early years of the decade oscillated around 10 per cent. At RCMA in 1953, net profits even reached 28.5 per cent of gross turnover but this is likely to have been exceptional (*Antara*, 8-6-1954). Scattered

6 It is important here to distinguish between temporary and permanent settlements, as well as between planted area and land held under concession by the estates. This may explain deviations compared to higher figures mentioned in the literature, for instance, a loss of control over 145,000 hectares suffered by the estates when agreeing to land partition in 1951 (Pelzer 1982:152).

and incomplete data on permits to transfer net profits from Indonesia to foreign owners regularly include leading North Sumatra estates of both Dutch and non-Dutch nationality. RCMA, for instance, dispatched Rp 5.3 million in August 1955 and Rp 7.3 million in October 1956, whereas the small Cultuur-Maatschappij Oostkust (Cultivation Company 'East Coast [of Sumatra]') sent Rp 1.6 million in November 1955 and Rp 2.6 million in March 1956. Among foreign non-Dutch estate owners, Goodyear was frequently granted permission to transfer substantial amounts of profits, for instance Rp 9.1 million in September 1955, Rp 4.3 million in January 1956, Rp 6.0 million in November 1956, Rp 7.8 million in December 1956 and Rp 27.3 million in November 1958.[7] As late as in 1958, a gross profit margin of 66 per cent was reported in the Indonesian rubber industry (Pelzer 1971:165). Short-tem profits took precedence above investment in long-term efficiency in business strategies pursued at foreign-owned estates, both in Deli and elsewhere in Indonesia.

A separate management issue concerned the elevation of Indonesians into staff functions, that is, Indonesianisasi in the narrow sense of the term. The Finec (Financieele en Economische Overeenkomst, Financial and Economic Agreement), attached to the conditions under which the Netherlands acknowledged Indonesian Independence in 1949, required Dutch enterprises to include 'qualified Indonesians in management and staff (also boards of directors) of the companies as soon as possible' with the aim that, after 'a reasonable time', the majority of the supervisory management staff of the firms would consist of Indonesian citizens (*Round Table Conference* 1950). But no targets or timetables were laid down and virtually the sole means of the Indonesian authorities to enforce implementation was by restricting entry permits for staff employees recruited overseas. According to international observers, the rate of Indonesianisasi at Dutch-owned estates was disturbingly low.[8] This was to have far-reaching repercussions for the management of the estates after the takeovers.

No survey of the economic situation in North Sumatra during the 1950s is complete without mentioning the controversy surrounding the refinery at Pangkalan Brandan, owned by the Anglo-Dutch oil giant BPM (Bataafsche Petroleum Maatschappij, Batavian Petroleum Company). With consent of the Allied command, the refinery facilities had been surrendered by the Japanese army to the PERBOEMI (Persatoean Boeroeh Minjak Indonesia, Union of Indonesian Oil Workers) in July 1946. Operations were continued, albeit far below capacity, by the Indonesian military forces under the name of Tambang Minjak Sumatera Utara (TMSU, North Sumatra Oil Mining). The

7 Bank Indonesia, Jakarta: LAAPLN (Lembaga Alat-Alat Pembajaran Luar Negri) 13, no. 41.
8 Mackie 1971:34. See also Van de Kerkhof 2005 and his contribution to this volume.

BPM demanded the property back but the government refused, claiming that BPM had forfeited its rights when ordering the facilities to be destroyed in the face of the Japanese invasion in 1942. In 1952, an official advice to return the Pangkalan Brandan refinery to BPM met with indignation in Parliament and was followed by negotiations that remained fruitless, as a joint venture was not considered a sensible option by BPM. By 1954, the labour force had declined to 1,200 workers, excluding over 700 on non-active status, which was far less than the 3,000 reported in 1946. In 1956, a serious conflict erupted between the labour union and management about alleged abuse of authority by superintendent Djohan, who had been appointed by the government. Djohan was said to secretly favour a surrender of TMSU to BPM and his wife was even rumoured to obtain consumer goods directly through the BPM office at Medan.[9] Djohan was replaced by Ibnu Sutowo, the later chief executive of the Indonesian state oil company Pertamina. Although the oil refinery at Pangkalan Brandan contributed only marginally to the economic performance of North Sumatra, the long-drawn and unresolved dispute between the Indonesian government and BPM worsened a sphere already infected by confrontation and conflict.

Pengambilalihan and afterwards

The actual takeover of estates in North Sumatra began on 7 December 1957, and was modelled on the action taken by the local trade union at the Jakarta office of the Koninklijke Paketvaart Maatschappij (KPM, Royal Packet Company) four days earlier. The government was conspicuously quick to wrest the initiative from the unions and ordered all seized estates to be placed under direct military supervision. The purpose was twofold, namely to legalize the 'temporary' takeovers retroactively and to forestall control over vital economic assets by communist-inspired trade unions (Feith 1962:584). In a very short time span, effective command of operations at hundreds of agricultural estates passed from the Dutch managers to local trade union leaders and from there to local military authorities. The seized estates were brought under the umbrella of the Pusat Perkebunan Negara-Baru (PPN-Baru, New Centre for State Estates). The Minister of Agriculture, Sadjarwo, emphasized that all should be done 'to safeguard the continuity of operations' (*untuk kepentingan kelangsungan perusahaan* (*Merdeka*, 11-12-1957).

There was a massive exodus of Dutchmen from North Sumatra during the first several months of 1958. Management of daily operations was by and

9 ANRI, Jakarta: Kabinet Presiden RI 1950-1959, 1531, 1533, 1574.

large taken over by senior Indonesian employees, usually men with records of long standing with the estate. The GAPPERSU or SPA, which replaced AVROS with an Indonesian of Batak origin as its chairman, hastened to organize crash courses in estate management, but it can safely be assumed that much of the following managerial decisions were improvised.[10] One international observer concluded that 'the new managers performed quite commendably, but excessive bureaucracy and deteriorating conditions have evidently undermined their morale recently [in the early 1960s]' (Mackie 1971:34; see also Mackie 1961).

Approximately the same volume of rubber was exported in 1958 as in 1957 and no 'large-scale decline' was reported in production during the first quarter of the year (Table 2; Bank Indonesia 1958:14). For the year as a whole, however, GAPPERSU statistics show a decline of 7 per cent in output, from 158,433 tons in 1957 to 146,957 tons in 1958, as well as a dramatic 25 per cent decline in export revenue.[11] The decline in revenue occurred despite maintaining export volumes by utilizing built-up inventories. Rubber prices had started to fall in late 1957 and continued to do so throughout the first two quarters of 1958. Main culprit was slackening demand in the United States and, to a lesser extent, in Western Europe, whereas demand in for instance China was increasing (Bank Indonesia 1959:11-8). The poor export performance for Deli estate rubber in 1958 was caused by an external factor, the fall in international prices, rather than by internal factors related to changes in management.

A separate problem with potential long-term repercussions was the decline in output in 1958, which was not halted by the recovery of international prices during the third and fourth quarters of the year. Meanwhile, the share of Deli in total estate rubber production in Indonesia remained the same at around 60 per cent, which implies that problems in production were not significantly different in North Sumatra compared to rubber estates elsewhere in Indonesia (Bank Indonesia 1959:184-5). The unfavourable performance in production must be attributed to the adjustments accompanying the transfer of management of estates all over Indonesia in 1958.

The analysis can be extended to the other two main export commodities of North Sumatra. Production in palm oil also fell, by 8 per cent, but, again, export volumes remained by and large constant whereas export revenues dropped by 13 per cent. The Netherlands remained the largest buyer although its share had fallen from 66 per cent in 1957 to 52 per cent in 1958 (Table 2;

10 For a rare but brief description of a similar situation at a seized Dutch-owned sugar factory, see Pipit Rochijat 1985.

11 Bank Agro, Medan: GAPPERSU, statistical document marked 'Secret' (*Rahasia*), Dec. 1958.

The main office of the organization of rubber estate owners, AVROS (Algemeene Vereeniging van Rubberplanters ter Oostkust van Sumatra), later GAPPERSU (Gabungan Pengusaha Perkebunan Sumatera Utara), in downtown Medan (KITLV 14101)

Bank Indonesia 1959:205, 1960:163-4). The situation in the palm oil industry in 1958 thus resembled the one prevailing in the rubber industry. In both cases, it is worth noting that a large number of estates, that is, those with non-Dutch foreign owners, were not at all affected by a transfer of management.

The situation in tobacco was a peculiar one. Exports were partially entrusted by PPN-Baru to the Deli Maatschappij and Senembah, but these two firms insisted on holding capital offshore as the produce originated from estates which were still their legal property. As a consequence, the auctioning of Deli tobacco was transferred from Amsterdam to Bremen (Bank Indonesia 1959:205). According to the planters' organization, in 1958 output fell by 23 per cent; other sources cite an even greater decline, corresponding to one-third of the level of production in 1957. Reported losses in export revenue corresponded to an average of the two figures quoted, namely 26 per cent (Bank Indonesia 1960:177-9). Here poor export performance was largely caused by internal factors generated by the takeover of the Dutch-owned estates.

A decline in output reflects less input of factors of production or a lower productivity. In the region's agricultural estate sector as a whole, the labour force declined only marginally, from 195,900 workers in January 1958 to 192,250 by January 1959. Almost all people laid off were female workers which raised the number of dependants to be supported by the male workers provided the women stayed on the estate. Interestingly, the number of children to be fed from the estates increased at the same time. The sudden and unprepared transfer of management brought a drop in efficiency and productivity in the course of 1958.

Qualitative assessments about estate management immediately after the takeovers are invariably highly negative and corroborate the documented decline in production and export incomes. Yet, as the cases of rubber and palm oil show, there were also important adverse external factors at play which bore no relation at all to the takeovers. In addition, it is important to assess whether the adverse internal factor, associated with the transfer of management, was of a short- or long-run nature. At the end of 1958, Bank Indonesia optimistically concluded that 'the control of Dutch enterprises and new channels for foreign trade do not present a great obstacle anymore' (Bank Indonesia 1959:20).

Although under Indonesian military supervision, the estates remained legally under Dutch ownership throughout the entire year of 1958. The law on nationalization of appropriated Dutch property was promulgated on 27 December 1958 and applied retroactively back to 3 December 1957. It covered 98 estates in North Sumatra, including 54 in rubber, 22 in tobacco and 13 in palm oil. The Deli Maatschappij, HVA, NHM, RCMA and Senembah were among those affected (Pelzer 1982:169). A second wave of nationalization was legally effectuated in February 1959, when numerous estates of the Deli Maatschappij became the property of the Indonesian state. The list included Bandar Klippa, Helvetia, Kwala Bingei, Mariendal, Rotterdam, Saentis, Tandom and Timbang Langkat (*Antara*, 25-2-1959).

Adverse conditions continued to haunt production also in 1959 but international prices now rose, especially for rubber in the recovering American market. Production and distribution remained under tight control of local military authorities. Significantly, three British-owned estates were also seized when their concessions came up for renewal (*Antara*, 16-2-1959). Harrisons & Crosfield, one of the managing agencies affected, did not seem particularly discouraged but resumed operations at another estate, Aek Tarum, which had been closed for several months due to problems with security (*Antara*, 2-10-1959).

Export volumes of rubber and palm oil fell by respectively 7 and 9 per cent in 1959, despite the improved market conditions abroad. Continuing 'setbacks' in production at the rubber estates and 'disturbances of law and order' in the region were held responsible for the failure of supply to react more vigorously to the improvement in demand conditions. The downward trend in production for a favourable market was declared a matter of 'concern' to the Indonesian authorities (Table 2; Bank Indonesia 1960:11, 151-7, 163-4). In the tobacco industry, persistent legal disputes with the one-time Dutch estate-owners overshadowed performance, but it was later reported that output under control of PPN-Baru in Deli had increased by as much as 14 per cent in 1959 compared to the year before (Bank Negara Indonesia 1968:209).

In 1959, a legal court case in Germany became the test case for the international recognition sought by Indonesia with respect to the nationalization of Dutch-owned estates. The Deli Maatschappij and Senembah had protested against intended auctioning in Germany of tobacco from their one-time estates, and the case now came before the *Oberlandesgericht* (high court) in Bremen. Three experts on international law (one British, one Belgian and one from Switzerland) were called in by the Dutch side to assert that the nationalizations could not be connected to the Round Table Conference agreements of 1949, which had been unilaterally abrogated by Indonesia in 1956. The Dutch party therefore demanded a restoration of ownership rights rather than compensatory payment in compliance with what was envisaged in the law of nationalization of 27 December 1958.

The Indonesian side responded with a 200-page elaboration on why the nationalization should be seen in the context of decolonization. The response included a reprint of Van den Brand's booklet on colonial exploitation from 1903, *De millioenen uit Deli*, a chapter by former *Reichsbank* President Hjalmar Schacht on current economic problems in Indonesia and referenced cases where German property in the Netherlands had been nationalized without compensation (*Antara*, 21-7-1959 and 1-8-1959). The high court in Bremen interpreted the nationalizations of Dutch estates 'in the context of liberation from the colonial power' (*dalam rangka usaha melepaskan diri daripada kekuasaan kolonial*). Nationalization (*onteigening*) of property of 'those who before formed part of the colonial regime' (*mereka jang dahulu termasuk golongan pendjadjah (Kolonialherren)*) served the interests of 'a change in the social and economic structure of a new nation' (*perubahan struktur sosial dan ekonomi negara jang baru*) (*Antara*, 26-9-1959). The Dutch had lost their case, the Indonesian tobacco fetched a good price and revenues accrued to PPN-Baru and its local associate, the Deutsch-Indonesische Tabaks-Handelsgesellschaft (German-Indonesian Tobacco Trading Company). In April 1960, Deli tobacco was for the first time sent directly from the port of Belawan near Medan to Bremen.

In December 1959, the Dutch government officially protested against the nationalizations demanding that the matter should be submitted to jurisdiction under the International Court of Justice in The Hague, as the Indonesian actions were in violation of the principles of international law. This was not acceptable to the Indonesian government, which felt strengthened by the ruling in Bremen (*Antara*, 21-12-1959).

There is an extreme paucity of information about management practices in the years immediately after the takeover and nationalization of Dutch estates. In 1960, the Indonesian authorities acknowledged that 'the transfer of management resulting from nationalization had to go through a consolidation stage, consuming in effect, a period of one to two years' (Bank Indonesia 1960:15). Due to a lack of more detailed information, we must review the global dimensions of the estate industry in North Sumatra in 1960, that is, two full years after the takeovers.

In 1955, the estate labour force had numbered about 212,000 persons but, as mentioned above, by early 1959 this number had fallen to 192,000. In 1960, however, a partial restoration of the labour force had taken place as the total number was now 202,000. The increase in the labour force suggests that conditions in production were returning to normality. A similar impression may be gathered from data on planted area where rubber and tobacco continued to gain at the expense of palm oil. In 1960, the total planted area in North Sumatra was back at approximately the same level as in 1938, that is, before any land occupations had taken place (AVROS 1956: Tables I and VIII; GAPPERSU 1960: Tables I and IX).

Major changes had, of course, occurred in patterns of ownership. Three-fifths of the estate industry, measured by numbers or planted area, were now controlled by the Indonesian state (Table 5). Dutch ownership had vanished altogether but the Belgian share in total was largely the same as in 1958. British and American estates had become slightly less important as some rubber estates had passed into the hands of the Indonesian government upon expiration of concessions. Emphasis had shifted away from single large estate-owning enterprises to managing agency networks. Foremost in the former category were US Rubber and Goodyear, whereas Socfin and Harrisons & Crosfield took the lead in the latter category. Between them, these four estate groups accounted for 22 per cent of all estates and 30 per cent of total planted area.

The new dominant player was the Indonesian government. PPN-Baru assumed responsibility for 104 estates and a planted area of more than 200,000 hectares. The estates in North Sumatra were arranged so as to form nine clusters labelled SUMUT (Sumatera Utara, North Sumatra) I through IX. They varied considerably in size, ranging from the huge SUMUT I, with nearly 42,000 hectares, to the small SUMUT VIII, which covered a mere 3,000 hectares.[12] The clustering resembled previous ownership patterns even if the correspondence was less than perfect. SUMUT I was all tobacco, dominated by one-time Deli and Senembah estates, but former Deli plantations were also found in SUMUT II, SUMUT V and SUMUT VII. Most HVA estates ended up in SUMUT III, whereas SUMUT IV largely comprised former RCMA estates. Several of the older state-owned estates (PPN-Lama, 'Old PPN') were squeezed into SUMUT IX together with additional RCMA plantations. The clustering represented considerations of continuity for administrative convenience and geographical proximity.

In 1961, the structure of PPN-Baru was altered and a regrouping was carried out based on type of crop. As a result, the correspondence with one-time Dutch patterns of ownership disappeared. On this occasion, a series of complaints was lodged with the central authorities in Jakarta concerning management abuses. The situation at the estates was said to have become so chaotic that it all amounted to a power struggle for personal gain (*keadaan perkebunan begitu chaosnja sehingga objek ini mendjadi rebutan kekuasaan untuk mendapat kekajaan*).[13] Such statements corroborate the impressions created above that the morale of the Indonesian managers was already in decline during the early 1960s.

As it turned out, the downward trend in production of the region's major export items was not continued into the 1960s. Total output of all rubber estates in Indonesia was at about the same level in 1964 as in 1959 whereas exports of palm oil had risen by 30 per cent over the same period. Deli tobacco suffered severe setbacks in production in 1960 and 1961, but from 1962 roughly the same volume was produced as in 1959 (Bank Indonesia 1968:162-4, 177-8, 204-5).

12 Bank Agro, Medan: GAPPERSU, 'Rapat umum anggota-anggota', 10-5-1962.

13 ANRI, Jakarta: BAPEKAN, 43 ['Verslag ringkas perkembangan/pertumbuhan PPN-Baru Sumatera Utara oleh majoor Abd. Moeis'].

Conclusion

By building a bridge between the situation before and after the takeover and nationalization of Dutch estates in North Sumatra, we gain a fuller understanding of the process of economic decolonization at the regional level in Indonesia. Various continuities and discontinuities may be identified and it is useful to distinguish between external and internal factors determining economic performance in the immediate aftermath of the takeovers.

The estate sector of North Sumatra remained a highly profitable branch of export agriculture and one of the foremost earners of foreign exchange for Indonesia. Total production capacity, as indicated by planted area and labour force, was restored relatively soon after the dramatic transition of management and ownership in the late 1950s. The structure of the production apparatus remained oligopolistic with a relatively small number of conglomerates or clusters. Problems of labour unrest and conflicts about land use also survived the expulsion of Dutch estate owners. Even the clustering of estates for administrative purposes after the takeovers displayed some continuity with the earlier situation.

The discontinuities were far more visible, especially for estate owners in the Netherlands and Dutch management and supervisory staff. From being a minor player in the industry, the Indonesian state now emerged as the most powerful estate owner. Management and supervision at the formerly Dutch-owned estates were done by Indonesian nationals, military men and senior employees at the estates. Management practices are said to have deteriorated sharply but the evidence is scant and biased. Exports of tobacco and palm oil, finally, were redirected to new destinations whereas rubber continued to be supplied to the international market at large.

Economic performance was determined by a juxtaposition of external and internal factors. Prospects in foreign markets were generally favourable with the notable exception of the period between 1956 and mid-1958, when lower prices caused a drop in export revenues for rubber and palm oil. Internal problems led to a stubborn downward tendency in production from the mid-1950s, which was aggravated by the transfer of management in 1958, but did not continue far into the 1960s. The external factors were best for rubber and the internal factors were worst for tobacco, whereas palm oil occupied an intermediary position. It is no coincidence that the tobacco estates, where we encounter the highest concentration of Dutch ownership, encountered the greatest difficulties even before the takeovers. The transfer of management in 1958 brought a sharp but short-lived disruption that cannot easily be directly associated with the extreme predicaments in the Indonesian economy several years later, in the mid-1960s.

Table 1. Estates in North Sumatra in 1958 by nationality

Nationality	Estates number	%	Planted area hectares	%
Dutch	94	40	161,444	43
British	59	25	69,120	18.5
Belgian	38	16	62,062	16.5
Indonesian	23	10	29,597	8
American	9	4.5	41,682	11
Other	10	4.5	11,303	3
Total	233	100	375,208	100

Source: Bank Agro, Medan: GAPPERSU, 'Inquiry into the nationality of individual SPA-member companies', 5-11-1958.

Table 2. Production of major crops at the estates in North Sumatra, 1938-1959

(tons)

	Rubber	Palm oil	Tobacco
1938	82,437	217,841	13,786
–			
1948	55,931	55,565	1,175
1949	98,732	116,829	5,587
1950	91,301	126,247	4,192
1951	99,379	117,057	4,000
1952	147,808	140,644	2,539
1953	156,555	154,588	3,588
1954	145,888	162,971	3,211
1955	137,225	165,413	3,457
1956	139,204	164,569	3,052
1957	130,149	160,123	3,260
1958	130,038	147,528	2,518
1959	120,474	134,826	

Sources: AVROS 1956: Tables II, III; GAPPERSU 1960: Tables II, III.
Note: Post-Independence data and data from 1938 are not fully comparable due to the change in territorial designations. Post-Independence data include Aceh and Tapanuli. Comparison with other data suggest that these figures, despite begin designated as production statistics, actually refer to exports (Bank Agro, Medan: GAPPERSU, statistical document marked 'Secret' (*Rahasia*), December 1958). No data on tobacco output for 1959.

Table 3. Labour unrest at the estates in North Sumatra, 1952-1959

	No. of strikes	Working days lost
1952	65	193,990
1953	115	341,481
1954	287	356,866
1955	500	445,700
1956	729	559,665
1957	231	90,349
1958	25	9,110
1959	84	23,430

Sources: AVROS 1956: Table XII; GAPPERSU 1960: Table XII.

Table 4. Permanent occupation by local inhabitants of estate lands in North Sumatra, 1954-1960

Date	Area (hectares)	Date (hectares)	Area
12 June 1954	79,850	31 Dec. 1958	126,266
31 Dec. 1955	92,796	31 Dec. 1959	131,418
31 Dec. 1956	114,234	30 Sept. 1960	123,711
31 Dec. 1957	122,801		

Source: GAPPERSU 1960: Table XIII.

Table 5. Estates in North Sumatra in 1962 by nationality

Nationality	Estates number	%	Planted area hectares	%
Indonesian	149	61	236,122	60
British	45	18	52,250	13
Belgian	35	14	57,844	14.5
American	9	3.5	43,000	11
Other	8	3.5	6,516	1.5
	246	100	396,000	100

Source: Bank Agro, Medan: GAPPERSU, 'Rapat umum anggota-anggota GAPPERSU', 10-5-1962.

Note: The seven estates of US Rubber, for which planted area is not given, are assumed to be of the same size as in 1958, about 24,000 hectares.

References

AVROS
1956 *Statistische gegevens*. Medan: Algemeene Vereeniging van Rubberplanters ter Oostkust van Sumatra.

Bangun, Tridah
1987 *Dr. T.D. Pardede 70 tahun; Pejuang-patriot*. Jakarta: Haji Masagung.

Bank Indonesia
1956-1960 *Report for the year 1955/1956 ... 1959/1960*. Djakarta: Kolff.
1968 *Laporan tahun pembukuan 1960/1965*. Djakarta: Gita Karja.

Bank Negara Indonesia (Unit I)
1968 *Report for the financial years 1966/1967*. Djakarta: Pertjetakan Negara.

Feith, Herbert
1962 *The decline of constitutional democracy in Indonesia*. Ithaca, NY: Cornell University Press. [Reprint Jakarta: Equinox, 2007.]

GAPPERSU
1960 *Angka-angka statistik*. Medan: Gabungan Pengusaha Perkebunan Sumatera/Sumatra Planters' Association.

Goedhart, A.
1999 *Eerherstel van de plantage; Uit de geschiedenis van de Handels Vereeniging 'Amsterdam', 1879-1983*. Amsterdam: Albini.

Hadinoto, Soejono
1949 *Ekonomi Indonesia; Dari ekonomi kolonial ke ekonomi nasional*. Djakarta: Jajasan Pembangunan.

Kerkhof, Jasper van de
2005 '*Indonesianisasi* of Dutch economic interests, 1930-1960; The case of Internatio', *Bijdragen tot de Taal-, Land- en Volkenkunde* 161:181-209.

Lindblad, J. Thomas
2002 'The importance of *Indonesianisasi* during the transition from the 1930s to the 1960s', *Itinerario. European Journal of Overseas History* 26-3/4:51-72.
2008 *Bridges to new business; The economic decolonization of Indonesia*. Leiden: KITLV Press.

Mackie, J.A.C.
1961 'Indonesia's government estates and their masters', *Pacific Affairs* 34:337-60.
1971 'The Indonesian economy, 1950-1963', in: Bruce Glassburner (ed.), *The economy of Indonesia*, pp. 16-69. Ithaca, NY: Cornell University Press. [Reprint Jakarta: Equinox, 2007.]

Pelzer, Karl J.
1971 'The agricultural foundation', in: Bruce Glassburner (ed.), *The economy of Indonesia*, pp. 128-61. Ithaca, NY: Cornell University Press. [Reprint Jakarta: Equinox, 2007.]
1982 *Planters against peasants; The agrarian struggle in East Sumatra, 1947-1958*. 's Gravenhage: Nijhoff. [KITLV, Verhandelingen 97.]

Pohan, Syafruddin
1992 *Achmad Bakrie; Sebuah potret kerja keras, kejujuran dan keberhasilan.* Jakarta: Kelompok Usaha Bakrie.
Rochijat, Pipit
1985 'Am I PKI or non-PKI?', *Indonesia* 40:37-56.
Round Table Conference
1950 *Results as accepted in the second plenary meeting held on 2 November 1949 in the Ridderzaal at The Hague.* The Hague/Djakarta: Kolff.
Sutter, John O.
1959 *Indonesianisasi; A historical survey of the role of politics in the institutions of a changing economy from the Second World War to the eve of the general election, 1940-1955.* PhD thesis, Cornell University, Ithaca, NY.
Zwaag, J. van der
1991 *Verloren tropische zaken; De opkomst en ondergang van de Nederlandse handel- en cultuurmaatschappijen in het voormalige Nederlands-Indië.* Meppel: Feniks Pers.

Tri Chandra Apriyanto

Decolonization in the Jember estate economy

On every brick
neatly structured each European building
for certain there are drops of sweat and tear of
the peasant from South countries

The expression quoted above was apparently used at an International Youth Conference in Yugoslavia in the 1950s.[1] It succinctly expresses the direct link between the colonial past and the post-colonial situation in the agricultural estate sector of the Indonesian economy. This contribution reviews the development of Western, mainly Dutch-owned private estates in East Java during the Revolutionary and immediate post-Independence period against the historical background of the policies pursued by the Dutch colonial government prior to the Japanese occupation. Our focus is on the fundamental changes which took place as a logical consequence of the proclamation of Indonesia's Independence on 17 August 1945. Insight into the development of the estates is deepened by a case study about the tobacco and coffee plantations in Jember, the southern half of Besuki, the region in the easternmost corner of Java.

Decolonization in the estate economy of Jember implied, amongst others, the takeover and subsequent nationalization of Dutch-owned properties. The successive movement towards such radical measures reflected the views of the founding fathers of the Republic of Indonesia with respect to the future role of foreign-owned estates in the national economy. The public debate at the time of the Indonesian Revolution and shortly afterwards was not only about future social and economic developments in Indonesia, but also about

1 Interview with Syamsir Muhammad, former secretary-general of Barisan Tani Indonesia (BTI, Indonesian Peasant Front), 26-4-2005.

political substance and its ideological foundation.[2]

This contribution consists of three sections, apart from a brief introductory note on the historical background. The first section surveys the public debate on estate agriculture during the Indonesian Revolution and traces the ideological roots of the various strands of the debate to the late colonial era. The following section pays attention to peasant movements in the late 1940s and early 1950s, demonstrating that attitudes of radical labour often deviated from the strategies adopted by the Republican government. The third and final section is devoted to the case study about estate agriculture in Jember and draws on information from a variety of primary sources.

The historical background can be sketched briefly as follows. Initially, private Dutch estate companies rented land for five years only from local residents for the cultivation of so-called post-harvest (*naoogst*) tobacco, simultaneously buying up tobacco from the local population. At a later stage, the Dutch firms requested planting (*opstal*) rights.[3] In 1870, the Dutch colonial government issued new legislation on land use and ownership (Agrarische Wet). Eventually, all owners of private estates acquired *erfpacht* rights (Landbouw-Maatschappij Oud Djember 1909; *Regeerings-Almanak* 1879, 1882, 1889).

From 1870, large parts of Besuki, in particular in Jember, were increasingly dominated by estates (*ondernemingen*) and a new colonial town emerged in Jember (Tri Chandra Apriyanto 2005). There were two groups of entrepreneurs or tobacco planters in the region. The first one consisted of planters known as *ondernemers*, who ran their business in cooperation with local peasants. They began by renting land from local residents, while also employing the owners of the land as labourers. Later, they provided seed and equipment to producers among the local peasant population. The harvest was acquired and exported by the *ondernemer*. This system differed markedly from the practice applied by the second group of planters, known as *opkopers* (purveyors), who had been less long involved in production. They bought tobacco harvested by local peasants, enabling drying and storage of the tobacco before being exported internationally. The practice of *opkoper* gave rise to a new, separate category of agents working on commission, the so-called *borgen* (security), in Madurese labelled *bandols*.[4] The two groups competed about 'exploiting' land in Besuki. Nevertheless, all estate business, whether carried out by *ondernemer*

2 This draws on critical comments by Professor Taufik Abdullah.

3 Arsip Nasional Republik Indonesia (ANRI), Jakarta: Gouvernementsbesluiten 52, 29/2 1860 no. 50; 54, 3/4 1860 no. 26; 57, 1863: no. 46.

4 De Jonge 1984:188-96. The presence of agents implies that a system of 'colonialization' took place that altered the social structure of the mass of peasants (Memmi 1967). A modern organization of cultivation also emerged, which included research institutes and labour recruitment agencies (Edy Burhan Arifin 1989).

or *opkoper*, involved a large sum of capital and was conducted in compliance with the policies pursued by the colonial government. Such was the situation at Independence.

Public debate during the Indonesian Revolution

Before the proclamation of Independence, there was no serious discussion among the Indonesian political elite about the future role of the agricultural estate sector. The desire for Independence dominated the discourse, whether this discourse was about social, economic or political matters. Yet the problems facing the estates in the late colonial and Japanese periods were manifold and urgently needed to be addressed. The sector was not only hit by the worldwide economic depression in the 1930s, but also suffered severe damage during the Japanese occupation. The total damage was estimated at 680 million guilders.[5]

In its attempt to rehabilitate the estate economy, the Republican government initially relied on the legal system inherited from the Dutch. Although Independence had been proclaimed, the political administration still made use of the old colonial legal system. Article 2 of the Republic's constitution even prescribed that the old system of government remain in effect as long as public institutions and regulations had not been altered. The legal and administrative inheritance also surfaced in the establishment on 19 August 1945 of twelve state departments, including one for Prosperity (*Kemakmoeran*) under Soerachman Tjokroadisoerjo, by the conference of the Panitia Persiapan Kemerdekaan Indonesia (PPKI, Committee for the Preparation of Indonesian Independence). The Department for Prosperity was scarcely different from the Departement van Economische Zaken in the colonial bureaucracy. During the first months after Independence, the main task was to execute routine duties performed by the Japanese military government.

During the years immediately after Independence, rehabilitation and recovery of the estates were seriously disturbed by political violence and Dutch military actions. Meanwhile, the Dutch naval blockade prevented access to international trade routes, thus seriously impairing the export trade. The output from the estate companies could not be exported in full and some estates

5 Based on prices of 1942, the government estimated the total war damage at 2,308 million guilders, specified as follows: mining 814 million, estate 680 million, manufacturing 193 million, public transport 172 million, shipping 150 million, real estate and business properties 134 million, port facilities 80 million guilders. The total estimate of the cost of rehabilitation of Dutch companies eventually increased threefold, reaching 5,968 million guilders as expressed in prices of 1947 (Bisuk Siahaan 1996:133).

had stopped producing altogether whilst under Japanese military control.[6] This caused material disadvantage and also had a demoralizing impact.

The task of the government was not easy. During the Indonesian Revolution, there were in fact two state administrations in Indonesia, the Republican government in Yogyakarta and the Dutch-controlled Federal government in Jakarta. This dualism created a fundamental difference in the approach to economic problems, including the future of the Western estates. In February 1946, the Republican government held several conferences to discuss economic matters. The meetings were chaired by Minister of Prosperity Darmawan Mangoenkoesoemo, who had replaced Tjokroadisoerjo. The three key issues concerned food production and distribution, the need for clothing and the status and administration of the estates. This was the first time that the problem of the estates was seriously discussed. At the same time, many peasants around the plantations began occupying estate land, assuming that the owners would not return since they had been defeated in the war.

In May 1946, yet another conference was held in Solo about fundamental economic and political issues such as public finance, price controls, distribution and allocation of labour. The war damage at plantations was again discussed, in particular efforts by the government to rehabilitate the sugar factories. Following this conference, the newly appointed Minister of Prosperity, A.K. Gani, devised a procedure for formulating economic development plans in the medium and long term, respectively two or three and ten years. Such plans also included measures with regard to foreign-owned estates.[7] In April 1947, the Committee of Scholars for Economic Research (Panitia Pemikir Siasat Ekonomi) was formed, with Vice President Moh. Hatta as its chairman. The task of the committee was to advise the government about planning in eight specified areas of economic development. The overall aim was to formulate a 'fundamental basis' for an Indonesian Economic Plan in accordance with Article 33 of the 1945 Constitution, stating that all vital economic activities were to be controlled by the government.[8]

6 The Japanese authorities closed 34 sugar factories in Java in 1943 and another 14 in 1944. This brought severe damage to the rural economy, which so far had been highly dependent on sugar exports. In Besuki, the Japanese closed four sugar factories: Pradjekan (Bondowoso), Djatiroto (Jember), Asembagoes (Situbondo) and Semboro (Jember).

7 Bisuk Siahaan 1996:138. These measures were: takeover of all formerly Dutch government property, nationalization of foreign-owned property considered to be vital, confiscation of Japanese companies as compensation for war damage, return of Dutch companies to their lawful owners after agreement had been reached between the Indonesian and Dutch governments, creation of opportunities for foreign capital investment in Indonesia, and abolition of restrictions on use of private land.

8 Bisuk Siahaan 1996:138-9. The eight areas were: (1) the economy in general, (2) estates, (3) industry, mining and oil, (4) foreign property rights, (5) finance, (6) electricity and public transport, (7) labour, (8) problems in Dutch-occupied territories.

Meanwhile, negotiations about the Linggadjati Agreement (15 November 1946) failed, as the Dutch interpretation remained different from the Indonesian one. On 21 July 1947, in the midst of recovery and rehabilitation, Dutch forces attacked the territory of the Republic by land, sea and air. This military intervention, known in Dutch historiography as the first police action (*eerste politionele actie*), was a long-planned military campaign serving to restore estate areas in Sumatra and Java and retake Dutch companies, thus giving Dutch planters a chance to recover their estates. Besuki was directly affected by the Dutch military attack.[9]

The Republican government had turned to diplomacy, including negotiations with the Dutch about the terms of transfer of sovereignty. This approach was fiercely criticized by Tan Malaka, who strongly opposed diplomacy since Indonesia had already proclaimed its Independence. Tan Malaka designated a new historical era labelled 'Collapsed Diplomacy Season' (*Musim Runtuh Berunding*) as a follow-up to the era known as 'Glorious Battle Season' (*Musim Djaja Bertempur*), which had lasted from 17 August 1945 until 17 March 1946. Two important political negotiations had taken place during the former period, resulting in the Linggadjati and Renville Agreements. According to Tan Malaka, diplomatic negotiation meant 'searching peace at the cost of sovereignty, independence, residence and economic area' (Tan Malaka 2000:14-5). During the 'Glorious Battle Season', all estates, whether property of enemy or friend, became the property of the Republic; during the 'Collapsed Diplomacy Season', however, all foreign estates occupied by peasants were supposed to be returned to their foreign owners.

Peasants were occupying estates that had been abandoned by the owners, tilling the land in order to meet subsistence needs. Although seemingly spontaneous and through local initiative without any national organization, the occupations were supported by nationwide peasant organizations such as Barisan Tani Indonesia (BTI, Indonesian Peasant Front), which aimed at nationalizing all estate land in Indonesia. The Dutch estate companies and the colonial government considered this occupation of land illegal and stigmatized the peasants as political activists. The peasants, however, saw the takeover of estate land as a manifestation of the Republic's sovereignty.

According to Tan Malaka, the Indonesians should fight, just as in the 'Glorious Battle Season', until all estates, mines, transport facilities, factories

9 According to Syamsir Muhammad, there were rumours at the time about financial problems in NICA (Netherlands Indies Civil Administration), resulting in a shortage of money to perform government duties. NICA did not get any loans from Great Britain or the United States. Therefore, the targets of military aggression were areas with a potential for quick gain, that is, estate areas such as Besuki. Syamsir Muhammad regretted the diplomacy that offered the Dutch an opportunity to 'survive'. Interview with Syamsir Muhammad, 26-4-2005.

and banks were owned by the Republic. Only then would Indonesia be liberated from economic problems. At a conference in Purwokerto on 4-5 January 1946, Tan Malaka delivered a speech, his first in 24 years in Indonesia. He spoke about the Volksfront or Persatoean Perdjoeangan. He suggested a minimum programme of seven pillars as basis of the Volksfront that would unite the Indonesian people in its struggle to obtain full Independence.[10] In dealing with the Dutch, he suggested two measures of economic warfare. The first one was to take such economic action as to cause economic loss to the Dutch. Tan Malaka wrote:

> Rakyat revolusioner merupakan rakyat yang sama sekali tidak membantu memperbesar produksi dan perdagangan (distribusi) Belanda. Sebenarnya lebih efektif lebih besar hasilnya, kalau di daerah pendudukan Belanda, kaum buruh sama sekali tiada mau bekerja dalam kebun, tambang, atau pabrik dan kantor Belanda. Ditambah pula kalau rakyat sama sekali tiada mau membeli barang dari saudagar Belanda dan tiada mau bekerja dengan Belanda. Memang tidak bisa dipungkiri, Perusahaan Belanda itu juga bisa dimasuki dengan maksud mengadakan penyabotan dari dalam atau mendirikan barisan terpendam. Tetapi tak ada orang yang bisa menyangkal bahwa boikot kerja dan boikot membeli senjata adalah paling efektif terhadap Belanda ceroboh itu! (Tan Malaka 2000:69).

The translation is as follows:

> Revolutionary people do not contribute at all to enlarging the production and trade (distribution) of the Dutch. In fact, it is more effective, with greater results, if workers in areas occupied by the Dutch altogether refuse to work on estates, in mines or factories or offices of the Dutch. The effect is even greater if the people completely refuse to buy products from Dutch traders and refuse to work with the Dutch. Dutch companies may also be entered with the intention to sabotage these from within or set up secret fronts. But no one can dispute that a work boycott and a purchasing boycott are most effective weapons against these vile Dutch.

The second measure was to bring economic advantage to the people in the revolutionary struggle:

> Maka semua sikap dan tindakan harus diambil untuk memperbesar produksi dan memperbaiki distribusi bagi rakyat kita sendiri. Haruslah pula terutama dipikirkan, bahwa petani tidak akan menghasilkan lebih daripada keperluannya sendiri, kalau berlebihan hasilnya itu tiada dapat ditukarkan dengan pakaian, cangkul, garam, minyak dan lain-lain. Jika petani tiada dapat membeli keperluan yang harus dibelinya itu, maka dia tiada akan menghasilkan lebih baik dari pada

[10] Tan Malaka 2000:32-7. The seven pillars were: (1) negotiating for recognition of 100 per cent independence after foreign armies had left Indonesian territory and waters, (2) government by the people, (3) people's army, (4) disarmament of the Japanese, (5) handling prisoners of war, (6) confiscation of estates and (7) confiscation of factories and industrial enterprises.

> keperluan keluarganya sendiri. Dengan demikian hasil tani akan susut, merosot! (Tan Malaka 2000:69-70).

In translation:

> Therefore, all must adopt an attitude and take measures to increase output and improve the distribution to our own people. In addition, the premise must be that peasants will not produce more food than to cover their own needs if a surplus cannot be exchanged for clothes, hoes, salt, oil and other goods. If the peasants cannot buy what they need, then they will not produce more than what their families require. Consequently, agricultural output will slip into decline and eventually collapse.

In this conception, the Indonesian economy was to be run by the Indonesians themselves. Indonesian labourers, peasants and merchants should make plans for production, distribution and structural change. Planning should not be confined to a small group of educated people with the view that peasants and workers are expected to toil diligently in order to taste the fruits of economic planning.

During the negotiations about the transfer of sovereignty, the Republican government decided to follow a different course. In July 1949, it ordered the return of the estates to their legal owners with the prospect that agrarian rights were to be aligned to the new economic policy. This meant that land would only be returned if foreign capital or technological knowledge and management were urgently needed. In July 1949, a national programme was launched requesting that those with a long-term lease should respect and uphold the ambitions of the new government with regard to the prosperity of labourers (Pelzer 1982:23-4). Foreign enterprises were supposed to support the government in improving the life of peasants and labourers and should not victimize people or the state when seeking to make a profit.

Following the Finec (Financieele en Economische Overeenkomst, Financial and Economic Agreement) of the Round Table Conference (RTC) of November 1949, the Republican government issued an instruction concerning the return of planters to those estates which had not yet been claimed by their lawful owners. The government declared that the governor of the province in question had the authority to issue a temporary permit to inspect and/or reopen an estate (Pelzer 1982:24). In July 1950, the government issued another regulation concerning estates deemed economically important, where the lease was to expire before 1970. The government did not give an extension beyond eight years but estate companies could apply for a new long-term contract. This pragmatic policy did not meet with approval of either extreme nationalists or communists (Pelzer 1982:25).

Peasant movements

Peasant organizations responded swiftly to Tan Malaka's call to occupy land and till the soil on abandoned estates. At a congress in Jember on 29 December 1946, BTI pressed the government to abolish the planters' conversion rights, which permitted planters to use half of the village land for another fifty years in exchange for surrendering the 'right' to compulsory unpaid labour services (Pelzer 1982:18-20). BTI insisted that the government appropriate all private estate companies, whether on concession or long-term lease. This demand was reiterated at a congress in Blitar on 16 December 1947. BTI accepted a resolution to abolish conversion rights and all other special rights enjoyed by foreign planters. Similar steps were also taken elsewhere by other branches of BTI. Demonstrations were held in East and Central Java in support of these demands and the demands were endorsed by the Sarekat Tani Islam Indonesia (STII, Association of Indonesian Islamic Peasants).

According to the Committee on Land Conversion (Panitia Tanah Konversie), the demands by peasant organizations were reasonable, since rights based on a feudal system were against democratic principles and violating Articles 27 and 33 of the 1945 Constitution. The committee declared that conversion rights in particular should be abolished since they offended social justice. These rights in the past had rendered the foreign planters a very substantial profit. BTI then launched a campaign for the nationalization of land.

As a result of pressure from mass organizations and occupations by peasants, President Sukarno on 21 May 1948 issued the regulation Surat Penetapan Presiden No. 16 and installed the Panitia Agraria J(Y)ogjakarta (PAY, Yogyakarta Agrarian Committee), which initiated the formulation of a new agricultural legislation coming into effect in 1960 (Budi Harsono 1970:94). The chairman of this committee was Sarimin Reksodihardjo and among the 16 members were officials from state ministries, representatives of peasant organizations (BTI and STII), members of Parliament, representatives of estate labour organizations and legal experts, especially experts on *adat* law. On 3 February 1950, a litte more than one month after the transfer of sovereignty, PAY delivered a report to the president, although its task had actually been to draft a new agrarian law and formulate a programme of agrarian policy. One of the issues considered in the report was the abolishment of the special status of a particular category of private estate companies in West Java (*particuliere landerijen*).

The committee was dissolved after delivering its report. Its terms of duty had expired and the government was returning to Jakarta. On 9 March 1951, PAY was replaced by the Panitia Agraria Dj(J)akarta (PAJ, Jakarta Agrarian Committee). PAJ had nearly the same task as PAY and the chairman was again Sarimin Reksodihardjo.

The agrarian committee had indeed a heavy task as its progress was watched closely by at least three political groups concerned with the position of private estates in Indonesia. The first one consisted of moderates arguing that the estates had an important role as a source of foreign exchange. They worried about the position of the estates in the future. This group was content with legislation restricting public ownership of vital resources (Pelzer 1982:26). In their view, agricultural policy measures would have to guarantee the existence and position of the estate companies. Such measures included higher wages for Indonesian workers, participation by Indonesians in managing the plantations and a higher tax rate for Western firms. The moderates emphasized the necessity to attract capital from the private sector.

The second group consisted of right-wing nationalists, who resented foreign owners of estates and advocated their expulsion through financial compensation. They thought the plantation sector should be managed by Indonesians and argued that plantation companies ought to be retained as an institution, but with all management done by Indonesians. Even so, this group agreed about the importance of obtaining capital and technical skills from foreigners and was prepared to accept capital investment from foreign sources.

The third group demanded expulsion of all foreign estate owners in Indonesia without compensation. This was the group of left-wing nationalists or Marxists. The communist faction argued for 'abolition of the landlord system replacing it with observation of farmers for land and abolition of feudalism' (*Soeara Tani* 1958). This was regarded as a firm basis for genuine Independence.

These three groups dominated the public debate on agrarian policy in Indonesia until the Agrarian Law was ratified by President Sukarno on 24 September 1960. As in other former colonies, the discussion was also influenced by the international debate on agrarian change in developing countries and the role of private landownership. In Indonesia the debate was increasingly dominated by left-wing nationalists. Some intellectuals spoke of an 'agrarian strategy', others about a 'path of agrarian change' (Harris 1982:37-43).

There are three points in agrarian by which policy we can identify a system of political ideology: land ownership, labour and management of the production process. In an agrarian strategy oriented towards capitalism, the land is owned individually by non-tillers. The tiller is the labourer paid by the land owner. Land ownership and land tilling are separated from each other. The labourer sells his or her work to the land owner. At this point, workers become a commodity. Management of the production process is in the hands of the land owner. In a strategy oriented towards socialism, land and other productive assets are owned by a public organization, usually the state. The

Tan Malaka, here in his late twenties, was an important source of ideological inspiration for trade union activists in Jember, East Java, in the early 1950s (KITLV 17800)

workers are paid at wage rates set by the labour union. Responsibility and decision-making about production, accumulation and investment are in the hands of the organization. Between these two views, there is a third strategy known as populism, where the family business is the dominant business unit. Land ownership is spread over the majority of the peasant families and the workers themselves come from the family. Production is the work of the entire family, although responsibility on accumulation is usually regulated by a state-organized cooperation. This third option was in fact a variation on the left-wing nationalist strategy.

The power of left-wing nationalists had increased since the transfer of sovereignty, also in relationship to matters concerning agrarian production and estates. The Madiun uprising in 1948 forced the left-wing nationalists to become more moderate and altered opinions among elite leaders. The difference of opinion between the Aidit group of the PKI (Partai Komunis Indonesia) and Sutan Sjahrir of the Socialist Party, PSI (Partai Sosialis Indonesia) encouraged Sjahrir to set up a separate peasant organization called Gerakan Tani Indonesia (GTI, Indonesian Peasant Movement). Unfortunately, this organization did not expand into rural areas like other nationalist left-wing peasant organizations. It resembled the Rukun Tani Indonesia (RTI, Indonesian Peasant Cooperation) although merging into the BTI in the 1950s. There were also some smaller leftist peasant organizations, notably the Sarekat Kaum Tani Indonesia (SAKTI, Peasants' Organization of Indonesia), close to the ideology of Tan Malaka, and therefore also stamped as Trotskyite (Ina Slamet 1965:20).

SAKTI was founded in Jakarta in 1949. At first, SAKTI was led by Tabrani Notosidirdjo, vice mayor of metropolitan Jakarta. The peasant organization expanded rapidly not only in Java, but also in Sumatra and Sulawesi. There were numerous activities such as demonstrations for a fairer distribution of land. SAKTI also supported actions by peasants to occupy and use estate land abandoned by the owner because of the war. At the second congress of SAKTI, Tabrani Notosidirdjo was replaced by Sidik Kertapati, who was assisted by Syamsir Muhammad as secretary-general.

Despite differences of opinion, in 1949 all peasant organizations gathered at a conference to discuss the problem of land that had been abandoned by its Dutch owners as well as the effort of the colonial power to return to the plantations. In January 1951, around the time when D.N. Aidit became chairman of the PKI, this party set up a network with several peasant organizations, in particular those oriented to the left. As a consequence, it is assumed in the literature that RTI was being observed overtly by the PKI, while the BTI was observed covertly and SAKTI was being infiltrated (Hindley 1966:165). However this impression is wrong. Among the elite leaders of the BTI was Mohammad Tauchid, a former member of PSI.

In July 1951, the three leftist-oriented peasant organizations BTI, RTI and SAKTI formed the Front Persatuan Tani (FPT, United Peasants' Front). In November 1951, PKI announced the importance of alliances between peasants and labourers for the Revolution (*Bintang Merah,* December 1951). In 1953, one of the communist leaders of RTI proposed a merger with the other peasants' organizations. The proposal was rejected by SAKTI, although several SAKTI leaders had been involved in the preceding discussion about a merger. Nevertheless, BTI and RTI continued to discuss a coalition. In September 1953, the BTI and RTI held a congress in Bogor during which they agreed to continue under the name of BTI. A SAKTI congress in June 1955 finally approved unification with BTI (Pelzer 1982:45).

In 1953, Aidit insisted that PKI should seek continued support from peasants. But because of a lack of knowledge about the peasants' dissatisfaction, PKI not only failed to run a successful agrarian programme in the rural communities, it also enraged peasants with slogans such as 'nationalization of the land' and 'state rights of the land' (*Bintang Merah,* July 1953). It seems that the left-wing politicians had an ambiguous attitude towards the estate companies. They wanted to confiscate estate companies and give the land to the peasants but nationalization implied that the confiscated estates become state-owned. In the words of Pelzer (1982:28): 'The confiscation of the foreign landlord's land does not mean that the modern plantations should be confiscated to be distributed to the peasants. Technically, modern plantations and forests should be controlled by the state.'

The PKI and BTI initially leant towards nationalization. Their standpoint reflected the idea, voiced by Professor Soepomo, that Indonesia should learn from the Soviet Union when formulating agrarian legislation. According to Soepomo, the state could regulate the agrarian rights on tilled land and forests and designate unused land as free land under state control, a practice usually followed by the Netherlands Indies government.

SAKTI criticized PKI on this point. For SAKTI, the nationalization of land was a political action meant to bring agrarian resources under direct state control. The entire process of agrarian exploration and exploitation was henceforth to be done by the state under the umbrella of a political regime affiliated with communism. SAKTI insisted on its former principle: land for the peasants. Critics of communism referred to the experiences of nations such as China, South Africa and East Germany, arguing that peasants could not be separated from their land. They applied slogans such as 'land for the peasants', 'private ownership of land for the peasants' and 'wage rise for farm labour'. Aidit took over these slogans to gain support from peasants, while a long list of other slogans referred to the suffering of peasants, high rents for land, heavy taxes and the obligation to work for the village.[11]

11 *Bintang Merah,* July 1953; Pelzer 1982:30. Interview with Syamsir Muhammad, 26-4-2005.

According to SAKTI, strategies propagated by PKI through BTI and RTI tended towards centralist communist ideas, which made it difficult for other organizations to join a peasant mass organization. The first offer of a merger by the communist group did not only get a disappointing response, but also elicited open criticism from members of SAKTI, especially with respect to issues of agricultural centralization.

SAKTI was critical of policy measures taken by the Republican government. After the Round Table Conference in 1949, SAKTI faced a political dilemma. It disagreed with government policies and felt offended by the Republic of the United States of Indonesia (RIS, Republik Indonesia Serikat), as it had been constituted in accordance with the wishes of the Dutch. On the other hand, urging people to protest meant opposing Sukarno, who was very popular. Consequently SAKTI was increasingly criticized from various sides and its members were accused of being traitors and opportunists.

SAKTI continued to hold organized actions. One of the actions was a demonstration in Tanjung Morawa, North Sumatra, that caused the death of two SAKTI members, Darmo and Sudarmo. It was rumoured that the victims were BTI members, but PKI and BTI declared that the victims had both been members of SAKTI (Pelzer 1982:70-5).

Aidit tried to unite all peasant organizations oriented to the left. With a proposal entitled 'The future of the Indonesian Peasants' Movement', the importance of land for the peasants was acknowledged. This was the second time that PKI offered SAKTI to join a peasant mass organization. Before the merger, Sidik Kertapati, Burhan, and Sasongko (a relative of Sultan Hamengku Buwono IX of Yogyakarta) met to discuss the matter. Burhan explicitly refused the offer. According to Syamsir Muhammad, Burhan could not forget the PKI uprising in Madium. Sasongko said it was better to be a drawing teacher in a Taman Dewasa (School for Adults) than to merge with PKI. Despite holding ideological reservations, Syamsir Muhammad was forced to agree with the idea after Sidik Kertapati had accepted it.[12] From that time onwards, the BTI network continuously urged for termination of *erfpacht* and *opstal* rights. All private land should be converted into land held by Indonesian peasants.

Actions to end rights inherited from colonialism began soon after the proclamation of Independence and were increasingly accompanied by the takeover of foreign estates. The actions were motivated by both the political situation in Indonesia in 1949 and the changes in international politics. The failure to develop a national economic policy was seen by many as a failure to end the domination of Dutch capital in Indonesia. Tan Malaka reasserted that

12 Interview with Syamsir Muhammad, 26-4-2005.

the economy should be dominated for 100 per cent by the Republican government. At least 60 per cent of production, distribution, exports and imports should be handled directly by the government, and it was important to draw up a plan for an economic war against the Dutch (Tan Malaka 2000:72-3). In reality, the government's diplomatic strategy by definition constrained efforts to find a quick solution to the economic problems.

The RTC agreements of November 1949 laid down guarantees for foreign capital operating in Indonesia, not only in main sectors of the economy such as agricultural estates, but also in matters of economic policy. As a result, up to 1958 almost 80 per cent of the estate output was sent to Europe to be auctioned in Amsterdam or Rotterdam. The foremost commodity from Indonesian estate agriculture was tobacco, with a value reaching 200 million guilders per year. It was followed by tea at a value of 65 million guilders, further by palm oil, rubber, coffee, copra and tapioca. Besuki was one of the main suppliers (*Warta Niaga dan Perusahaan*, 21-2-1958).

Based on the RTC agreements, Indonesia was obliged to take over most of the debts of the colonial government, to an amount of 4.5 billion guilders. According to the Dutch, it was reasonable that Indonesia as legal heir to the Netherlands Indies inherited the debt. The economist Sumitro Djojohadikusumo, however, argued that the Dutch government should pay the debt. The proclamation of Independence had implied the transfer of power from the Japanese to the Indonesians, whereas the Dutch had twice launched a military campaign in order to re-colonize Indonesia. Sumitro Djojohadikusumo proposed to recalculate the debt and asserted that the Dutch government should pay back $ 540 million to Indonesia (Mestika Zed 1997:258). The United States promised to help Indonesia to pay the debts, but the loan amounted to only $ 100 million in the form of export-import credits (Kahin and Kahin 1995:34).

The leftist nationalist groups continuously called for a takeover of Dutch companies, including estates. Actions to urge the government to abrogate the RTC agreements were organized by several peasant organizations and included demonstrations and strikes. At a congress in Malang on 6-9 June 1956, the Sarbupri (Sarekat Buruh Perkebunan Republik Indonesia, Union of Indonesian Estate Workers) insisted that the government confiscate all Dutch property as a punishment for holding onto western New Guinea.

The demands voiced by Sarbupri anticipated the takeover of Dutch-owned estates throughout Indonesia by local labour unions in December 1957 and the following months. Although directly linked to the Dutch-Indonesian conflict over western New Guinea, the takeovers resembled similar actions elsewhere, notably against Belgian estates in Congo and British estates in Malaysia. The pattern was the same everywhere. Labour unions and youth organizations openly broke the law by seizing foreign property; the government criticized these acts but then authorized a central organization of state-owned estates (Pelzer 1982:38).

Between late 1957 and early 1960, the Indonesian government issued various decrees and regulations to meet demands made by PKI. The PKI claimed the victory over Dutch estates in December 1957 and early 1958 and called for the abolition of the so-called *particuliere landerijen* in West Java where European and Chinese landowners still enjoyed privileges inherited from the era of the Dutch East Indies Company, VOC (Vereenigde Oost-Indische Compagnie). At the time of the transfer of sovereignty, there were about 200 such estates, together measuring 32,000 hectares (Pelzer 1982:35).

The case of Jember

The golden age of private estate agriculture in Jember came to a conclusion during the period of Japanese occupation. All energy was mobilized for the war. Estate production with an export quality became part of the war effort and planters had to abandon their properties looking for a safe escape. Even more estate land was abandoned at the time of the proclamation of Indonesian Independence, resulting in a power vacuum. The local population began to cultivate abandoned land in order to meet needs of subsistence. Almost all estates in the Jember area were occupied and used by the local population, including various plantations owned by the Landbouw-Maatschappij Oud-Djember (LMOD, Estate Company Oud-Djember) for which George Birnie had acquired *erfpacht* rights in the nineteenth century, for instance Djenggawah, Sukoredjo (355 hectares), Ketadjek I (126 hectares), Ketadjek II (352 hectares) and the coffee estate in Tjurah Wangkal (4,500 hectares).

Historical narratives tell us how the estates abandoned by their owners attracted the population living nearby. The actions taken by the peasants cannot be understood just as a measure to occupy production facilities; they should also be understood as a demonstration of Independence after the oppression that they had experienced under colonialism. The power vacuum also attracted foreign estate companies returning in the wake of the Dutch military aggression. Dutch planters reoccupied most of the areas in Besuki, including sugar factories and tobacco, coffee, cacao and rubber estates in Jember.[13] They claimed that they still enjoyed rights of *erfpacht*. In Sukoredjo, for example, the *erfpacht* rights held by the LMOD were scheduled to end in February 1954 whereas elsewhere, at the estates Ketadjek, Djenggawah and Tjurah Wangkal, the date of expiration was in the 1960s.

The return of the planters signified the continuation of conflict between

13 Dison Mulyadi no year. Interview with Ibrahim, 13-9-2004.

the *ondernemer* and the surrounding population. Most conflicts were about the control of agricultural resources. The *ondernemer* assumed that cultivation of land by the local population under *erfpacht* rights formed an illegal action, whereas the local population saw such action as a manifestation of Independence and sovereignty (Lyon 1970:46).

The occupation of estate land appeared spontaneous lacking any local coordination. In reality, such initiatives did get strong support from national organizations such as BTI. As mentioned above, the second BTI congress in Jember in December 1946 had demanded abolishment of conversion rights, urging the Republican government to speed up the purchase of estate assets, whether in concession or long-term lease.

Conflict and seized estate land

The transfer of sovereignty on 27 December 1949 did not reduce conflict in the plantation area, as most planters made an effort to re-occupy the estate land. In July 1949, the Indonesian government ordered the return of estates to the owners and in September 1950, the government entrusted management of state-owned estates to the Pusat Perkebunan Negara (PPN, Centre for State Estates), an institution based on Indonesian company law (Indonesische Bedrijven Wet) dating from 1927. All formerly foreign-owned estates should be managed by PPN. The Tjurah Wangkal coffee estate, for example, had been occupied by local dwellers since 1945, and in 1956 the planters resumed cultivation. There were some estates that at the time of the transfer of sovereignty were occupied by planters with headquarters in the Netherlands, for instance Gunung Madjang, Glantangan, Kali Badjing, Pasewaran, Mangli and Penataran in the southern part of Jember.[14]

Since the estates had been abandoned by their owners, there was a perception among local dwellers that the planters got their land back through manipulation of Dutch colonial legislation, in particular *erfpacht* rights. There seemed to be a grand design for agrarian reform among the founding fathers of the Republic, which would include the abolition of *erfpacht* rights and allow control over land to be shared between peasants and the state (Mochammad Tauchid 1992, II:112). Such perceptions triggered conflicts in the state companies in the 1950s. In November 1954, the military arrested 342 peasants from Banpasir, Bandjaragung, Gentong and Gladakputih upon request by the planters (*Trompet Masjarakat*, 30-11-1954). Just as in the case of Tanjung Morawa in the preceding year, the peasants were accused by the

14 Interview with Jacob Vredenbregt, 18-9-2004.

planters of performing illegal and 'wild' actions when occupying and cultivating estate land still under *erfpacht* rights. In December 1954, a conflict erupted between the peasants and the planters at the Kotta Blater estate in Kalisat in the northern part of Jember. All peasant actions were supported by BTI, which assumed that the actions taken by peasants were correct. Another conflict occurred in Tjurah Damar, also in Kalisat, where more than 100 peasants were accused by planters of illegally occupying estate land (*Trompet Masjarakat*, 24-12-1955 and 18-6-1957).

In 1954 the government passed emergency legislation, Undang-Undang No. 8 Darurat Tahun 1954, in order to solve the problem of occupations of estate land. By this law, not all peasant actions were designated unlawful. Conflict could be resolved in two ways. One was by ruling of the Department of Agriculture whenever the occupied land was owned by planters but held under state control. The other way was to initiate round table negotiations with planters whose land had been occupied without permission. In the latter case some conditions had to be met, including the formation of a committee for conflict resolution consisting of both peasants and planters. This legislation was labelled a 'victory' for Indonesian peasants (Anu Lounela and R. Yando Zakaria 2002:41).

In the internal management of the estate companies, the labourers proved very dynamic and capable, which surprised the planters. In this period the estate labourers were vigorously pressing for better material conditions. Such actions had never taken place before. The labourers even pursued a dialogue with the planters. This militancy was a result of the increasing power of Sarbupri. The leftist or communist labour movement was keen on organizing the estate labourers in Jember. Per hectare of tobacco estate, the planters needed 1,069 persons: 697 for cultivation, 92 for preparations of seedlings, 231 for drying, 30 for maintenance and 19 for other tasks. The LMOD alone needed 30,000 labourers and this number would double during the harvest season (*Surabaja Post*, 4-2-1958).

In the early 1950s, Sarbupri also became a pioneer in negotiating Memorandums of Understanding (MoU) between labourers and planters. The MoU could force planters to improve labour conditions by measures ranging from rice sharing to health services. The MoU could also force the main employers' organization in Java, the Algemeen Landbouw Syndicaat (ALS, General Agricultural Syndicate), to implement ideas from the labour force. The outcome of the negotiations was laid down in a Collectieve Arbeids Overeenkomst (CAO, Collective Labour Agreement).[15] The rise of the estate labour movement came as a surprise. Apparently the planters, who were 90

15 Interview with Jacob Vredenbregt, 18-9-2004.

per cent Dutch, were just not mentally ready for it. They had never encountered militancy like this before. Next to 'radical' organizations such as Sarbupri and BTI, the Sarekat Buruh Islam Indonesia (SBII, Union of Indonesian Islamic Workers), affiliated with Masjumi, gained ground in Jember but it was less conspicuous. In practice, SBII was more concerned with the profits the planters had to make in order not to cause any financial loss to the labour force.[16]

Efforts at Indonesianisasi

When the planters had successfully reoccupied estate lands, they attempted to minimize resistance by peasants and labour. In order to achieve this, the planters began recruiting local (*bumiputera*) employees to participate in the management of the estate. The situation at LMOD in early 1958 was described in the regional press as follows:

> Pada hakekatnja usaha Indonesianisasi dikalangan LMOD sudah dilakukan sedjak Safiudin memegang pimpinan LMOD mulai tahun 1955. Sehingga waktu sebelum diambil alih, keadaan pegawai LMOD sudah terdiri dari Indonesia 78% dan Belanda 22%. Usaha Indonesianisasi ini dilakukan dengan secermatnja dengan *screening* jang selama waktu kurang dari 2½ thn sedjak tahun 1955. Dari pegawai Indonesia jang ada sekarang adalah 41 orang dari SPMA dan *cultuurschool*. Sehingga waktu diadakan ambil alih-ambil alih dan kemudian pegawai Belandanja sama minta pulang ke negeri Belanda, LMOD tidak mengalami *schokking* jang besar. Tidak seperti perkebunan jang sebelumnja tidak melakukan usaha Indonesianisasi dikalangan pegawainja. Beberapa waktu sebelumnja diambilalihkan itu dengan djalan Indonesianisasi keadaan situasi pegawai LMOD dengan perintjian, untuk tenaga Administratir 5 orang dari Indonesia, 14 orang dari Belanda, sedang untuk Hfd. Employe 4 orang dari Indonesia, 12 orang dari Belanda, sementara untuk Employe sebanjak 55 orang dari Indonesia dan 11 orang dari Belanda, dan untuk Ass. Employe 70 orang dari Indonesia sedang dari Belanda tidak ada. (*Surabaja Post*, 4-2-1958.)

In translation:

> In reality, the process of Indonesianisasi of the LMOD staff had been implemented since Safiudin had taken over the leadership of the LMOD in 1955. Before the takeover, staff at LMOD consisted for 78 per cent of Indonesians and for 22 per cent of Dutchmen. The Indonesianisasi process was executed conscientiously with screening during less than 2½ years starting in 1955. Out of the current Indonesian staff, 41 persons have graduated from SPMA and *cultuurschool* [agricultural training]. So that at the time of the takeovers, when the Dutch staff asked to be repatriated to the Netherlands, LMOD did not experience a major shock. [This was] dissimilar

16 Interview with KH Mursyid, 2-2-2002.

> to estates where no previous Indonesianisasi of the staff had taken place. Shortly before the takeover, the situation in terms of Indonesianisasi may be specified as follows: among the supervisors 5 from Indonesia, 14 from the Netherlands; among senior staff 4 from Indonesia, 12 from the Netherlands; among regular staff 55 from Indonesia and 11 from the Netherlands; and among junior staff 70 from Indonesia and none from the Netherlands.

Similar develop;ments took place at the Cultuur-Maatschappij Djelboek (CMD, Estate Company Djelboek) in Soekokerto Adjong and at the Besoeki Tabak Maatschappij (BTM, Besoeki Tobacco Company) estate in Tamansari in Bondowoso. Before the takeover, some employees of BTM in Bondowoso worked as estate inspectors, for instance Endung Soetardjo (Plindungan, Bondowoso), Akhmad Soebandi (Besuki) and Djoko Pramudito (Probolinggo).[17]

The recruitment of Indonesians also had a political background. The planters wanted to weaken the radical labour movement, especially Sarbupri. In the 1950s and 1960s, however, the position of Sarbupri was very strong and could not be ignored. The strategies of the planters were of course opposite to the nationalist or leftist ambitions in Indonesia. The planters only wished to reduce radical labour influence and in reality most *pribumi* worked as coolies, preparing areas for cultivation, maintaining tobacco fields, cleaning the building and sorting the tobacco.[18]

Confiscation

With the Indonesian attempt to put the West Irian conflict before the United Nations in late November 1957, yet another strategy was chosen. A couple of days after the vote in the General Assembly, local labour unions began taking over foreign assets. The acts of confiscation underscored national sovereignty in economic and political terms. The actions had been preceded by mass meetings, including one in Jakarta on 18 November 1957.[19]

Sudibjo, then Minister of Information and chairman of the Action Committee for Liberation of West Irian (Panitia Aksi Pembebasan Irian Barat) instructed the workers in Dutch companies to go on strike. This instruction was broadcast by Radio Republik Indonesia (*Indonesia Raya, Suluh Indonesia, Pedoman*, 2-12-1957). In Jember, Sarbupri, BTI and the SOBSI (Sentral Organisasi

17 Interview with Ibrahim, 14-9-2004.

18 Interview with Sahid, 13-5-2004.

19 ANRI, Jakarta: Kabinet Presiden RI 1950-1959, 1545, 30-6-1958. The term 'confiscation' was used by the Sarekat Buruh Gula (SBG, Union of Sugar Labourers) in preference to 'nationalization' or 'Indonesianization', as the latter terms would downplay the element of struggle.

Buruh Seluruh Indonesia, Central Organization of Workers in All Indonesia) organized labourers to join the strike in support of the government's plan to force the Dutch to abandon West Irian. All workers in Jember were on strike for three days. Local people in Jember assembled in a demonstration. The target of the demonstration was the Dutch *sociëteitsgebouw*, currently part of the University of Jember. From there, they walked to the Dutch residential area and confiscated and occupied everything owned by Dutch nationals. All seized property was surrendered to the local government.[20]

Some Dutch citizens in rural areas were arrested by estate workers and interned. In Kotta Blater, two Dutch citizens were arrested, handed over to the local authorities and then permitted to leave Jember. At BTM, at least three Dutch families had to leave the estate area. The same happened in Tamanan in Bondowoso, where at least four Dutch citizens had to depart. The evictions were triggered by statements by Minister Sudibjo requesting all Dutch citizens to leave Indonesia, except for a selected group of experts who would continue working. The eviction of Dutch citizens occurred in stages affecting different groups: jobless Dutchmen, those of the middle class and experts. Before the takeovers, there were about 50,000-60,000 Dutch citizens in Indonesia. By mid-1959, there were only 6,000 left (Oey 1991:388).

During the takeover, there were actions of scratching walls of estate buildings. Slogans on estate buildings in Wono Djati, Pondok Suto and Kotta Blater included 'property of the Republic' (*milik Republik*), 'already appropriated by the Republic' (*sudah dikuasai Republik*) and other formulations that would appeal to feelings of national identity.[21] The legal basis of the actions of confiscation was laid down in a military order (Surat Keputusan [SK] Penguasa Militer/Menteri Pertahanan 1063/PTM/1957) dated 9 December 1957 (*Surabaja Post*,11-12-1957). On 10 December 1957, the military authorities issued an instruction to confiscate all Dutch companies, including private estates (SP/PTM/077/1957), which was endorsed by the Minister of Agriculture (SK 229/UM/1957). The confiscated estates were placed under control by the military authorities of East Java acting on behalf of the Indonesian government. Ten Dutch firms were confiscated in East Java: Anemaet & Co., Handels Vereeniging 'Amsterdam' (HVA), Kooy & Coster van Voorhout, Tiedeman & Van Kerchem, Cultuurbank, Majanglanden, LMOD, Landbouw-Maatschappij Amsterdam, Kedawoeng Kawisredja and BTM.

All estate managers were invited by the local government in Jember for a gathering in the Ambassador Cinema (today's Kusuma Theatre) on 10 December 1958. There the regional government officially announced that

20 Interviews with Sumargo, 1-6-2004 and 2-6-2004; Sahid, 8-6-2004 and Kusdari, 10-6-2004.

21 Interview with Sahid, 8-6-2004.

some estates had been confiscated. Not all estate managers joined the meeting. Some directors, who had not been present, were later invited by General Major Sarbini, chief commander of the Brawijaya military territory, to come to Surabaya. Eventually they handed over all their assets to the government, voluntarily or coerced.

On 6 February 1959, the government set up a separate agency called Badan Nasional (BANAS, National Body) to coordinate and control estates in preparation of nationalization. The legal basis of this institution was a government regulation (Peraturan Pemerintah [PP] 3/1959, *Negara Republik Indonesia* 1959: 1731). On 23 February 1959, President Sukarno issued another government regulation (PP 4/1959) by which Dutch-owned estates became subject to nationalization on the basis of legislation adopted by Parliament in December 1958. Nine estate companies were nationalized immediately, four of them in Jember. The first one was LMOD with nine tobacco estates in Jember, including Adjong, Gambirono, Kertosari, Oost-Djember and West-Djember, and one in Bondowoso, Nangkaan. The second one was BTM with three tobacco estates (Modjo in Jember and Soember Djeroek and Tamansari in Bondowoso). The third estate company was Djelboek with two estates in Jember (Djelboek and Soekokerto/Adjong), whereas the fourth and final one was the Landbouw-Maatschappij Soekowono with its like-named estate in Jember.

Conclusion

This contribution focused on the economic decolonization, using the agricultural estate sector in Jember, East Java, as a case study. It described the public debate about the estate system during the Indonesian Revolution and in the early 1950s, tracing the background of strands of opinion which emerged at the time. In addition, a historical explanation was offered of the social process that united planters with the colonial state, creating a situation that was radically altered after Indonesia had gained Independence.

The contrast between official government-held views and the strategies of peasant mass organization illustrated the dilemmas confronting the Indonesian Republic in the late 1940s and 1950s. The guarantees given to Dutch estate firms and the need for foreign capital and know-how contradicted to the demand for full control of land and labour as expressed by the peasant organizations. The culmination of developments was the takeover and nationalization of Dutch-owned estates in the late 1950s. These dramatic events are particularly well illustrated by the account of what happened at the estates in Jember in late 1957 and 1958.

References

Apriyanto, Tri Chandra
2005 'Kota dan kapitalisme perkebunan; Jember dalam perubahan zaman 1900-1970', in: Freek Colombijn, Martine Barwegen, Purnawan Basundoro and Johny Alfian Khuysyairi (eds), *Kota lama, kota baru; Sejarah kota-kota di Indonesia*, pp. 359-83. Yogyakarta: Ombak.
Arifin, Edy Burhan
1989 'Emas hijau di Jember; Asal-usul, pertumbuhan dan pengaruhnya dalam kehidupan sosial ekonomi masyarakat, 1860-1980'. MA thesis, Department of History, Gadjah Mada University, Yogyakarta.
Harsono, Budi
1970 *Undang-undang pokok agraria; Sejarah penyusunan, isi dan pelaksanaannya hukum agraria di Indonesia.* Jakarta: Djambatan.
Harris, John (ed.)
1982 *Rural development.* London: Hutchinson University Library.
Hindley, Donald
1966 *The Communist Party of Indonesia, 1951-1963.* Berkeley: University of California Press.
Jonge, Huub de
1984 *Juragans en bandols; Tussenhandelaren op het eiland Madura.* PhD thesis, Katholieke Universiteit Nijmegen, Nijmegen.
Kahin, Audrey R. and George McT. Kahin
1995 *Subversion as foreign policy; The secret Eisenhower and Dulles debacle in Indonesia.* New York: Norton.
Landbouw-Maatschappij Oud-Djember
1909 *Een jubileum in de tabak.* Djember: Landbouw-Maatschappij Oud-Djember.
Lembaran Negara Republik Indonesia
1959 *Lembaran Negara Republik Indon*esia. Djakarta: Pertjetakan Negara.
Lounela, Anu and R. Yando Zakaria
2002 *Berebut tanah; Beberapa kajian berperspektif kampus dan kampung.* Yogyakarta: Insist Press.
Lyon, Margo L.
1970 *Bases of conflict in rural Java.* Berkeley: Center for South and Southeast Asian Studies.
Malaka, Tan
2000 *Gerpolek (Gerilya Politik Ekonomi).* Jakarta: Djambatan. [First published 1948.]
Memmi, Albert
1967 *The colonizer and the colonized.* Boston: Beacon Press.
Mulyadi, Dison
no year 'Agresi militer Belanda di Bondowoso.' [Research report, University of Jember.]

Oey Beng To
1991 *Sejarah kebijaksanaan moneter Indonesia; Vol. I. 1945-1958*. Jakarta: Lembaga Pengembangan Perbankan Indonesia.

Pelzer, Karl J.
1982 *Planters against peasants; The agrarian struggle in East Sumatra, 1947-1958*. 's-Gravenhage: Nijhoff. [KITLV, Verhandelingen 97.]

Siahaan, Bisuk
1996 *Industrialisasi di Indonesia; Sejak hutang kehormatan sampai banting stir*. Jakarta: Pustaka Data.

Slamet, Ina E.
1965 *Pokok-pokok pembangunan masyarakat desa*. Jakarta: Bhratara.

Tauchid, Mochammad
1952 *Masalah agraria; Sebagai masalah penghidupan dan kemakmuran rakyat Indonesia*. Jakarta: Tjakrawala.

Zed, Mestika
1997 'Indonesian economy in the revolutionary era; The struggle to find financial resources to fund the Revolution (1945-1950)', in: Taufik Abdullah (ed.), *The heartbeat of Indonesian Revolution*, pp. 181-98. Jakarta: Gramedia.

The international comparison

ANNE BOOTH

Indonesian colonial economic performance in an East Asian perspective

In the second part of the twentieth century, the two former Japanese colonies of Taiwan and the Republic of Korea have 'forged ahead' in the race for economic growth, and have achieved considerable success in narrowing the gap in per capita Gross Domestic Product (GDP) between themselves and both the United States and Japan.[1] Aside from the two city states of Hong Kong and Singapore, no other former colony in Asia has achieved the same success in catching up. In several cases, including Indonesia, India and the Philippines, per capita GDP was lower in relation to that of the United States (and in the case of India and Indonesia in relation to that of their former colonizer) in 2000 than it had been in 1913 (Booth 2007a:3-4). To many subsequent scholars seeking to find a reason for the superior performance of Taiwan and the Republic of Korea after 1960, Japanese colonialism did indeed appear more developmental in both its aims and achievements, in comparison with colonial regimes in other parts of Asia. Numerous authors have stressed the achievements of the Japanese in promoting new technologies in rice agriculture.[2] In the Korean context, Kohli has claimed that there was a striking degree of institutional continuity between colonial Korea and the South Korean state under Park Chung-Hee (Kohli 1994:1285).

It is not the purpose of this article to enter into the debate on the causes of rapid growth in Taiwan and South Korea after 1960. My purpose is rather to look at the record of other colonial regimes in Southeast Asia, with a particular focus on the Dutch legacy in Indonesia. The key questions I pose are the following: was the difference in economic performance, and in broader development indicators, between the various colonies in East and Southeast

1 This article draws on Booth 2007a (see also Booth 2003). I am very grateful to participants in the Leiden conference, and to two referees, for helpful suggestions; I accept full responsibility for all remaining errors of fact and interpretation.

2 See Myers and Ching 1964; Myers, Carr and Myers 1973; Hayami 1973; Myers and Yamada 1984.

Asia sufficiently striking at the end of the 1930s to provide a clear indication of their post-1950 economic trajectories? In particular, was Indonesia already lagging behind other parts of the region before the collapse of Dutch colonialism in 1942? If the answer is no, then that would support those who argue that it was the process of decolonization itself, or the policies adopted by post-Independence regimes in Indonesia and elsewhere (some of them intended to reverse rather than sustain colonial policies) that have determined the post-1950 outcomes. On the other hand, if the evidence suggests that the Japanese colonies were already ahead in terms of several development indicators in the late 1930s, and Indonesia was lagging behind, then the case for Japanese 'developmental colonialism' is supported.

I begin by examining the evidence on economic growth and structural change across colonial territories in East and Southeast Asia in the first four decades of the twentieth century. I then discuss policies relating to government revenue and expenditure and to trade, exchange rates and the balance of payments. I also look at some non-monetary indicators relating to living standards, including mortality rates and educational enrolments. The final section draws conclusions on the nature of the colonial state in East and Southeast Asia and the legacies bequeathed by these states to post-colonial governments.

Economic growth and structural change

By 1913, the United States had already become the world leader in terms of both total and per capita GDP (Maddison 2003: 262-3). Of all the major Asian economies, only Japan had a per capita GDP which was more than one-quarter of that of the United States; in most of the colonial territories and in China, per capita GDP was well below 20 per cent of that in the United States. After Japan, the highest per capita GDP in 1913 was in Hong Kong and Singapore, followed by the Philippines, Indonesia, Malaysia and Thailand. South Korea and Taiwan were below all these countries, and above only Burma (Table 1). By 1929, Taiwan and South Korea had overtaken Thailand, but were still below the other three Southeast Asian economies. It was only during the 1930s, a period of slow or negative growth in most parts of Southeast Asia, that the two Japanese colonies grew much faster than the Southeast Asian ones, although by 1938 the Philippines still had a per capita GDP above either of them.[3]

[3] It should be noted that the Maddison data have been challenged by Fukao, Ma and Yuan 2005, who argue that his method of adjusting GDP data for differences in purchasing-power was faulty for Japan, Taiwan and Korea. They argue that Korean real per capita GDP was lower compared to that of Japan, and Taiwan real per capita GDP higher than is indicated in Table 2.

As would be expected given the generally low levels of per capita GDP in 1913, most Asian economies were predominantly agricultural, with more than 40 per cent of GDP coming from the agricultural sector, except in Japan where the share had already fallen to under 30 per cent (Table 2). Agricultural growth was roughly similar in Taiwan, Korea and Indonesia between 1913 and 1929, although it was faster in the Philippines.[4] Over the 1930s, agricultural growth slowed in Indonesia and Burma, reflecting the severe impact of the world depression on these two economies. In most parts of Asia over these years, the non-agricultural sectors were growing faster than agriculture, so that by 1938 the agricultural share of GDP had fallen everywhere except in the Philippines and Thailand. In Indonesia by 1938, agriculture accounted for about one third of total GDP, compared with 35 per cent in Taiwan and 41 per cent in Korea. By the 1930s, non-agricultural employment in many parts of Asia had also become significant. In Japan, over half the economically active population was working outside agriculture; in Indonesia, Burma and the Philippines the proportion was around 30 per cent. This was a higher ratio than in Taiwan and Korea (Table 3).

The rapid agricultural growth in both Korea and Taiwan after 1913 was largely based on smallholder agriculture, albeit with a high incidence of tenancy. Estate agriculture was unfamiliar to the Japanese, and the colonial officials felt comfortable with the landlord-tenant regimes which existed in both colonies, and saw little reason to change them (Ho 1984:385). Government policy was directed towards increasing the supply of rice from both colonies to the Japanese mainland. By 1925, Korea was supplying Japan with over 5 per cent of its total rice consumption, and Taiwan added an additional 2.8 per cent to rice supplies available in Japan (Ka 1995:135). Taiwan also became an important supplier of sugar to Japan, displacing imports from Java, although the development of the Taiwanese sugar industry was assisted by a variety of direct and indirect subsidies (Ho 1971:320-3; Schneider 1998:164). There can be little doubt that the introduction of a 'Meiji agrarian strategy', including considerable investment in irrigation and rural infrastructure, and the large market in metropolitan Japan all served to accelerate the pace of agricultural growth in both Korea and Taiwan. By the late 1930s, rice yields were much higher than in other parts of Asia (Table 4). The impact of Japanese agrarian policies on the welfare of the rural populations in both colonies was more controversial, and will be discussed below.

In much of Southeast Asia after 1900, colonial governments were actively

[4] The very rapid growth in agricultural output in the Philippines after 1902 would seem to reflect, in part at least, recovery after the economic breakdown which occurred at the turn of the twentieth century as a result of war and occupation.

seeking to promote agricultural growth, both for home and foreign markets. The growth of rice production was quite rapid in the decades after 1910 in land abundant parts of Southeast Asia such as the Philippines, British Malaya and Thailand, and in southern Vietnam (Cochinchina), although nowhere was it faster than in Taiwan (Table 4). Much of this growth was due to the reproduction of traditional varieties and technologies over more of the land, although the Dutch colonial government in Java did try to develop new varieties which increased double cropping, and thus annual production (Barker, Herdt and Rose 1985:58; Van der Eng 1996:81-91). In Peninsular Malaya, in Sumatra and in southern Vietnam, the English, Dutch and French colonial authorities facilitated the acquisition of land by large estate companies to grow crops such as tobacco and rubber. The expansion of rubber estates after 1900 in Sumatra and Malaya in turn led to a rapid growth in smallholder production; by the 1930s, around 45 per cent of all rubber production in Indonesia came from smallholders (Booth 1988:201). Much of the rubber went not to markets in the metropolitan powers, but to the United States. This growth of both estate and smallholder export production, not just in Indonesia but in other parts of Southeast Asia as well, in response to the opportunities offered by world market demand had no counterpart in either Taiwan or Korea, where export growth was tightly geared to the requirements of the Japanese market.

Turning from agricultural to industrial growth, there were differences between the two Japanese colonies both in growth of manufacturing industry between 1911 and 1938, and in the size of the sector by the late 1930s. From a very small base in 1911, industrial growth in Korea was more rapid than in mainland Japan: between 1911 and 1938, there was an almost tenfold increase in value added in the mining and manufacturing sector. Growth was particularly rapid over the 1930s, and by 1938, manufacturing and mining accounted for around 16 per cent of Korean Net Domestic Product. In Taiwan, industrial growth was slower, especially during the 1930s. However, as the manufacturing and mining sector was larger to begin with, it accounted for a greater share of Net Domestic Product than in Korea, around 24 per cent by 1938.

It is sometimes asserted that, in comparison with the Japanese colonies, the industrialization which took place in Southeast Asia was limited in scope, and largely restricted to agricultural and mineral processing right up until 1942.[5] British, French and Dutch colonial regimes were supposedly intent on preserving colonial markets for their own manufactured products, and had little inter-

5 For example Huff (2007:131) argues that no Southeast Asian colony developed 'much manufacturing' before 1940. This statement seems at odds with the evidence from Indonesia, the Philippines and French Indochina.

est in encouraging either their own nationals or anyone else to establish industrial plants in their colonies. In fact, the evidence does not support these rather crude generalizations, especially in the inter-war era. The increase in national income which undeniably took place between 1900 and 1930 in Indonesia, as well as in British Malaya and the Philippines, and to a lesser extent in Burma and Indochina, did lead to increased demand for a range of manufactures, some of which by reason of high transport costs or perishability could profitably be produced in the home market, even without tariff protection.

The world slump of the 1930s had a serious impact on agricultural exports (both in terms of quantity and price) in most parts of Southeast Asia, and forced many colonial officials to consider economic diversification as a means of insulating their populations against the vagaries of world markets: 'Among the solutions offered none was seized upon with more enthusiasm than industrialisation' (Shepherd 1941:4). The flood of manufactured exports from Japan also served to increase official support for colonial industrialization; after all, if Japan could industrialize using its abundant supplies of cheap labour, why not Java, Luzon or Vietnam? Already in 1930, the industrial labour force accounted for more than 10 per cent of total employment in British Malaya, Burma, Indonesia and the Philippines (Table 3). It is probable that this proportion increased over the 1930s in Indonesia, as real output in the manufacturing industry over the decade grew rapidly, at around 8 per cent per annum (Booth 1998:41-5).

Much of the employment was in small-scale and cottage industry, but Van der Eng's estimates indicate that value added in the industrial sector (manufacturing, utilities and construction) in Indonesia comprised around 15 per cent of GDP in 1930 (Van der Eng 2002:171). During the 1930s, the Dutch made great efforts to attract foreign investment into the large-scale manufacturing sector, with considerable success.[6] Companies such as Goodyear, National Carbon, Unilever and Bata all built Indonesian plants during the decade, and in addition breweries, paper mills, canneries and several large weaving and spinning mills were established (Booth 1998:44). By 1941, the industrial sector (manufacturing, utilities and construction) accounted for around 20 per cent of GDP (Van der Eng 2002:72). There was also some development of industry in both French Indochina and the Philippines. Even under a tariff system which gave most American manufactures duty-free access to the local market, manufacturing industry in the Philippines accounted for 15 per cent of the colony's GDP in 1940 (Hooley 2005: Table A.1).

6 Dick (2003:267-9) argues that in Surabaya in the early 1920s, the metal/machinery sector was a very important component of the manufacturing sector in the city, mainly because of the demand from the sugar processing industry, railway workshops and shipbuilders. Also important were brick and tile manufacturing.

What was the government doing? The myth of the nightwatchman state

One of the enduring concepts of colonial states in many parts of Asia is that they were almost entirely concerned with maintaining law and order, and with raising the revenues necessary to support the costs of such activities. Colonial states were considered to be 'night-watchman states' with 'no self-conscious programme of active economic development' (Morris 1963:615). Writers who support Japanese exceptionalism argue that the Japanese colonies were characterized by more activist governments; in the case of Korea, it is argued that the 'colonial state in Korea was a busy state', actively involved in bringing about sustained economic change (Kohli 2004:40). But was such a policy agenda unique to Korea? In fact, by the first decade of the twentieth century, all the colonial powers in Southeast Asia and independent Thailand had established effective administrative structures which prioritized the centralization and reform of fiscal systems. Old practices of revenue farming were eliminated over the last decades of the nineteenth century, in favour of more diversified systems relying not just on land taxes but also on export and import duties, excises, sales taxes and in some cases corporate and individual income taxes.[7]

By 1910, government revenues per capita were highest in the Federated Malay States, at around $ 15 per capita, followed by the Straits Settlements and Taiwan, at $ 8 per capita. In the other colonies, including Indonesia, they were lower, at between $ 1 and $ 3 per capita (Table 5). In all colonies, revenues per capita in nominal dollar terms increased between 1913 and 1929. This did not necessarily mean a more progressive tax system, although it is probable that in those economies, including Indonesia, where more than 40 per cent of all government revenues were derived from income and land taxes and customs duties, the overall impact of the revenue system was more progressive.[8] Indonesia imposed income taxes on both personal and corporate incomes; neighbouring Malaysia did not, and instead relied more on indirect taxes, revenues from monopolies and excises, which were more regressive in their impact.[9]

In discussing the overall incidence of the fiscal system, it is essential to look at expenditures as well as revenues. During the first three decades of

7 On the demise of revenue farming across Southeast Asia, see Butcher and Dick 1993.

8 Kimura argues that the land tax in Korea was in theory a proportional tax, but in practice 'fundamentally regressive' (Kimura 1989:203). This contrasts with the situation in Java, where by the inter-war years the land tax was a tax on the presumptive income from agricultural land and broadly progressive in its incidence (Furnivall 1934).

9 For a more detailed discussion of the incidence of colonial taxes in Southeast Asia see Booth 2007b.

the twentieth century, most colonial regimes in Southeast Asia were devoting a considerable part of their budgets to education, health, agriculture and public works, including irrigation. A comparative study carried out by Schwulst in 1931 found that the Philippines, the Federated Malay States and French Indochina were all spending more than 40 per cent of total budgetary outlays on these sectors (Schwulst 1932:57). Administrative expenditures, together with defence and debt service, accounted for much of the rest. By 1931, Indonesia was devoting a lower proportion of total budgetary outlays to 'developmental' expenditures than any other Southeast Asian colony. This contrasted with the situation in the first two decades of the twentieth century, when expenditures on public works increased, and those on defence declined (Booth 1990:224). This decline in commitment to developmental expenditures after 1920 had serious consequences for infrastructural development, especially outside Java.

By the late 1930s, both Taiwan and Korea had high endowments of both roads and railways (relative to area) in comparison with most parts of Southeast Asia, although neither colony was better served than Java, which compared favourably with Taiwan in terms of transport infrastructure (Table 6). British Malaya did well in terms of both roads and electric power capacity. Nowhere in Southeast Asia was irrigation as extensive as in Korea and Taiwan, although colonial governments in both Indonesia and Vietnam did give irrigation development high priority, and devoted substantial budgetary resources to it up to the 1930s. But outside Java, transport infrastructure remained poorly developed in comparison with much of the rest of Asia, and this was to have serious consequences for post-Independence development.

Trade and exchange rate policies

An influential model of a colonial economy which was developed in the 1960s and 1970s, emphasizes an open economy which is tightly tied via both trade and investment flows to the metropolitan power, 'so that bilateralism may be a more approriate description than openness' (Ho 1984:381; also Paauw and Fei 1973). In such a model, exports were entirely agricultural and mineral and supplied from enclaves which were not tightly linked to the rest of the 'hinterland', where the great majority of the population lived. Imports were determined by the requirements of the export industries for both consumption and capital goods, and were usually well below exports in value, so that a large export surplus could be used to finance outward remittances of profits; part of the export surplus was accumulated as foreign reserves in the metropole. Such reserves were then used to maintain strict parity between the colonial currency and that of the colony via a currency board arrangement.

Ho argues that 'in many respects the Japanese colonies developed in the manner suggested by the model' (Ho 1984:382). In the case of Taiwan, exports to Japan only comprised around 20 per cent of total exports immediately after the Japanese occupation, but by the late 1930s this had risen to 88 per cent. Taiwanese exports were dominated by rice and sugar, almost all of which went to Japan. Korea was already quite tightly tied to the Japanese economy in terms of both exports and imports early in the twentieth century, and these tight links remained until 1940 (Table 7).

In colonial Southeast Asia, most economies were running large surpluses on the balance of trade from the 1890s onwards. The main exceptions were the Philippines and French Indochina where, until 1915, the trade balance was frequently in deficit (Booth 2007a: Tables 105, 107). However a surplus of exports over imports did not mean that the current account was necessarily in surplus, as the balance on services was almost always in deficit. We only have complete balance of payments estimates for two colonies for the period from 1890 to 1940: Indonesia and French Indochina. In both cases, when the balance of trade was large and positive, the current account balance was substantially lower. In Indonesia, on average the current account balance was positive for much of the period from 1901 to 1939 (Korthals Altes 1987: Table 1; Booth 1998:212). Given that the budget was often in deficit over these years, the current account deficit must have been the result of remittances on private account.

There was also considerable variation within East and Southeast Asia by the 1930s in the degree of dependence of the colony on the metropole for imports and exports. While the two Japanese colonies were very dependent on Japan for both imports and exports, only one colony in Southeast Asia demonstrated similar dependence. That was the Philippines, where exports of sugar in particular benefitted from preferential access to the American market. Elsewhere the degree of dependence on the metropole was not as high, and in Indonesia it fell over the last four decades of effective Dutch colonial rule (Table 7). The reason for the low dependence on metropolitan markets in both Indonesia and British Malaya by the late 1930s was the rising importance of other markets, especially the United States, for two of their principal exports: rubber and tin.

Trends in living standards in colonial Asia

A frequent criticism made of many colonial economic systems, in Asia and elsewhere, is that the economic growth which occurred did not benefit the great majority of the population. While exports may have boomed and government revenues expanded, nutritional intakes for the mass of the population did not improve, and access to health care and secular education was severely limited. As a result, mortality rates were high and many people were illiterate. In fact, an examination of the evidence for East and Southeast Asia shows considerable variation by the end of the 1930s in per capita rice availability, and in health and educational indicators (Tables 4 and 8). In Java, per capita availability of rice was only 85 kg by 1937-1939, and in the Philippines 97 kg, which was slightly higher than in Korea. This contrasts with 181 kg in Thailand, and 169 kg in Vietnam. In both Java and the Philippines, calorie intake was augmented by other foods, including corn, cassava and sweet potatoes. The time series produced by Mears on rice availability in Java shows some fluctuation between 1921 and 1941, but no discernible upward trend (Mears 1961:248).

Demographic indicators are also widely used by economic historians as a guide to changes in living standards over time. We do not have long time series on, for example, infant mortality rates for all parts of East and Southeast Asia for the early part of the twentieth century, but we do have figures for most countries by the 1930s. It seems clear that infant mortality rates were lower in Taiwan, the Philippines and British Malaya than in Indonesia, Indochina and Burma (Table 8). The data on crude death rates (which are probably less reliable, as they are derived from registration data) tell a similar story. There can be little doubt that infant mortality rates and crude death rates fell in Taiwan over the Japanese period, and life expectancy increased (Barclay 1954: Tables 36, 37 and 39). There was also a decline in death rates in Korea after 1920 (Kimura 1993:643). In the Philippines there was also some decline in both indicators over the American period (Zablan 1978: Tables 79 and 90). Infant mortality rates among the Vietnamese population in Hanoi show a rapid decline between 1925 and 1938, admittedly from a very high level (Banens 2000: Table 7), while in British Malaya the fall was estimated at around one-third in the Straits Settlements between 1911 and 1931 (Vlieland 1932:110; see also Manderson 1996:55). Hans Gooszen finds some evidence to support declining infant mortality rates in Batavia between 1919 and 1939, although she warns about the quality of the data (Gooszen 1999:192-3). No doubt in all cases, colonial governments would have attributed these declines to better access to modern health facilities and, especially in urban areas, to better provision of sanitation and clean drinking water.[10]

The final set of welfare indicators relate to education. Here the differences between colonies were quite stark by the 1930s. In spite of the assertions of

[10] Infant mortality rates were often higher in urban than rural areas, probably due to lack of clean water and poor sanitation. Gooszen (1999) cites Dutch research, which found very high infant mortality of more than 400 per 1,000 in parts of Batavia (Jakarta) in 1917-19, which were similar to those reported for Hanoi (Banens 2000:36). Vlieland (1932) found that infant mortality rates in urban Singapore were higher than in the more rural Federated Malay States.

The Daendels Building in central Jakarta housed, amongst others, the Department of Finance and may be considered a symbol of the bureaucratic apparatus introduced into Indonesia by the Dutch colonial authorities (KITLV 4101)

Maddison and others that the Japanese were more successful in increasing access to education than the other colonial powers (Maddison 1990:365), the evidence indicates that neither in Taiwan nor in Korea did the Japanese surpass the American achievement in the Philippines. By 1940/41 it was estimated that just over two million students were enrolled in public schools in the Philippines, and a further 180,000 in private schools. Of these a remarkable 40,000 were in tertiary institutions, a much larger figure than in Korea or Taiwan, or in any European colony (Bureau of Census and Statistics 1960:21-9). The Philippines and Taiwan were well ahead of most other parts of East and Southeast Asia in terms of the ratio of educational enrolments to total population by the end of the 1930s (Table 8).

At the other end of the scale was Indochina; both here and in Indonesia, provision of education to the indigenous population was still very limited by the end of the 1930s. In British Malaya the ratio of enrolments to population was above that of Korea, although there a disproportionate number of students were Chinese and Indian rather than Malay. In Indonesia, over 2.4 million pupils were enrolled in educational institutions by 1939/40; the vast majority of them (2.3 million) were indigenous Indonesians (Centraal Bureau voor de Statistiek 1947:22). However, most of these were in elementary schools teaching in the vernacular language of the region. Very few of the graduates from these schools were able to proceed to secondary education. In the 'Western advanced elementary and secondary schools', European and Chinese students outnumbered Indonesians. The 'plural society' which had been created by large-scale immigration from China and India to Malaya, Burma and Indonesia had led to a skewed access to education by race. Correcting this bias proved to be a major challenge for post-Independence governments.

Conclusion

To return to the question posed at the beginning of this article: was there already clear evidence by the late 1930s that Korea and Taiwan had benefitted from Japanese 'developmental colonialism' to a greater extent than elsewhere in Asia? In fact, it would appear from Table 8 that if a composite index of human development were to be constructed for 1938 on the basis of per capita GDP, demographic data and educational enrolments, the Philippines would have come out on top. Taiwan would certainly have been second, although we should bear in mind that the GDP data for Taiwan in 1938 computed by Maddison are probably underestimated; if Taiwanese per capita GDP was indeed substantially higher, then Taiwan could have been placed first, or first equal with the Philippines. Korea and Malaya had higher per capita GDP, at least according to the Maddison data, than Taiwan, and similar demographic data, but they scored less well on educational enrolments. It is likely that French Indochina would have been at the bottom of the ranking followed by Burma and Indonesia. Although per capita GDP was relatively low in Thailand, crude death rates were lower and enrolments higher than in French Indochina, Burma or Indonesia.[11]

Indonesia was behind all the countries in East and Southeast Asia in the late 1930s except French Indochina in terms of educational enrolments, although the figures for Thailand and Burma are boosted by the large numbers attending the monastic schools. The demographic indicators place Indonesia lower than all the other colonies except Burma, although the data are far from

11 The lack of reliable data on life expectancies and literacy for several parts of Southeast Asia make the computation of a Human Development Index for the late 1930s difficult. The one computed by Metzer (1998:57) for 36 countries in the late 1930s puts the Philippines at 22, above most Latin American countries, with the exception of Chile. Thailand was ranked at 26, and India bottom at 36. No other Asian countres were included.

complete for most regions. Indonesia, like most other parts of Southeast Asia, experienced an increase in mortality during the troubled years of the Japanese occupation, although the magnitude of the increase is controversial.[12] Some progress in both education and healthcare was achieved after Independence, but by the late 1950s, most parts of East and Southeast Asia were ahead of Indonesia in terms of both economic and social indicators, and fiscal weakness, leading to mounting inflation, impeded further progress for at least another decade. It was only in the 1970s, after more than two decades of political independence, that income and welfare indicators in Indonesia began to show an appreciable improvement. But by then other countries in the region were also forging ahead, and by the end of the twentieth century, Indonesia was still ranked lower in the United Nations Human Development Index than any other Southeast Asian country except Cambodia, Burma and Laos (UNDP 2003:238-9).

It may well have surprised the Philippine government in the late 1930s to have learnt of its top slot. Senior officials were conscious that in several sectors, especially agriculture, other parts of Southeast Asia were technically more advanced.[13] Surveys carried out in the late 1930s showed that many Philippinos were very poor, and it was argued that most of the gains from American rule had accrued to a small urban middle class.[14] Critics of American rule have pointed out that the result of American policies was to entrench this class in business, professional occupations, senior government positions and politics, where they remain dominant to the present day. American rule 'did little to transform the existing Philippine power structures' (Kang 2002:27). In Indonesia, it is also probable that the very modest gains in education and health care, as well as the more impressive progress in infrastructure, which occurred after 1900 benefited only a small proportion of the total population. It would certainly have disappointed those Dutch officials associated with the Ethical Policy to have learnt that, after four decades of government initiatives to uplift the indigenous population, Indonesia still lagged behind most other colonies in Asia, and indeed behind independent Thailand. In spite of the sincere efforts of the Dutch reformers at the beginning of the twentieth century, substantial improvements in living standards proved impossible to achieve

12 A critical discussion of the evidence on mortality rates in Indonesia in the 1940s is given in Widjojo Nitisastro 1970: 115-23.

13 Davis (1932:23-8) stressed the gap in yields of rice and sugar between Luzon and Java, and the more advanced development of experimental stations for sugar in Java, and rubber in Sumatra and Malaya. He also stressed that the Philippines was 'backward in adopting a definite plan of development extending over a period of years and in consistently carrying out that plan'. Davis was a Republican appointment as governor-general.

14 See Lava 1938 and Runes 1939 for detailed studies of living standards in rural areas in the Philippines in the latter part of the 1930s. See also Kurihara 1945:37-48.

with the limited fiscal resources available before 1942. This, combined with the slow progress after 1949, meant that economic and social progress in Indonesia has lagged behind most of the rest of Asia over the entire twentieth century.

Table 1. Per capita GDP for Japan, Thailand and colonies in East and Southeast Asia in 1913, 1929 and 1938

	Per capita GDP (1990 dollars)			Percentage growth rate	
	1913	1929	1938	1913-29	1913-38
Japan	1,387	2,026	2,449	2.4	2.3
Hong Kong	1,279	n/a	n/a	n/a	n/a
Singapore	1,279	n/a	n/a	n/a	n/a
Philippines	1,053	1,502	1,522	2.2	1.5
Indonesia	904	1,170	1,175	1.6	1.1
Malaysia	900	1,682	1,361	4.0	1.7
Thailand	841	793	826	-0.4	-0.1
Korea	820	1,014	1,459	1.3	2.3
Taiwan	747	1,146	1,302	2.7	2.2
Burma	685	n/a	740	n/a	0.3

Source: Maddison 2003:180-3.

Table 2. Index of growth of real value added in agriculture for Japan, Thailand and selected colonies in 1913, 1929, and 1938

Country	Index of value added in agriculture			Percentage annual growth	Agriculture as a % of NDP/GDP	
	1913	1929	1938	1913-1938	1913	1938
Japan	100	118	129	1.0	28.9	15.6
Korea	100	133	184	2.5	63.3	47.1
Taiwan	100	132	202	2.8	53.8	41.2
Philippines	100	200	245	3.7	38.5	38.1
Thailand	100	129	168	2.1	44.7	44.3
Indonesia	100	131	148	1.6	40.5	33.7
Burma	100	125	129	0.9	68.6	54.3

Note: Net Domestic Product (NDP) for Japan, Korea, Taiwan and Burma; Gross Domestic Product (GDP) for the Philippines, Indonesia and Thailand.

Sources: Japan, Korea and Taiwan: Mizoguchi and Umemura 1988:230-9; Philippines: Hooley 2005: 480-81; Thailand: Manarungsan 1989:251; Indonesia: Van der Eng 2002:171-2; Burma: Hlaing 1965:289.

Table 3. Occupational distribution of the employed population in Japan, Thailand and colonies, ca. 1930 (in %)

Country	Agriculture	Industry	Other
Japan (1930)	49.6	20.1	30.3
Taiwan (1930)	73.0	8.6	18.3
Korea (1930)	79.6	6.3	14.1
British Malaya (1930)	60.8	12.3	26.9
Burma (1931)	69.6	11.0	19.4
Indonesia (1930)	70.0	10.4	19.6
Philippines (1939)	69.0	12.2	18.8
Thailand (1929)	84.2	2.2	13.6

Sources: Taiwan and Japan: Grajdanzev 1944:33, 77; Korea: Suh 1978: Table 2; British Malaya: Vlieland 1932:99; Burma: Saito and Lee 1999: Table 1.6; Indonesia: Mertens 1978:51; Philippines: Kurihara 1945:16; Thailand: Ingram 1971:57, 144.

Table 4. Growth of rice production, 1916/20 to 1937/39, per capita availability and planted area per agricultural worker in East and Southeast Asia, 1937/39.

Colony/ country	Output growth 1916/20 to 1937/39[a] (% per annum)	Yield 1937/9 (tons/ha)[b]	Per capita availability (kg per year) 1937/39	Irrigation ratio[c]	Planted rice area per worker (ha)
Taiwan	3.4	2.1	129[d]	83.7	0.47
Korea	2.9	2.1	91	68.5	0.21
Malaya	2.7	1.1	178	n/a	0.24
Thailand	2.6	0.8	142	9.7	0.56
Philippines	2.3	0.8	97	24.8	0.57
Indochina	1.6	0.7	169[e]	n/a	n/a
Java	1.4	1.1	85	30.6	0.30
Burma	0.6	0.8	122	11.8	1.20

[a] Output growth for British Malaya: 1917/19 to 1937/39; Korea: 1917/18 to 1937/38; Indochina: 1916/18 to 1936/38.
[b] Milled rice; data for Indochina refer to 1937.
[c] Irrigated area as a percentage of harvested area of rice in the late 1930s.
[d] Average for 1938/39 and 1939/40
[e] 1937 only

Sources: Rose 1985 (supplemented by data from Van der Eng 1996: Tables A.3 and A.6); Saito and Lee 1999; Grajdanzev 1942:54, 1944:291; Boomgaard and Van Zanden 1990:96; Barnett 1947: Table 26. Data on per capita rice availabilities for Taiwan and Korea from Johnston 1953:270, for the Philippines from Mears et al. 1974:355, for Java from Mears 1961:246, for Burma from Richter 1976:6, for Thailand from Manarungsan 1989:210-1, for British Malaya from Grist 1936: Table 32.

Table 5. Government revenues per capita in Southeast Asia, Taiwan and Korea, 1910-1938

($)

Country	1910	1920	1929	1934	1938
Vietnam[a]	1	3	3	3	2
Indonesia	2	5	5	4	4
Philippines	3	6	6	4	5
Thailand	3	3	4	3	3
Burma	3	5	6	6	4
Unfederated Malay [b]	5	6	11	10	10
Straits Settlements	8	21	29	17	15
Federated Malay	15	24	28	19	18
Taiwan	8	16	16	8	12
Korea	1	4	6	4	7

[a] Data refer to 1913, not 1910. Local and (after 1931) provincial revenues and expenditures are included.
[b] Data refer to 1911 and 1921, not 1910 and 1920. 1911 data refer to Johore and Kelantan only.

Sources: Vietnam: Bassino 2000, Banens 2000; Indonesia: Creutzberg 1976: Table 4, Van der Eng 2002:171-2; Philippines: Birnberg and Resnick 1975: Table A.38; Thailand: Ingram 1971: Appendices B and C; Burma: Shein, Thant and Sein 1969: Appendix II; National Planning Commission 1960, Andrus 1948: Tables 37 and 38; British Malaya (Federated and Unfederated Malay States and Straits Settlements): Emerson 1937:135-311, with additional data from Lim 1967: Appendix 9.2, Fraser 1939: Appendix A. Exchange rates: Van Laanen 1980: Table 8; Direction des Services Economiques 1947:288; Ingram 1971:337, Emerson 1937:522. Taiwan and Korea: Mizoguchi and Umemura 1988:256, 288-93; exchange rates from Japan Statistical Association 1987.

Table 6. Infrastructure endowments in the late 1930s

Country	Roads (km per thous. sq. km)	Railways (km per thous. sq. km)	Electricity[a] (installed capacity)
Philippines (1939)	70.5	4.5	4.76
Indonesia (1940)	27.7	3.9	2.97
- Java	171.9	40.5	3.01
- Outer Islands	17.0	1.1	2.86
Indochina (1936)	38.8	5.7	2.39
British Malaya (1938)	100.1	12.5	36.06
Burma (1938)	45.2	3.4	3.69
Taiwan (1937)	94.4	43.3[b]	38.32
Korea (1938)	107.2	25.7	28.48

[a] Data refer to installed capacity in kilowatts per 1,000 population for the following years: 1938 (Philippines), 1937 (British Malaya) and 1940 (Indonesia and Taiwan). For Burma the data refer to the capacity of the large plants with an estimate for smaller plants.
[b] Data exclude 2,098 km of special track for the transport of sugar.

Sources: Philippines: Bureau of Census and Statistics 1941; 1947:279, 304-7; Indonesia: Centraal Bureau voor de Statistiek 1947:56, 97; Indochina: Robequain 1944:94-7, 285; British Malaya: Department of Statistics 1939; Burma: Andrus 1948:226, 237); Korea: Grajdanzev 1944:72-4, 135, 185-92; Taiwan: Grajdanzev 1942:118-9, Barclay 1954:42.

Table 7. Percentage of foreign trade with the metropolitan power

Country	Early 20th century		ca. 1939	
	Exports	Imports	Exports	Imports
Korea (1904-6)	84.6	73.3	73.2	88.5
Philippines (1902-4)	40.1	13.5	82.0	68.3
Indonesia (1900-4)	35.4	31.4	14.4	18.7
Indochina (1897-1901)	20.6	44.6	32.3	55.4
Taiwan (1896-1900)	19.6	27.0	86.0	87.6
British Malaya (1938)	n/a	n/a	14.1	18.2
Burma (1904-7, 1938/9)	9.2	26.7	12.7	18.2

Sources: Korea: Bank of Chosen 1920:166-8, Grajdanzev 1944:227; Philippines: Bureau of Census and Statistics 1947:347; Indonesia: Korthals Altes 1991: Tables 1B, 2B, 3B, 4B; Indochina: Doumer 1902:296-7, Bassino and Huong 2000:305-23; Taiwan: Grajdanzev 1942:144; British Malaya: Department of Statistics 1939:114; Burma: Office of the Prime Minister 1958, Andrus 1948:167-76.

Table 8. Development indicators for East and Southeast Asia in the late 1930s

Country	Per capita GDP, 1938 (1990 international, $)	Infant mortality rates	Crude death rates	Educational enrolments as % of total population
Philippines	1,522	139	23	11.5
Korea	1,459	n/a	23	5.8
Malaya[a]	1,361	147	21	7.8
Taiwan	1,302	142	21	11.4
Indonesia	1,175	225-250	28	4.0
Thailand	826	n/a	22	10.7
Burma	749	232	30	5.5
Indochina	n/a	190	24	2.5

[a] GDP and crude death rate data refer to Malaysia (British Malaya excluding Singapore). Infant mortality rates refer to the Federated Malay States only. Educational enrolments refer to British Malaya including Singapore.

Sources: GDP data: Maddison 2003:182-3; Educational enrolments: Furnivall 1943:111, with additional data on Korea from Grajdanzev 1944:264. Data on infant mortality rates and crude death rates for Indonesia: Widjojo Nitisastro 1970:113, Table 39 (Java only); Korea: Chang 1966:268; Philippines: Zablan 1978:100-5); Taiwan: Barclay 1954:146, 161; Thailand: Manarungsan 1989:35; Vietnam: Banens 2000:36-7 (crude death rates refer to Cochinchina; infant mortality rates to Hanoi only). Burma: Sundrum 1957:20, 52; British Malaya: Evans 1939: Table XV; crude death rates: Palmore, Chander and Fernandez 1975: Table 4.1.

References

Andrus, J.R.
1948 *Burmese economic life*. Stanford, CA: Stanford University Press

Banens, Maks
2000 'Vietnam; A reconstruction of its 20th-century population history', in: Jean-Pascal Bassino, Jean-Dominique Giacometti and K. Odaka (eds), *Quantitative economic history of Vietnam 1900-1990*, pp. 1-40. Tokyo: Hitotsubashi University, Institute of Economic Research.

Bank of Chosen
1920 *Economic history of Chosen*. Seoul: Bank of Chosen.

Barclay, George
1954 *Colonial development and population in Taiwan*. Princeton, NJ: Princeton University Press.

Barker, Randolph, Robert Herdt and Beth Rose
1985 *The rice economy of Asia*. Washington, DC: Resources for the Future.

Barnett, H.L.
1947 *Malayan agricultural statistics*. Kuala Lumpur: Department of Agriculture.

Bassino, Jean-Pascal
2000 'Public finance in Vietnam under French rule, 1895-1954', in: Jean-Pascal Bassino, Jean-Dominique Giacometti and K. Odaka (eds), *Quantitative economic history of Vietnam 1900-1990*, pp. 269-92. Tokyo: Hitotsubashi University, Institute of Economic Research.

Bassino, Jean-Pascal and Bui Thi Lan Huong
2000 'Estimates of Indochina's and Vietnam's international trade (1890-1946)', in: Jean-Pascal Bassino, Jean-Dominique Giacometti and K. Odaka (eds), *Quantitative economic history of Vietnam 1900-1990*, pp. 293-324. Tokyo: Hitotsubashi University, Institute of Economic Research.

Birnberg, Thomas B. and Stephen A. Resnick
1975 *Colonial development; An econometric study*. New Haven, CT: Yale University Press

Boomgaard, Peter and Jan Luiten van Zanden
1990 *Changing economy in Indonesia; Vol. X. Food crops and arable lands, Java 1815-1942*. Amsterdam: Royal Tropical Institute.

Booth, Anne
1988 *Agricultural development in Indonesia*. Sydney: Allen and Unwin.
1990 'The evolution of fiscal policy and the role of government in the colonial economy', in: Anne Booth, W.J. O'Malley and Anne Weidemann (eds), *Indonesian economic history in the Dutch colonial era*, pp. 210-43. New Haven, CT: Yale University Press.
1998 *The Indonesian economy in the nineteenth and twentieth centuries; A history of missed opportunities*. Basingstoke: Macmillan.
2003 'Four colonies and a kingdom; A comparison of fiscal, trade and exchange rate policies in South East Asia in the 1930s', *Modern Asian Studies* 37:429-60.
2007a *Colonial legacies; Economic and social development in East and Southeast Asia*. Honolulu: University of Hawai'i Press.
2007b 'Nightwatchman, extractive or developmental state? Some evidence from late colonial Southeast Asia', *Economic History Review* 60-2:241-66.

Bureau of Census and Statistics
1941 *Yearbook of Philippine statistics 1940*. Manila: Bureau of Census and Statistics.
1947 *Yearbook of Philippine statistics 1946*. Manila: Bureau of Census and Statistics.
1960 *Handbook of Philippine Statistics, 1903-1959*. Manila: Bureau of Census and Statistics.

Butcher, John and Howard Dick (eds)
1993 *The rise and fall of revenue farming*. London: Macmillan.

Carr, Carolle and Ramon H. Myers
1973 'The agricultural transformation in Taiwan; The case of ponlai rice, 1922-42', in: R.T. Shand (ed.), *Technical change in Asian agriculture*, pp. 28-50. Canberra: Australian National University Press.

Centraal Bureau voor de Statistiek
1947 *Statistical pocketbook of Indonesia, 1941*. Batavia: Kolff.
Chang Yunshik
1966 *Population in early modernization; Korea*. PhD thesis, Princeton University.
Creutzberg, P.
1976 *Changing economy in Indonesia; Vol. II. Public finance, 1816-1939*. The Hague: Nijhoff.
Davis, Dwight
1932 'Reports on good will trip', in: *Annual report of the Governor General of the Philippine Islands 1931*, Appendix 1. Washington, DC: United States Government Printing Office.
Department of Statistics
1939 *Malayan yearbook 1939*. Singapore: Government Printing Office for the Department of Statistics, Straits Settlements and Federated Malay States.
Dick, Howard W.
2003 *Surabaya, city of work; A socioeconomic history, 1900-2000*. Singapore: Singapore University Press.
Direction des Services Economiques
1947 *Annuaire statistique de l'Indochine, 1943-1946*. Hanoi: Direction des Services Economiques.
Doumer, Paul A.
1902 *Rapport; Situation de l'Indochine, 1897-1901*. Hanoi: Schneider.
Emerson, Rupert
1937 *Malaysia; A study in direct and indirect rule*. New York: Macmillan.
Evans, L.W.
1939 *Federated Malay States; Report of the Registrar General of births and deaths for the year 1938*. Kuala Lumpur: Federated Malay States Government Press.
Fraser, H.
1939 *Annual report on the social and economic progress of the people of the Federated Malay States for 1938*. Kuala Lumpur: Federated Malay States Government Press.
Fukao Kyoji, Debin Ma and Tangjun Yuan
2005 'International comparison in historical perspective; Reconstructing the 1934-36 benchmark purchasing power parity for Japan, Korea and Taiwan'. Tokyo: Hitotsubsashi University Research Unit for Statistical Analysis in Social Sciences. [Discussion Paper series 66.]
Furnivall, J.S.
1934 *Studies in the social and economic development of the Netherlands East Indies; Vol. IIID. The land revenue system*. Rangoon: Burma Book Club.
1943 *Educational progress in Southeast Asia*. New York: Institute of Pacific Relations.

Gooszen, Hans
1999 *A demographic history of the Indonesian archipelago, 1880-1942*. Singapore: Institute of Southeast Asian Studies.

Grajdanzev, Andrew J.
1942 *Formosa today; An analysis of the economic development and strategic importance of Japan's tropical colony*. New York: Institute of Pacific Relations.
1944 *Modern Korea*. New York: Institute of Pacific Relations.

Grist, D.H.
1936 *An outline of Malayan agriculture*. Kuala Lumpur: Department of Agriculture.

Hayami, Yujiro
1973 'Development and diffusion of high yielding rice varieties in Japan, Korea and Taiwan, 1890-1940', in: R.T. Shand (ed.), *Technical change in Asian agriculture*, pp. 9-27. Canberra: Australian National University Press.

Hlaing, Aye
1965 *An economic and statistical analysis of economic development of Burma under British rule*. PhD thesis, University of London.

Ho Samuel Pao-san
1971 'The development policy of the Japanese colonial government in Taiwan, 1895-1945', in: Gustav Ranis (ed.), *Government and economic development*, pp. 347-98. New Haven, CT: Yale University Press.
1984 'Colonialism and development; Korea, Taiwan, and Kwantung', in: Ramon H. Myers and Mark R. Peattie (eds), *The Japanese colonial empire, 1895-1945*. Princeton, NJ: Princeton University Press.

Hooley, Richard
2005 'American economic policy in the Philippines, 1902-1940; Exploring a dark age in colonial statistics', *Journal of Asian Economics* 16:464-88.

Huff, Gregg
2007 'Globalization, natural resources, and foreign investment; A view from the resource-rich tropics', *Oxford Economic Papers* 59:127-55.

Ingram, J.
1971 *Economic change in Thailand, 1850-1970*. Kuala Lumpur: Oxford University Press.

Japan Statistical Association
1987 *Historical statistics of Japan; Vol. III*. Tokyo: Japan Statistical Association.

Johnston, B.F.
1953 *Japanese food management in World War II*. Stanford, CA: Stanford University Press.

Ka Chih-Ming
1995 *Japanese colonialism in Taiwan; Land tenure, development, and dependency, 1895-1945*. Boulder, CO: Westview Press.

Kang, David C.
2002 *Crony capitalism; Corruption and development in South Korea and the Philippines*. Cambridge: Cambridge University Press.

Kimura, Mitsuhiko

1989 'Public finance in Korea under Japanese rule; Deficit in the colonial account and colonial taxation', *Explorations in Economic History* 26:285-310.

1993 'Standards of living in colonial Korea; Did the masses become worse off or better off under Japanese rule?', *Journal of Economic History* 53:629-52.

Kohli, Atul

1994 'Where do high growth political economies come from? The Japanese lineage of Korea's "developmental state"', *World Development* 22:1269-93.

2004 *State-directed development; Political power and industrialization in the global periphery*. Cambridge: Cambridge University Press.

Korthals Altes, W.L.

1987 *Changing economy in Indonesia; Vol. VII. Balance of payments 1822-1939*. Amsterdam: Royal Tropical Institute.

1991 *Changing economy in Indonesia; Vol. XIIA. General trade statistics 1822-1940*. Amsterdam: Royal Tropical Institute.

Kurihara, Kenneth

1945 *Labor in the Philippine economy*. Stanford, CA: Stanford University Press.

Laanen, J.T.M. van

1980 *Changing economy in Indonesia; Vol. VI. Money and banking, 1816-1940*. The Hague: Nijhoff.

Lava, Horacio

1938 *Levels of living in the Ilocos region*. Manila: University of the Philippines. [Philippine Council of the Institute of Pacific Relations Studies.]

Lim Chong-Yah

1967 *Economic development of modern Malaya*. Kuala Lumpur: Oxford University Press.

Maddison, Angus

1990 'The colonial burden; A comparative perspective', in: Maurice Scott and Deepak Lal (eds), *Public policy and economic development; Essays in honour of Ian Little*, pp. 361-75. Oxford: Oxford University Press.

2003 *The world economy; Historical statistics*. Paris: OECD Development Centre.

Manarungsan, Sompop

1989 *Economic development of Thailand, 1850-1950*. PhD thesis, University of Groningen.

Manderson, Lenore

1996 *Sickness and the state: Health and illness in colonial Malaya, 1870-1940*. Cambridge: Cambridge University Press

Mears, Leon A.

1961 *Rice marketing in the Republic of Indonesia*. Djakarta: University of Indonesia.

Mears, Leon, M. Agabin, T.L. Anden and R.C. Marquez

1974 *The rice economy of the Philippines*. Manila: University of the Philippines Press.

Mertens, Walter
1978 'Population census data on agricultural activities in Indonesia', *Majalah Demografi Indonesia* 9:9-53.

Metzer, Jacob
1998 *The divided economy of mandatory Palestine.* Cambridge: Cambridge University Press.

Mizoguchi, Toshiyuki and Mataji Umemura
1988 *Basic economic statistics of former Japanese colonies, 1895-1938.* Tokyo: Toyo Keizai Shinposhain.

Morris, D.
1963 'Towards a re-interpretation of nineteenth century Indian economic history', *Journal of Economic History* 23:606-18.

Myers, Ramon H.
1969 'Taiwan', in: R.T. Shand (ed.), *Agricultural development in Asia*, pp. 25-52. Canberra: Australian National University Press.

Myers, Ramon H. and Adrienne Ching
1964 'Agricultural development in Taiwan under Japanese colonial rule', *Journal of Asian Studies* 23:555-70.

Myers, Ramon H. and Saburo Yamada
1984 'Agricultural development in the empire', in: Ramon H. Myers and Mark R. Peattie (eds), *The Japanese colonial empire, 1895-1945*, pp. 420-52. Princeton, NJ: Princeton University Press.

National Planning Commission
1960 *A study of the social and economic history of Burma (British Burma); Vol. VIII. British Burma from the rebellion of 1931 to the Japanese invasion of 1941.* Rangoon: Ministry of National Planning.

Nitisastro, Widjojo
1970 *Population trends in Indonesia.* Ithaca, NY: Cornell University Press.

Office of the Prime Minister
1958 *A study of the social and economic history of Burma (British Burma); Vol. VIA. 1897-1913.* Rangoon: Office of the Prime Minister.

Palmore, James A., Ramesh Chander and Dorothy Fernandez
1975 *The demographic situation in Malaysia.* Honolulu: University of Hawaii. [East-West Population Institute Reprint Series 70.]

Paauw, Douglas S. and John C.H. Fei
1973 *The transition in open dualistic economies; Theory and Southeast Asian experience.* New Haven, CT: Yale University Press.

Richter, Hazel
1976 'Burma's rice surplus; Accounting for the decline'. [Working Paper 3, Development Studies Centre, Australian National University, Canberra.]

Robequain, Charles
1944 *The economic development of French Indo-China.* London: Oxford University Press.

Rose, Beth
1985 *Appendix to the rice economy of Asia.* Washington, DC: Resources for the Future.

Runes, I.T.
1939 *General standards of living and wages of workers in the Philippine sugar industry*. Manila: Institute of Pacific Relations.
Saito, T. and Lee Kin Kiong
1999 *Statistics on the Burmese economy; The 19th and 20th centuries*. Singapore: Institute of Southeast Asian Studies.
Schneider, Adam
1998 'The Taiwan government-general and prewar Japanese economic expansion in South China and Southeast Asia, 1900-1936', in: Harald Fuess (ed.), *The Japanese empire in East Asia and its postwar legacy*, pp.161-82. Munich: Iudicium.
Schwulst, E.B.
1932 'Report on the budget and financial policies of French Indo-China, Siam, Federated Malay States and the Netherlands East Indies', in: *Report of the Governor General of the Philippine Islands 1931*, pp. 42-59. Washington, DC: United States Government Printing Office.
Shein Maung, Myint Myint Thant and Tin Tin Sein
1969 '"Provincial contract system" of British Indian empire, in relation to Burma; A case of fiscal exploitation', *Journal of the Burma Research Society* 53-12:1-27.
Shepherd, Jack
1941 *Industry in South East Asia*. New York: Institute of Pacific Relations.
Suh Sang-Chul
1978 *Growth and structural changes in the Korean economy, 1910-1940*. Cambridge, MA: Harvard University Press.
Sundrum, R.M.
1957 'Population statistics of Burma', *Economics Research Project Statistical Papers* 3. Rangoon: University of Rangoon.
UNDP
2003 *Human development report 2003*. New York: Oxford University Press.
Van der Eng, Pierre
1996 *Agricultural growth in Indonesia*. Basingstoke: Macmillan.
2002 'Indonesia's growth performance in the 20th century', in: A. Maddison, D. Rao and W. Shepherd (eds), *The Asian economies in the twentieth century*, pp. 143-79. Cheltenham: Elgar.
Vlieland, C.A.
1932 *British Malaya; A report on the 1931 census and on certain problems of vital statistics*. London: Crown Agents.
Zablan, Z.C.
1978 'Trends and differential in mortality', in: *Population of the Philippines*. Bangkok: United Nations Economic Commission for Asia and the Pacific.

Daan Marks

The economic consequences of decolonization
The 'special' case of Indonesia

> Decolonization was among the most significant phenomena of the twentieth century. Indeed, it helped shape the history of the past century, and in one way or another, either directly or indirectly, affected the lives of nearly everyone, all across the globe. In its shape and duration, decolonization varied from place to place. Furthermore, it has been evaluated in many different ways. But in any case, its importance is beyond question.[1]

While there is a large body of literature on the political aspects of decolonization, economic literature that directly addresses this topic has been relatively scarce. Bertocchi (1994) and Bertocchi and Canova (2002) form a notable exception.[2] Graziella Bertocchi and Fabio Canova highlight empirically the channels through which the colonial heritage has influenced growth. In particular, they find evidence that colonization did have a direct effect on the growth pattern in African countries. Moreover, for a restricted number of countries their results suggest that there was a significant break in the growth pattern at Independence, with post-Independence growth rates exceeding pre-Independence and forecasted post-Independence growth rates.

Although Bertocchi and Canova focus on African countries this pattern seems to hold for Asian countries as well. Figure 1 shows that for four selected Asian countries per capita GDP was at a modest level before decolonization. The figures also suggest a break in the growth pattern following decolonization in three out of these four countries, which is in line with Bertocchi and Canova's findings. Whereas per capita GDP levels remained by far the lowest

1 Interview with Prasenjit Duara at: http://www.international.ucla.edu.

2 Other economic studies on this subject include Acemoglu, Johnson and Robinson 2001, Alam 1994 and Grier 1999.

in India, average annual growth rates (Table 1) do support this notion also for India with higher rates after Independence. Only Indonesia appears to have followed a different path. Except for some initial growth immediately after Independence, there was economic stagnation up to the mid-1960s.

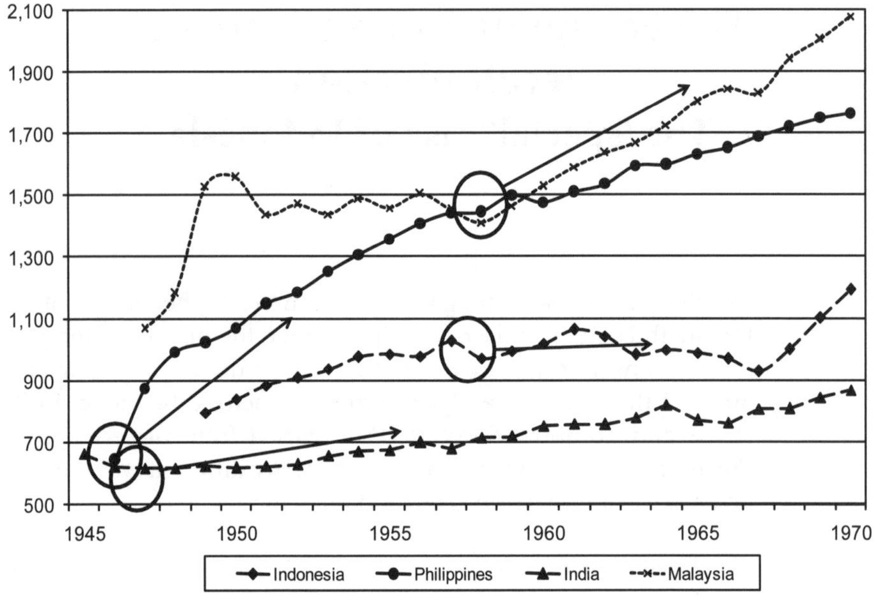

Figure 1. Per capita GDP in India, Indonesia, the Philippines and Malaysia, 1945-1970 (Maddison 2003:180-7)

Table 1. Average annual per capita GDP growth (%)

	India	Indonesia	Philippines	Malaysia
1900-1939	0.3	1.1	2.2	2.5
1949-1957	2.5	2.6	4.1	0.2
1957-1964	1.7	0.4	1.5	2.5

Source: See Figure 1.

Table 2. Country, colonizer and year of independence

Country	Colonizing country	Independence
India	United Kingdom	1947 (14 August)
Indonesia	Netherlands	1945 (17 August)
Philippines	USA	1946 (4 July)
Malaysia	United Kingdom	1957 (31 August)

When trying to distinguish between colonial and post-colonial regimes one should be aware that political independence does not necessarily coincide with economic independence (Bertocchi and Canova 2002:1857). The process of economic decolonization may predate the end of political control, while features of colonial dependence may persist well past the end of colonial times. The dates of decolonization in Table 2 are the dates Independence was granted or proclaimed in the various countries. Indonesian Independence was declared on 17 August 1945, but only on 27 December 1949 was sovereignty transferred by the Netherlands.[3]

The same point is also made by Lindblad (2002a). He states that most studies of the decolonization of Indonesia have paid surprisingly little attention to economic ties as opposed to political and military aspects. However, when economic ties are taken into account, can it then be argued that Indonesia followed a 'normal' path? The period between December 1957 and the first half of 1959 marked the end of direct Dutch involvement in the Indonesian economy with the takeover and subsequent nationalization of Dutch-owned private business firms. According to Bertocchi and Canova's 'model', this should be a breaking point in economic development. But the take-off to high rates of economic growth did not take place until the late 1960s or even early 1970s. This suggests that the process of decolonization in Indonesia differed from other countries in the region. This article explores the causes of such an 'abnormal' path of development. It argues that the institutional damage caused by decolonization forms a key aspect in understanding the poor macroeconomic performance of Indonesia at a later stage.

This article is structured in three layers that complement one another. It starts at the world level, then zooms in, first on Asia, and finally on Indonesia. At first, a macro perspective is chosen in which economic theories on colonialism, decolonization and economic growth are discussed and applied to the Indonesian experience. Then we descend to a second layer depicting differences in the process of decolonization in Asia. At the third layer, economic decolonization in Indonesia is analysed using the Dutch-owned shipping concern KPM (Koninklijke Paketvaart Maatschappij, Royal Packet Company) as a case study.

3 It took until the 2005 celebration of Independence Day in Indonesia for the Minister of Foreign Affairs of the Netherlands, Ben Bot, to formally accept 17 August as the true day of Indonesian Independence. In his speech, Bot stated that: 'The most important thing about today is that we are finally speaking openly to the Indonesians. For many years there have been Dutch representatives at the celebrations of Indonesia's independence on 17 August. With the support of the government, I can make it clear to the people of Indonesia that the Netherlands understands that the independent Republic of Indonesia in fact began on 17 August 1945 and that we – sixty years later – fully accept this both morally and politically.' Ben Bot, http://www.minbuza.nl.

Colonization and economic growth in theory

The prevailing view in the mainly historically oriented literature is that colonization was bad for colonial economies (Bertocchi and Canova 2002:1852). According to the 'colonial drain' literature, most of the colonial surplus was extracted by colonizing countries in the form of interest payments on loans, repatriated profits, salaries and pensions. This reduction of indigenous capital accumulation had a negative effect on the colonies' future growth prospects. Direct exploitation also included taxes, tariffs, restrictions on trade and foreign investment, forced labour and even enslavement of the indigenous population. Such distortions hampered the growth potential of the one-time colonies. Colonization could also create disincentives to human capital accumulation, affecting the growth potential adversely via an indirect channel. Finally, colonial domination may have been responsible for generating societies with dysfunctional institutions, rent-seeking elites and ethnic conflict (Engerman and Sokoloff 2005).

An alternative point of view emphasizes the positive development impulses provided by the colonizing powers. According to the 'modernization' thesis, colonial rule was legitimized by the fact that it promoted the integration of the colonies into the world economic system, channelling foreign capital to the colony and fostering modernization. Supporters of this hypothesis therefore stress that colonialism was beneficial to economic growth.

The issue of colonization has received little attention from professional economists. Exceptions are Lucas (1990) and Grossman and Iyigun (1995), who developed static models of a colonial economy in which the scale of foreign intervention is endogenously and optimally determined from the vantage point of the colonizer.

Another line of research emphasizes the importance of institutions. La Porta et al. (1999) perform an empirical analysis of legal systems that emphasizes colonial heritage. Acemoglu, Johnson and Robinson (2001) elaborate this argument. They claim that there were different types of colonization policies, which created different sets of institutions. The colonization strategy was influenced by the feasibility of settlements. In places where disease was virulent and potentially fatal to European settlers, an extractive state was more likely to be established. Settlements were a major determinant for early institutions. The colonial state and its institutions persisted even after Independence and formed the basis of current institutions.

By exploring differences in European mortality rates as an indication of current institutions, Acemoglu, Johnson and Robinson find substantial effects of institutions on income per capita levels. In other words, colonies where Europeans faced higher mortality rates are today substantially poorer than colonies that were healthy for Europeans. The theory is that this relationship reflects the effect of settler mortality working through the institutions brought by Europeans. It is difficult to apply this type of argument to the Indonesian case. A high mortality rate did not prevent Dutchmen from settling in the Indonesian archipelago. Moreover, they were heavily involved in the construction of institutions.[4] With respect to the four decades up to 1942, Anne Booth writes:

> There was also increasing intervention on the part of the government to attain objectives which would not have been achieved had product and factor [of production] markets been left to the vagaries of national and international trends. In this aspect of their behaviour, the last generation of colonial civil servants foreshadowed many of the policies which would be enthusiastically adopted by newly industrializing countries in many parts of the world after 1945. (Booth 1998:155-6.)

This does not mean, however, that the Dutch succeeded in establishing lasting, efficient institutions. While involved in creating institutions serving their own interests in particular, the Dutch failed in terms of 'indigenization' or *Indonesianisasi* of these institutions. The Dutch created institutions but did not succeed in getting indigenous Indonesians involved.[5]

At this stage, it is worth mentioning a study by Alam (1994), who compares growth rates in sovereign countries and colonies. He concludes, although on fairly weak statistical grounds, that colonial policies after the Second World War showed signs of a developmental orientation which had been missing before. On the other hand, some of the recently decolonized countries wasted their potential for rapid growth because of hasty indigenization and excessively interventionist policies in support of industrialization. In other words, these opposite tendencies make it difficult to predict whether decolonization would lead to faster growth rates, and also whether decolonized countries would grow faster than those that were still under colonial rule.

For Indonesia one could very well argue that the hopeful developments in the late 1930s, when colonial Indonesia showed modest growth rates and the first steps towards industrialization were taken, were cancelled out by the Japanese occupation, the struggle for Independence and the difficult process of Indonesianisasi (Dick et al. 2002:155-62).

Another interesting study on the relationship between colonization, decolonization and economic growth is offered by Grier (1999). He studies the relationship between the length of colonial rule and long-run economic growth. In a sample of 63 ex-colonial states he finds that the length of colonization is

4 For mortality rates see Acemoglu, Johnson and Robinson 2001:1398.

5 For an extensive discussion of the term Indonesianisasi, see Sutter 1959 and Lindblad 2002b.

positively and significantly correlated with economic growth. This means that colonies that were held for relatively long periods of time as opposed to short periods tend to perform better, on average, after Independence. However, his sample only includes former British, Spanish and French colonies. Also here Indonesia would be a special case, since Indonesia was a colony for a (very) long time, while economic growth after decolonization was slower than in many other countries in the region.

The most comprehensive studies on the relationship between decolonization and economic growth were performed by Bertocchi (1994) and Bertocchi and Canova (2002). Bertocchi first analysed the historical determinants of underdevelopment by introducing colonization in an otherwise standard growth model of the colonial economy. In this model, she showed that colonization can promote output growth, but at the same time can depress living standards in the colonies. More importantly for our purposes, the model also predicts that decolonization may deliver disappointing, or even disastrous, economic performances when investment withdrawal is accompanied by persistent economic and institutional damage. In a later study Bertocchi and Canova find evidence that there is a significant break in the growth pattern at Independence, with post-Independence growth rates exceeding pre-Independence and forecasted post-Independence growth rates. Unfortunately, Bertocchi and Canova do not relate their findings to Bertocchi's earlier empirical study.

My hypothesis runs as follows: There is likely to have been a significant break in the growth pattern at Independence, with post-Independence growth rates exceeding pre-Independence and predicted post-Independence growth rates, unless decolonization was accompanied by persistent economic and institutional damage.

This hypothesis could help explain the specific case of Indonesia where decolonization seemed to hamper economic growth, whereas in comparable countries in the region decolonization proved the starting point for accelerated economic growth.

Indonesian decolonization in a regional perspective

This section gives a short overview of how in different countries in the region the process of decolonization took place. Admittedly, the discussion here remains incomplete in terms of both coverage of countries and depth of analysis, since an exhaustive treatment would go well beyond the scope of our study. It does aim to show, however, that in former colonies such as the Philippines, Malaysia and India decolonization was a relatively gradual process. In these cases relatively good and close ties with the former colonizing country were retained, which reduced economic and institutional damage. Indonesia does not fit this pattern. It went through a highly disruptive process during which the relationship with its former colonial rulers the Netherlands was tense and successively deteriorated to a total breakdown. The case of Burma is not discussed here but is likely to provide yet another illustration of how decolonization occurred.

In the Philippines decolonization was already planned before the Pacific War broke out. Soon after American colonial rule was established in the first decade of the twentieth century, the process of devolving power to Filipinos was set in motion. The executive and judicial branches of government were 'decolonized' and already in 1935 the Philippines' Commonwealth became colonial Southeast Asia's first self-governing state headed by an indigenous president. Remaining American-controlled fields of policy, notably foreign relations, finance, immigration and the governance of minority ethnic groups, were surrendered when the Philippines became independent in 1946.

The orientation of foreign policy in the Philippines was heavily geared towards the alliance with the former colonial power. Apart from the fact that the country's political elite had been educated in America, economic ties with the United States favoured a continuation of close Philippine-American relations. For example, the Filipino landowners and exporters had for decades been reaping the benefits of a protected American market. Protection was extended into the post-Independence era by the United States, albeit on a lesser scale. At the same time, the Philippines had to extend so-called 'parity' rights to American firms, which allowed free operations on Philippine soil, identical with those enjoyed by local enterprises (Lindblad 2003:41-2). The Philippines also granted territorial leases for American bases, originally for a 99-year period. All this meant that in the process of decolonization in the Philippines, the Philippine-American relations remained close.

The situation in British Malaya was quite different. In the immediate years after the Pacific War near-anarchy prevailed in Malaya (Bastin and Benda 1968:173). This stood in stark contrast to the relative tranquillity of the country's earlier evolution under British rule. After a quick restoration of British authority it took a sizeable effort by combined Commonwealth contingents, coupled with the forced resettlement of Chinese squatters, to subdue the communist challenge. The 'Emergency' (the official name of the insurrection) officially ended only in 1960, three years after Malaysia had become a sovereign nation. Progress towards independent nationhood had actually proceeded swiftly in an endeavour to counter communist propaganda appeals to fight for the liberation of the country from British colonialism.

British wartime plans for the future of her Malayan possessions had digressed markedly from the colonial pattern. Considerations of rapid economic reconstruction, reinforced by the desire to simplify, centralize and modernize the cumbersome administrative machineries, led colonial officers in London to urge a unitary structure for post-war Malaya. The plan which they had devised eradicated the separate constitutional entities. They were to be incorporated into a centralized Malayan Union.

But almost at once opposition was aroused. In Britain, former colonial administrators waged a successful campaign against such a departure from the principles of indirect rule through Malay sultans. In 1948 the Federation of Malaya was born, which reflected a clear victory for the Malay population. The new constitutional arrangement altered the basic pattern of government. The traditional rulers and sultans retained their prerogatives, while their English-educated descendants came to occupy high positions at the centre of authority. In 1957 the Federation of Malaya, the West's last major dependency in Southeast Asia, attained Independence.

In 1963, the Federation was expanded to include the remaining British colonial enclaves of Singapore and the territories Sarawak and Sabah on the island of Borneo. The sultanate of Brunei remained a British colony. Yet only two years after its founding, Singapore left – or was forced to leave – the federation, and became an independent Republic.

The federation involved a constitutional monarchy with the Malay sultans employing a rotation method to elect a king. The leadership represented the intrinsically conservative elements of the Malay aristocracy and the well-established Chinese commercial middle class. Retention of close ties with Britain and the Commonwealth and a favourable climate for foreign investment were other features of the gradual nature of decolonization in Malaya (Lindblad 2003:45).

India, another former British colony, is described by John Springhall as 'the prototype for the evolution of the rest of the British Empire' (Springhall 2001:66). Cautious British attempts to respond to the aspirations of Indian nationalists can be chartered from the Montagu-Chelmsford reforms (1919), usually known as the Montford reforms, through to the Simon Commission (1927-1929) and then the government of India Act (1935). The end of British rule was accelerated by the Second World War, which was crucial in determining the timing of departure.

Once the war ended, cost effectiveness suggested to Labour politicians in the United Kingdom that the expense in trying to control a reluctant Indian empire by far outweighed the commercial benefits. India's economy stalled and ceased balancing its metropolitan trade with other parts of the world, failing to provide a protected market for British goods. Imperial protection and patronage were no longer necessary for British businesses. The general conclusion was that Great Britain would not lose out and could possibly gain in prestige and power by handing over the country to the Indians. An important proviso was that a friendly and united India would become a member of the British Commonwealth. Arrangements were also made for defence links.

Clearly, the process of decolonization in the countries described here differed in several respects from each other. The cases have one thing in common though: in both cases ties with the former colonizers were gradually removed. This resulted in a slower economic reorientation and a gradual indigenization of economic institutions. The Indonesian story is quite different in this respect.

On 17 August 1945, Sukarno and Hatta declared Indonesia independent. But it took another five days before the Japanese commander in Java officially announced Japan's capitulation (Hall 1981:890). What followed was a period of turmoil with the Dutch refusing to hand over sovereignty and the Indonesians struggling for international recognition of Independence.

After many attempts and considerable pressure from abroad, the so-called Linggadjati agreement was reached on 15 November 1946. The Dutch government recognized the Sukarno administration of the Republic of Indonesia as exercising de facto authority over Java, Madura and Sumatra. The two governments were to cooperate in establishing a sovereign democratic state on a federal basis, to be called the United States of Indonesia. The United States of Indonesia was in turn to form part of a Netherlands-Indonesian Union, together with the Netherlands, Surinam and Curaçao. This would promote joint interests in foreign relations, defence, finance and economic and cultural matters. Although this was a good plan in theory, it turned out very difficult to put it into practice. The main reason for this was lack of mutual trust.

The Dutch accused the Republic of not honouring the Linggadjati Agreement and proceeded to restore order by military intervention, a so-called 'police action', in July-August 1947. Under pressure of the United Nations, a new conference was held on 17 January 1948 on board the American warship Renville. The subsequent Renville Agreement, however, was no more successful than the one negotiated at Linggadjati. Both sides accused the other of violating the truce. In December 1948, negotiations broke down and the Dutch again resorted to 'police action'.

The second military intervention caused serious agitation, not only in the ranks of the United Nations, but also throughout Asia. When the Dutch realized that their solution by force had failed, they felt aggrieved at the extent to which their actions had turned world opinion against them. There was a strong revulsion of feeling in the Netherlands in favour of a round-table settlement which would satisfy the aspirations of the Indonesian people. Dutch policy now was to grant Independence, not grudgingly, but 'with good grace and liberality' (Hall 1981:895). Eventually on 27 December 1949, the provisional government of the new federal state was constituted.

Relations remained tense between Indonesia and the Netherlands well into the 1950s. This was mainly caused by the dispute over the fate of western

A vessel of the shipping company KPM (Koninklijke Paketvaart Maatschappij) anchoring at Hollandia, Netherlands New Guinea, in 1955. This was just two years before all KPM ships were expelled from adjacent Indonesian waters. (KITLV 54710.)

New Guinea (West Irian). The Dutch argued that recognition of Indonesian Independence did not necessarily involve handing over all territories of the former Netherlands Indies to Indonesia. They reasoned that western New Guinea was no part of Indonesia, geographically or ethnically. The Indonesians, on the other hand, saw Netherlands New Guinea as a European colonial outpost at their doorstep.

The agitation intensified in 1952, when the Netherlands refused further negotiations on the matter. The losses both sides suffered from the affair were enormous, both in terms of economic recovery and the bitterness it engendered (Hall 1981:937). Eventually, again under pressure from the United Nations, the matter was resolved in 1962, when the region was transferred via the United Nations from the Netherlands to Indonesia. An important consequence of the dispute about western New Guinea formed the measures taken by the Indonesian government to take over and eventually nationalize private Dutch business firms still operationing in Indonesia in the late 1950s. Agreement was eventually reached on payment of compensation for the takeover, but the sum paid was considered grossly inadequate.

The process of decolonization in Indonesia clearly developed in a different way compared to several other countries in the region. While the Philippines and Malaysia in Southeast Asia and India in South Asia gradually gained sovereignty with relatively little conflict, it took a great deal of struggle for Indonesia to achieve full political and economic sovereignty. The political and economic conflicts explain why decolonization in Indonesia hampered economic growth instead of marking the take-off into rapid economic growth, as elsewhere in the region. This is in line with the theoretical literature discussed above and our hypothesis that Independence marks a negative break in growth performance if decolonization is accompanied by persistent economic and institutional damage. In Indonesia the Dutch at first refused to grant Independence whereas the indigenization of institutions failed. In the next section we will, at a micro level, look more closely at the troublesome transfer of institutions by discussing the case of the Dutch shipping company KPM.

The Koninklijke Paketvaart Maatschappij (KPM)

The following statements[6] illluminate the turbulence in the Indonesian economy immediately after the transfer of sovereignty, in general and specifically in interisland shipping:

> It is true that the Dutch lion is dead, but it still has its claws in the body of Indonesia. The earlier foreign capital and non-Indonesians leave Indonesia, the better. (Meijer 1994:349.)

> The development of global shipping lines was part and parcel of late nineteenth-century imperialism, and many great national shipping companies remained mainstays of colonialism throughout the first half of the twentieth. As decolonization gained momentum after World War II, the maritime empires were also forced into retreat. Many new states promoted national shipping as a means to secure economic independence, a tactic which induced friction with vested interests. The role of Dutch shipping in the colonization and decolonization of Indonesia fits fairly well into this overall pattern. (À Campo 1998:1.)

Mainly due to the severe losses incurred by KPM during the Pacific War, maritime transport immediately after the declaration of Indonesian Independence was affected by urgent demands and acute tonnage shortages. In 1939 the KPM fleet had contained 136 ships, but in 1945 only 26 remained, scattered

6 This section is largely based on À Campo 1998 and À Campo's website (http://www.fhk.eur.nl/websites/kpm, accessed in February 2006.

across the Pacific and Indian Oceans. The initial impulse was to reconstruct the fleet completely and to resume all former operations.

After the war, the colonial government stated that priority should be given to the reconstruction of shipping 'above any other single sector of the economy' and demanded that ranks be closed (À Campo 1998:13). There were economic, technical and political reasons for much closer cooperation and the avoidance of any conflict. From a commercial perspective Dutch shipping faced much stronger competition than before. If Dutch companies wanted to survive, they had to compete against American, British, Chinese, Norwegian and other foreign firms. Closer cooperation could also yield economies of scale by lowering operating costs per ton. The political motive, however, was predominant. From a commercial point of view, KPM fared well in 1948 and in 1949 because it was well prepared to reap the benefits of the general economic recovery.

At the end of 1946, KPM operated 22 regular lines, a number that doubled within five years, while total route mileage rose from 46,000 to 160,000 geographical miles (À Campo 1998:6). Despite the protection guaranteed to Dutch companies under the agreements reached at the Round Table Conference in (RTC) 1949, in 1952 the Indonesian government established a shipping company of its own, PELNI (Pelajaran Nasional Indonesia, National Indonesian Shipping). Its ultimate aim was to usurp the role of KPM in interisland and short-range sea transport. PELNI started operations with 13 ships but within five years its fleet had grown to 38 ships totalling 38,000 tons. As most vessels clearly were too small for long-distance shipping, PELNI incurred heavy losses, which contrasted painfully with KPM's continuing profits (À Campo 1998:26; Dick 1987:17).

Freight rates were set by the government and PELNI tended to conform to KPM's levels – undercutting would have increased losses and overcharging would have reduced its market share – but it did not enter into arrangements on routes or schedules. PELNI usually consigned new ships to existing KPM routes without prior notification, which resulted in sub-optimal allocation of tonnage. Contacts at a personal level were pleasant, but the Indonesians did not accept offers for advice or support: 'They prefer to take their own line. In the Asian perception, consultation by the Dutch seems to amount to loss of face.' (À Campo 1998:27.)

It became increasingly clear that cooperation was not the Indonesian goal. In the Indonesian cabinet political sentiments increasingly overruled economic considerations, much to the despair of pragmatic and competent Indonesian officials.

KPM had little choice but to continue its pre-Independence policy of internal contraction and external expansion. KPM went on shrinking its Indonesian activities by reducing personnel, transferring shipments from its own agencies to commissioned agencies and outsourcing other activities. Unprofitable lines were discontinued, while the government no longer allowed KPM to operate foreign charters on regular lines. Despite lavish profits, KPM hardly undertook any new investment in Indonesia.

The KPM-PELNI conflict rested on the opposing interests of a large profit-making colonial corporation and a poorly performing national company. With the substitution of KPM by PELNI being only a matter of time, KPM's attitude towards the Indonesian economy became 'to get as much out of it as long as it lasted' (À Campo 1998:29). The battle was fought over the recurrent issue of rising costs and raising rates. The relative price stability of the previous years was spoiled by inflationary measures taken by successive cabinets. KPM insisted the rising costs must be offset by rising freight rates. Regulations, however, made it nearly impossible to pass costs on to shippers.

In the meantime, the Indonesian press increasingly urged for nationalization. The development of a national shipping industry through the nationalization of KPM had been considered since 1945, but Indonesian politicians never succeeded in mapping out a viable procedure. Proposals for a mixed company had been rejected. The idea of nationalization, however, had not been dropped altogether and was revived after the unilateral renunciation of the 1949 RTC agreements by Indonesia in February 1956.

Strained with social unrest and political tensions, the situation became rather paradoxical. The Indonesians wanted to get rid of KPM, yet feared its departure. KPM wanted to stay, but was prepared to relocate. As both sides were acting adversely to their own interests, the relationship was inherently unstable. Sunar Suraputra characterized it as '[a]n equilibrium in which both are equally strong, or rather both are equally weak, an equilibrium lacking a solid foundation' (quoted in À Campo 1998:33-4). KPM calculated that strong measures against it would do more harm to Indonesia than to itself. At least until the middle of 1957, KPM remained confident that the Indonesian government assessed the situation the same way. Still, it took two important precautionary measures. First, it insured its entire fleet with Lloyds in London against seizure. Second, in November 1957 all captains received a sealed letter containing instructions in case of emergency, to be opened if they received a coded message.

The breakthrough was triggered by a wave of political protest and trade union action, which resulted in the nationalization and eviction of Dutch post-colonial capital. KPM bore the brunt. On 3 December 1957 radical trade unionists occupied KPM's head office in Jakarta. Having lost effective control, the directors immediately instructed all ships to flee to foreign ports. Thirty-four ships managed to escape, but 29 were held in Indonesian ports by crews or military guards. Another 11 were seized on the high seas. The Indonesian government, which most probably had approved of and, according to some, even coordinated the action, legalized the takeover in retrospect.

In the period immediately following the expulsion of KPM it seemed that water transport was not as negatively affected as first feared. The newly created vacuum was filled quite swiftly (Ali 1966:35). Within two years, total shipping capacity was at a level comparable to that before the expulsion of KPM (Tables 3 and 4).

Table 3. Interisland freight (in tons) and productivity of KPM and PELNI, 1950-1960

	KPM			PELNI		
	Transported goods	Total gross tonnage	Productivity	Transported goods	Total gross tonnage	Productivity
1950	3,610,000	176,602	20.4			
1951	4,079,000	185,945	21.9			
1952	3,835,000	178,460	21.5		20,450	
1953	3,630,000	170,065	21.3		36,750	
1954	3,312,000	184,881	17.9	437,659	51,100	8.6
1955	3,176,000	187,306	17.0	720,212	36,400	19.8
1956	2,999,000	190,547	15.7	968,358	46,300	20.9
1957				1,006,339	58,020	17.3
1958				808,169	89,687	9.0
1959				1,254,673	134,554	9.3
1960				1,514,946	154,242	9.8

Note: Productivity is measured by dividing transported goods by total gross tonnage of the fleet.
Source: BPS 1958, 1961.

Table 4. Interisland fleet, cargo (in tons), and productivity, 1957-1964

Year	Tonnage owned			Tonnage chartered			Total tonnage	Total cargo	Fleet productivity
	PELNI	Private	Total	PELNI	Private	Total		000 tons	
1957	30,500	21,100	51,600	18,900	28,300	47,200	98,800	n/a	n/a
1958	57,700	28,000	85,700	38,400	24,800	63,200	148,900	n/a	n/a
1959	80,800	58,800	139,600	61,100	47,200	108,300	247,900	2,797	11.3
1960	93,400	71,100	164,500	77,600	56,100	133,700	298,200	2,713	9.1
1961	108,800	125,700	234,500	116,100	60,900	177,000	411,500	3,027	7.4
1962	132,100	113,200	245,300	100,800	43,500	144,300	389,600	2,281	5.9
1963	154,000	158,900	312,900	90,200	43,900	134,100	447,000	2,800	6.3
1964	144,200	191,500	335,700	29,600	20,600	50,200	385,900	3,300	8.6

Source: Dick 1987:28.

However, the most important finding here is the significant decline in productivity at PELNI in Indonesian interisland transport after KPM had been banned from Indonesian waters in 1957. Where KPM had recorded productivity rates, as measured by tons of goods transported divided by total gross tonnage, of 15 or more, this rate dropped below 10 for PELNI and the entire Indonesian fleet after 1958 and 1960 respectively. One could attribute the decline in productivity to a fall in total trade. This is not the case. Domestic trade actually increased from 10.3 million tons in 1957 to 11.0 million tons in 1962 (Singgih Tri Sulistiyono 2003:237). It was not a lack of capital investment in the form of new ships which slowed down developments in the water transport sector, but rather a lack of organizational knowledge and skills, both lost as a result of the way in which nationalization took place in this important sector. The Dutch can be held partly accountable. At first they refused to hand over sovereignty, then they attempted to delay economic decolonization. With the expulsion of KPM an institution was lost. In the first few years following the nationalization of KPM, bottlenecks in interisland transport could be alleviated but in the long run the organizational inefficiencies in this sector came to light.

The importance of institutions for economic growth is often stressed in the development literature.[7] This theory can be readily applied to the Indonesian situation in general and KPM in particular. While the Dutch created institutions, they did not employ enough indigenous Indonesians at a supervisory level. So when the Dutch were forced to leave, this resulted in the deterioration of these institutions. As shown above, macroeconomic performance in Indonesia was reasonably good between 1949 and 1957, but then deteriorated significantly (Table 2). The institutional argument can serve to connect the deterioration in macroeconomic performance to the process of economic decolonization, a connection which so far has not been sufficiently acknowledged in the literature on the economic development of Indonesia.[8]

Conclusion

In many decaying empires, decolonization was a multi-staged process in which political decolonization sooner or later was followed by economic withdrawal. In Indonesia, political independence was achieved between 1945 and 1949, but the decisive step towards economic decolonization was not

7 The standard work in this field is North 1990. See also Bertocchi 1994; Acemoglu, Johnson and Robinson 2001, and Bertocchi and Canova 2002.

8 Divergent opinions can be found in Lindblad 2006 and Singgih Tri Sulistiyono 2003:251-2 and 2006:123, who conclude that the economic slowdown only began to gain ground in the early 1960s, while the takeover and nationalization of Dutch firms took place in 1957-1959.

taken until 1957-1958. In the interim period, Dutch corporations in Indonesia operated in a state of post-colonial turmoil, and this applies to the shipping company KPM as well. Because indigenous Indonesian shipping was not yet equipped to take over interisland shipping, the new national government had to accept continuing operations by KPM also after the transfer of sovereignty.

Just as in the colonial state, the course of KPM's post-colonial history was very much determined by government action. During the Indonesian Revolution, the colonial government was the driving force behind the reconstruction of the KPM fleet, which had been largely destroyed during the war. Pressure by the colonial government was essential in the transfer of local shipping to Indonesian control. Although some colonial officials advocated a liberal attitude towards *Indonesianisasi*, KPM was reluctant to make concessions, wishing to preserve its Dutch identity.

The expulsion of KPM from Indonesian waters in 1957/1958 marked the failure of both Dutch foreign policy and KPM's quest for continuity. Being part of the general breakdown in Dutch-Indonesian relations, the expulsion cannot be attributed to a failure of Dutch foreign policy or Indonesian nationalism alone. In its dealings with the government on rate policy, KPM's policy of toughness verging on brinkmanship no doubt aggravated the instability and thus accelerated the crisis of decolonization.

While on a world and regional level it was already suggested that Indonesia's process of economic development was different from that of other countries in the region, the case study of KPM shows some explanatory elements at a micro level. This evidence reaffirms my hypothesis that there is likely to have been a significant break in the growth pattern at Independence, with post-Independence growth rates exceeding pre-Independence and predicted post-Independence ones, unless decolonization is accompanied by persistent economic and institutional damage. The persistent economic and institutional damage that rises from the KPM case study was observed to a far lesser extent in other countries in the region. Using an expression of Booth, it was 'a missed opportunity' to forestall such serious institutional damage (Booth 1998).

References

Acemoglu, Daron, Simon Johnson and James A. Robinson
2001 'The colonial origins of comparative development; An empirical investigation', *American Economic Review* 91:1369-1401.

Alam, M.S.
1994 'Colonialism, decolonization and growth rates; Theory and empirical evidence', *Cambridge Journal of Economics* 18:235-57.

Ali, Shamsher
1966 'Interisland shipping', *Bulletin of Indonesian Economic Studies* 2:27-51.
Bastin, John S. and Harry J. Benda,
1968 *A history of modern Southeast Asia*. Englewood Cliffs, NJ: Prentice-Hall.
Bertocchi, Graziella
1994 'Colonialism in the theory of growth'. Working Paper, Brown University, no. 94-14.
Bertocchi, Graziella and Fabio Canova
2002 'Did colonization matter for growth? An empirical exploration into the historical causes of Africa's underdevelopment', *European Economic Review* 46:1851-71.
Booth, Anne
1998 *The Indonesian economy in the nineteenth and twentieth centuries; A history of missed opportunities*. Basingstoke: Macmillan.
BPS
1958 *Statistical pocketbook of Indonesia 1958*. Djakarta: Biro Pusat Statistik.
1961 *Statistical pocketbook of Indonesia 1961*. Djakarta: Biro Pusat Statistik.
Campo, Joseph N.F.M. à
1998 'Business not as usual; Dutch shipping in independent Indonesia, 1945-1958', *International Journal of Maritime History* 10-2:1-39.
Dick, Howard W.
1987 *The Indonesian interisland shipping industry; An analysis of competition and regulation*. Singapore: Institute of Southeast Asian Studies.
Dick, Howard W., Vincent J.H. Houben, J. Thomas Lindblad and Thee Kian Wie
2002 *The emergence of a national economy; An economic history of Indonesia, 1800-2000*. Crows Nest, NSW: Allen and Unwin.
Engerman, Stanley L. and Kenneth L. Sokoloff
2005 'Colonialism, inequality and long-run paths of development'. [NBER Working Paper, no. 11057.]
Grier, R.M.
1999 'Colonial legacies and economic growth', *Public Policy* 98:317-35.
Grossman, Herschel I. and Murat Iyigun
1995 'The profitability of colonial investment', *Economics and Politics* 7-3:229-42.
Hall, Daniel G.E.,
1981 *A history of South-East Asia*. Basingstoke: Macmillan
La Porta, Rafael, Florencio Lopez-de-Silanes, Andrei Shleifer and Robert W. Vishny
1999 'The quality of government', *Journal of Law, Economics and Organization* 15:222-79.
Lindblad, J. Thomas
2002a 'Politieke economie en de dekolonisatie van Indonesië', in: J. Thomas Lindblad and Willem van der Molen (eds), *Macht en majesteit; Opstellen voor Cees Fasseur*, pp. 132-46. Leiden: Opleiding Talen en Culturen van Zuidoost-Azië en Oceanië.
2002b 'The importance of *Indonesianisasi* during the transition from the 1930s to the 1960s', *Itinerario. European Journal of Overseas History* 26-3/4:51-72.

2003 'The economic impact of decolonization in Southeast Asia; Economic nationalism and foreign direct investment, 1945-1965', in: Marc Frey, Ronald W. Pruessen and Tan Tai Yong (eds), *The transformation of Southeast Asia; International perspectives on decolonization*, pp. 35-51. London: Sharpe.

2006 'Macroeconomic consequences of decolonization in Indonesia'. [Paper, Conference of the International Economic History Association, Helsinki, 21-25 August.]

Lucas Jr., Robert E.

1990 'Why doesn't capital flow from rich to poor countries?', *American Economic Review* 80-2:92-6.

Maddison, Angus

2003 *The world economy; Historical statistics*. Paris: OECD Development Centre.

Meijer, Hans

1994 *Den Haag-Djakarta. De Nederlandse-Indonesische betrekkingen 1950-1962*. Utrecht: Aula.

North, Douglass C.

1990 *Institutions, institutional change and economic performance*. Cambridge: Cambridge University Press.

Springhall, John O.

2001 *Decolonization since 1945; The collapse of European overseas empires*. Basingstoke: Palgrave.

Sulistiyono, Singgih Tri

2003 *The Java sea network; Patterns in the development of interregional shipping and trade in the process of national economic integration in Indonesia, 1870s-1970s*. PhD thesis, Leiden University.

2006 'The expulsion of KPM and its impact on the inter-island shipping and trade in Indonesia', *Itinerario. European Journal of Overseas History* 30:104-28.

Sutter, John O.

1959 *Indonesianisasi; A historical survey of the role of politics in the institutions of a changing economy from the Second World War to the eve of the general election, 1940-1955*. PhD thesis, Cornell University, Ithaca, NY.

JASPER VAN DE KERKHOF

'Colonial' enterprise and the indigenization of management in independent Indonesia and Malaysia

Indonesia stands out among the Southeast Asian countries for the rapidity with which it eradicated the economic institutions implanted by the former metropolitan power during the era of colonialism (Paauw 1963:155).[1] In December 1957, the government-sponsored campaign to free West Irian (present-day Papua) from Dutch rule 'spontaneously' induced labour unions to take over virtually all Dutch companies in the archipelago.[2] In the following weeks, Dutch employees were repatriated and their functions taken over by senior indigenous personnel under the supervision of the Indonesian military. The promulgation of the Nationalization Act in December 1958 all but eliminated Dutch business in the archipelago, ushering in the final phase towards the complete dismantlement of the Dutch empire in Southeast Asia in 1962/1963.[3]

Obviously, there were other newly independent Southeast Asian countries – notably Burma and Vietnam – which also experienced abrupt and dramatic transitions from a colonial to a national economy. Yet this was certainly not typical of the region. In the Philippines, for instance, the dissolution of the colonial economy was 'rapid and occurred without overt expropriation of the alien communities' whereas the political leadership of independent Malaysia 'recognize[d] an interest in maintaining a large Western share in the economy'

1 The author would like to thank Prof. Leonard Andaya (University of Hawaii), Dr J. Thomas Lindblad (Leiden University) and Dr Peter Keppy for commenting on earlier versions.

2 Whether the takeover of Dutch enterprise was planned or not remains a matter of speculation. Jakarta's reaction to the workers' actions was characterized by improvisation, which supports the idea that the takeovers caught the government unprepared. Yet a number of high-ranking Indonesian officials, including Sukarno himself, later claimed that the takeovers took place with prior government knowledge and consent.

3 The BPM (Bataafsche Petroleum Maatschappij,), a subsidiary of the Anglo-Dutch oil giant Royal Dutch/Shell, and the Anglo-Dutch soap and margarine producer Unilever were not considered as Dutch enterprises and therefore permitted to stay in Indonesia.

(Golay et al. 1969:101, 346). The course of events in Indonesia is therefore in sharp contrast with the overall gradual and non-violent withdrawal of 'colonial' enterprise elsewhere in Southeast Asia.

Why is this so? Oversimplifying a little, the literature has brought forward two explanations, which are not mutually exclusive, for the confrontational nature of the relationship between Dutch enterprise and the government of independent Indonesia. One explanation is that the political legacy of decolonization, in particular the Dutch refusal to negotiate the status of the disputed territory of West Irian, hindered fruitful cooperation between Dutch capital and the Indonesian government.[4] Dutch enterprise was merely a scapegoat for Indonesian annoyance over the obstinacy of the Netherlands government in The Hague (Golay et al. 1969:184-92; Sluyterman 2003:219).

The second explanation emphasizes that Indonesians saw continued economic supremacy by the Dutch as an intolerable relic of colonial rule. According to this argument, Dutch enterprise in Indonesia was by and large insensitive to justified Indonesian demands for a larger share of the country's economic pie, thus fuelling Indonesian frustration and contributing significantly to its own demise. This argument implicitly assumes that Dutch enterprise could have escaped expropriation of its Indonesian assets had it taken a more cooperative stance in dealing with independent Indonesia (Schmitt 1962:289; Robison 1986:62-5; Meijer 1994:637).

This article examines the validity of the second explanation by comparing the responsiveness of Dutch enterprise in Indonesia and British business in Malaysia to the plea for a distribution of economic power in line with the new nations' aspirations. The focus is on one specific aspect of the relationship between 'colonial' firms and the decolonized countries, that is recruitment, training and advancement of indigenous personnel to management and expert positions within 'colonial' enterprise. This so-called indigenization was a declared aim of virtually all newly independent nations in their efforts to create a national economy. It was also a yardstick for the sensitivity of 'colonial' firms to the ambitions of the decolonized peoples. Finally, it was an area in which forms of formal and informal racial discrimination that had been characteristic of the colonial system appeared to survive into the era of Independence.

'Colonial enterprise' is no clearly defined entity, but rather an umbrella term encompassing a highly heterogeneous set of firms, large and small, old and new, centrally and locally managed, 'free standing' and multinational, with either capital- or labour-intensive lines of production, and so forth. Their

4 West Irian (today Papua) was part of the Netherlands Indies but was excluded from the transfer of sovereignty in 1949 since the Dutch insisted that its definitive status be decided later. The dispute continued to sour Indonesian-Dutch relations until, in 1962, the Dutch finally gave in to heavy international pressure.

response to the challenges of decolonization was likewise diverse (Baudet and Fennema et al. 1983; Meijer 1994:349-54; White 2004). The findings presented here, based on research in the archives of a large number of Dutch firms representing most important sectors of the Indonesian economy as well as British government and business records, reflect the overall process of indigenization in the Western-controlled corporate sectors of both countries.

Notwithstanding numerous and obvious differences between post-colonial Indonesia and Malaysia, there are also several parallels. Both countries achieved Independence while their economies were still overwhelmingly controlled by nationals of the former colonial power (Sutter 1959:107-8; Puthucheary 1960:27-8; Harper 1999:363). The economic structure in Indonesia and Malaysia was also similar in the sense that the modern, capital-intensive and export-oriented sectors were owned and managed by Western firms, whereas the indigenous population provided the bulk of the requisite labour but little capital or management skills. In both countries the ethnic Chinese community played a crucial role as an intermediary between the Western apex of the economic system and its indigenous base.

The presence of commercially powerful Chinese (and to a lesser extent Indian and Arab) minorities adds to the complexity of economic decolonization in Indonesia and Malaysia. A distinction needs to be made between the economic advancement of the indigenous population (*pribumi* in Indonesia, *bumiputra* in Malaysia)[5] and the process of improving economic conditions for all nationals, including those of Chinese and other non-Western descent. In this article, the former process is referred to as 'indigenization', or *pribumisasi* and Malayanization when referring explicitly to one of the two nations. The latter process is termed Indonesianization or Malaysianization.

Dutch enterprise in independent Indonesia

The newly independent nations of Southeast Asia encouraged 'colonial' firms to provide training and expand career opportunities for their citizens, especially indigenous ones. The rationale was threefold. First, the indigenization of leading and presumably well-paid functions would lead to a transfer of income from foreigners to nationals. Second, relocation of responsibilities

5 Both terms mean literally 'earlier son of the soil'. *Bumiputra* and Malay are often used interchangeably with regard to peninsular Malaysia where the vast majority of *bumiputra* are Malays. By contrast, Sabah and Sarawak in East Malaysia contain several indigenous ethnic groups that are not Malay. The term *pribumi* actually came into usage in Indonesia only under the New Order government of Soeharto replacing the previous term *asli* ('original people'). It is used here to avoid confusion.

from foreigners to nationals would raise commercial, technical and management skills of the population through 'learning by doing' and thus pave the way for economic emancipation. Third, economic advancement at the expense of nationals of the former colonizer would generate 'psychic' income in terms of nationalist satisfaction, especially if highly prestigious jobs were involved (Breton 1964:376-9; Johnson 1965:177).

In Indonesia, the 1930s saw the first, if modest, effects of the preceding Ethical Policy as increasing numbers of educated Indonesians entered the labour market (Kahin 1952:29-33). The available evidence, however, suggests that in the late-colonial period Dutch firms 'virtually never took Indonesians or Chinese into the top echelons of their companies' (Sutter 1959:95-6). The local population provided manual labour for the Dutch-owned estates, mines and factories, but hardly any technical, commercial or management skills. Educated Indonesians rarely advanced to supervisory posts. Most were absorbed by the colonial bureaucracy or bitterly turned away from Dutch rule.[6]

Immediately following the Japanese conquest of the Netherlands Indies in March 1942, some branches of Dutch companies came under management of experienced indigenous personnel. The Japanese authorities tolerated this, pending the arrival of their own experts.[7] In most instances, however, Dutch managers and technicians were required to stay at their jobs to forestall economic dislocation. Yet by mid-1943 almost the entire Dutch community had been interned and all important positions were occupied by Japanese. To enhance its anti-imperialist credentials, the Japanese authorities from 1944 urged Japanese-run private companies in Indonesia to include indigenous personnel in their staff. This policy, however, produced few tangible results before Japan surrendered in August 1945 (Sutter 1959:133-6, 265).

Indonesia's proclamation of Independence on 17 August 1945 left the Indonesians once more briefly in control of a large share of the country's productive assets, including the principal estate and oil-producing areas in Java and Sumatra. Unfortunately, little is known about the performance of the Indonesian managers of Dutch estates, mines and factories during this period.[8] When the Dutch regained control of their possessions after their first 'police action' (*agresi pertama* in Indonesian historiography), launched in July-

6 In 1931, only 816 Indonesians in the service of Western firms received a salary higher than 100 guilders, compared to 833 'foreign Orientals' (mainly Chinese) and 3,300 Europeans. (Hollandsch-Inlandsche Onderwijs Commissie 1931:46).

7 Unfortunately, little is known about the management of Dutch firms (and other 'enemy property') during the Japanese occupation (see further Keppy 2006).

8 Van Doorn rightly observes that 'we hear a lot about the mess [on the liberated Dutch estates] and even more about rehabilitation, but remarkably little about enterprises that were found in full operation under Indonesian management' (Van Doorn 1994:289).

August 1947, they found the buildings, equipment and crops in a desolate state. It is difficult to establish to what extent this was the result of deliberate destruction, neglect or mismanagement.

From early 1948, when it became apparent that the Dutch were unable to restore colonial rule in Indonesia, the training and promotion of Indonesians to key positions in Dutch enterprise was from time to time discussed in various Dutch business organizations. The chairman of the Ondernemersraad voor Nederlands-Indië (ORNI, Employers' Council for Netherlands Indies), the principal organization of private Dutch enterprises operating in Indonesia, warned that the Dutch 'should not remain entirely passive in this matter [...]. It is likewise inevitable to appoint Indonesians to functions for which they still lack competence'.[9] However, despite such accommodating utterances, little was achieved prior to the transfer of sovereignty in December 1949 (Van de Kerkhof 2005b:190).

Article 12d of the Finec (Financieele en Economische Overeenkomst, Financial and Economic Agreement), by which the Netherlands in 1949 recognized Indonesian sovereignty, obliged Dutch firms to bring 'as quickly as possible [...] skilled Indonesians into executive (including top managerial) and staff positions' (*Round Table Conference* 1950). However, no time schedule was given nor did the agreements specify the percentage of Indonesians to be promoted to management positions. In order to overcome the severe shortage of qualified Indonesian personnel, a fact recognized on either side, the Dutch companies were to train Indonesians for key functions and to increase their experience through 'learning by doing'.

The Indonesian authorities wished Dutch companies to take the initiative in this matter. Prime Minister Moh. Natsir stated in September 1950 that 'the existing foreign enterprises will be urged to open ample and actual opportunity for Indonesian personnel to obtain training up to the top ranks' (Donnithorne 1954:27). The chairman of the Dutch Federation of Upland Estates cautioned that 'it would be wise for us to carry out Article 12 of the Finec as quickly as possible'.[10] In some sectors, notably the oil industry, extensive training schemes were set up to prepare Indonesians for key functions. The Dutch estate companies and sugar producers collectively financed technical and commercial courses in several Indonesian cities whereas some firms, for instance Unilever and the trading firm Borsumij, organized their own in-company training.[11]

9 Nationaal Archief, The Hague: Ondernemersraad voor Nederlands- Indië/Indonesië (ORNI) 18, 3-11-1949.

10 Nationaal Archief, The Hague: Federabo (Federatie van Vereenigingen van Bergcultuurondernemingen in Indonesië) 5, 16-1-1950 (Opening address).

11 Meijer 1994:354; Fieldhouse 1978:297. Golay et al. (1969:136) conclude that there was 'sig-

But the results of these efforts were inconspicuous and failed to satisfy Indonesia's national aspirations. Dutch companies routinely stated that they strived for the advancement of Indonesians to higher functions, but typically added that there were not enough experienced and sufficiently educated candidates and that it therefore remained necessary to employ Europeans. Although in the intermediate ranks Indonesians rapidly replaced the Dutch employees, the top positions remained the exclusive domain of expatriates. The only exceptions were the joint ventures between Dutch firms and the Indonesian government in which the latter formally held the majority, such as the Billiton tin mining concern, GMB (Gemeenschappelijke Mijnbouwmaatschappijen Billiton). Also here, however, actual operations stayed in Dutch hands.[12]

Several factors contributed to the sluggishness of indigenization in the Dutch companies. The one most frequently aired in Dutch business circles was that there were simply not enough qualified Indonesians to replace all European expatriates in key positions (Meijer 1994:352). This may have been a convenient excuse but nonetheless contained much truth, as is illustrated by the fact that only one in every ten Indonesians had received any rudimentary education and only a few hundred held a university degree.[13] In fact, Dutch enterprise in independent Indonesia remained confident about its future in the archipelago precisely because it reckoned that Indonesia could not do without Dutch expertise.

However, defensible Dutch claims that numbers of educated and experienced Indonesians were inadequate and that training Indonesians for key positions would take time intermingled with inflated notions of Western superiority and the alleged unsuitability of the indigenous population for such posts.[14] As late as January 1957, the personnel manager of the large Dutch trading firm Internatio, himself in favour of indigenization of the personnel corps, asserted that 'the Indonesian staff performs to a certain extent well to very well but it lacks the capacity to lead. It is the same story

nificant compliance by Western enterprises' with demand for training courses and the advancement of Indonesians to managerial positions.

12 Van de Kerkhof 2005c:132. The Indonesian government held 62.5 per cent of equity and the Dutch Billiton Company the remainder in GMB. The company continued to rely almost exclusively on Dutch management and supervisory personnel until its concession expired in March 1958 and operations were taken over by a state mining company.

13 According to contemporary observation, 'the new state [Indonesia] began its career with a dangerously small elite of persons with Western education' (Allen and Donnithorne (1957:283). Independent Indonesia awarded high priority to mass education and with some success.

14 I am not referring here to the bigotry exposed by many Europeans during colonial rule, but to the far more subtle forms of discrimination, often cloaked in paternalist views about the inability of indigenous people to take care of their own affairs, which persisted after Independence.

everywhere' (Van de Kerkhof 2005b:197). His observation epitomized the sentiment of many Dutch managers in Indonesia.

Also, whereas most Dutch firms considered the incorporation of indigenous employees into the leading echelons a potential advantage in their relations with Indonesian officials and labour unions, some were reluctant to leave Indonesians in charge of Indonesians. Administrators of the leading Dutch estate company HVA (Handels Vereeniging 'Amsterdam'), for instance, claimed that indigenous workers were generally loathed to accept the authority of another Indonesian (Van de Kerkhof 2005a:121, n. 17). The few Indonesians who were promoted to higher functions within Dutch firms had usually been in their service since before the Pacific War and had, in the eyes of their employer, sufficiently demonstrated their unconditional loyalty to the company.[15]

In addition, Dutch firms were averse to invest large sums of money in the preparation of Indonesians for key positions, since many after completion of their training opted for a more respectable career in the government service. For instance, of the twenty graduates of the trading concern Borsumij's course for talented Indonesians only three actually continued to work for the company (Meijer 1994:354). For that same reason, the interisland shipping company KPM, widely regarded as a prime symbol of Dutch economic domination, felt itself forced to abandon its time-honoured recruitment grounds in Java and Sumatra in favour of 'areas with little or no political agitation and relatively poor regions'.[16]

From 1952, the Indonesian authorities restricted entry of Dutch expatriates in an attempt to speed up indigenization within Dutch enterprise. Increasingly, Dutch firms needed to prove that the vacancy for which they wanted to engage an employee from overseas could not be filled locally. This turned out to be a much more serious nuisance for the Dutch firms than previous indigenization measures which, after all, were largely voluntary. In November 1952, the HVA complained that the immigration restrictions threatened 'to break up our already stretched personnel formation'. To meet the shortage of Dutch personnel, the firm proceeded to advance Indonesians to the rank of assistant planter.[17]

Bureaucratic pressures to speed up indigenization prompted Dutch firms

15 For instance, by the mid-1950s Internatio had promoted only two indigenous employees to decision-making positions. At the time, both were in their mid-forties and had over twenty years of experience in the firm (Van de Kerkhof 2005b:196).

16 Nationaal Archief, The Hague: Koninklijke Paketvaart Maatschappij (KPM) en Koninklijke Java-China-Paketvaartlijnen (KJCPL) 503, 4-1-1950 (Abstract of letter from the directors in Indonesia).

17 Nationaal Archief, The Hague: Handels Vereeniging 'Amsterdam' (HVA). 8, 7-11-1952.

to experiment with means to increase the number of Indonesians in key functions. In 1954, the trading firm Internatio set up a group labelled *Staf Indonesia* (Indonesian Staff) consisting of talented local employees next to the expatriate staff. The aim was to inspire Indonesian 'high potentials' to assume positions of responsibility more rapidly. The *Staf Indonesia* group grew swiftly and by January 1957, locally recruited employees occupied 37 per cent of all staff functions at Internatio. However, over half of the group consisted of Indonesians of Chinese descent, who were considered to be more suitable for such positions, whereas less then one-third were pribumi. Virtually all top functions remained in the hands of Dutch expatriates (Van de Kerkhof 2005b:196).

Dutch companies also ingeniously created staff functions for Indonesian personnel by 'upgrading' the stature of existing jobs, although this frequently failed to convince local functionaries. For instance, in 1954 the Landbouw-Maatschappij Oud-Djember (LMOD, Estate Company Oud-Djember) in Jember, East Java, attempted to earn goodwill with the Indonesian authorities by pointing out the high percentage of Indonesians in its staff. In response, a senior Indonesian official told the company directors that he was not at all interested in 'a listing of *mandur* [foremen] and petty clerks which you just happen to call employee'. He insisted, successfully, on the employment of five graduates of the Indonesian agricultural colleges in exchange for leniency in immigration matters.[18]

A complicating factor was that the local population not always thought highly of the few Indonesians in leading positions within Dutch 'colonial' enterprise, especially after public and political discourse took a radical turn following Indonesia's unilateral repudiation of the RTC agreements in February 1956. The Indonesian chief administrator of the LMOD, who occupied one of the two top functions within the firm, complained in July 1957:

> My position as an Indonesian representative of a large Dutch company is not easy in today's society in which sentiment reigns supreme and common sense is hard to find. In particular the parties and organizations of the left, which have gained much influence of late, give me a hard time. They call me a *kaki tangan kapital asing* [puppet of foreign capital].[19]

The process of indigenization within Dutch firms in Indonesia up to the takeover of December 1957 can be summed up as follows. In the late 1940s

[18] Gemeente Archief, Deventer: Landbouw-Maatschappij 'Oud Djember (LMOD) 138, 8-3-1954 (Report of a visit to Mr. Amien Tjokrosoeseno, head of the estates section at the Jakarta office).

[19] Gemeente Archief, Deventer: LMOD 51, 27-7-1957 (Confidential letter by chief administrator Safioedin).

and early 1950s, Dutch managers generally declared their readiness to prepare Indonesians for higher functions, and to that effect a number of training schemes was set up.[20] However, results were unsatisfactory due mainly to the paucity of educated Indonesians and the reluctance of Dutch companies to invest heavily in training schemes that served the ranks of government more than the companies themselves. Persistent Dutch notions of Western superiority and the alleged inability of Indonesians to assume responsibility also hampered progress.

The introduction of immigration controls in 1952 forced Dutch companies to step up the pace of Indonesianization. The mid-1950s saw extensive Indonesianization of the lower and intermediate levels of Dutch companies and by 1957 the Indonesian element in their personnel corps was typically over 70 percent. Yet, this failed to satisfy Indonesia's aspirations for two reasons. First, the positions vacated by the Dutch were often taken over by Chinese Indonesians rather than indigenous employees. It was Indonesianization rather than *pribumisasi*. Second, the top management level turned out to be an almost impenetrable bastion that remained firmly in Dutch hands.

The indigenization of top level positions only gained momentum after the takeover of Dutch enterprise in December 1957. By the end of that month all Dutch firms had been placed under 'military custody', but army officers commonly delegated day-to-day management to the handful of Indonesians who had already obtained executive experience under the Dutch.[21] The Dutch employees and their families were repatriated with the exception of a small number of senior expatriate staff members who were, as the trading concern Internatio put it, 'the last stayers, or perhaps the first beginners [...] the guardians of our interests [...] on the spot'.[22]

The labour unions, however, demanded 'radical and immediate Indonesianization through the promotion of Indonesians to staff functions and the handing over of key positions to Indonesian staff'.[23] Remaining Dutch managers in Indonesia soon realized that their presence in the archipelago was no longer wanted and that the curtain was about to fall. '[T]he clock cannot be turned back and for most [Dutch employees] it has been

20 Larger Dutch-based multinationals took more initiative in this respect than traditional 'colonial' firms. This is also observable in other post-colonial societies and is probably related to the more flexible corporate culture in multinational enterprise.

21 In this sense the degree of continuity was much higher than is generally assumed. The Indonesian military only gradually took effective control of the nationalized Dutch businesses.

22 Van de Kerkhof 2005b:203. The Anglo-Dutch companies BPM and Unilever were permitted to retain their Dutch personnel but nevertheless decided to replace many of them with British and German managers (Meijer 1994:592).

23 Nationaal Archief, The Hague: N.V. Billiton Maatschappij: Nederlands Indische/Indonesische activiteiten 388, 7-12-1957 (Serikat Buruh Tambang Timah to Billiton Maatschappij).

Chinese students constructing a radio in a workshop in Kuala Lumpur in 1960. Differences in educational background by ethnic origin played an important role in policies of Malayanization in newly independent Malaysia. (KITLV 29142.)

quite enough', wrote the Jakarta manager of Internatio in late December 1957 to the company's head office in Rotterdam (Van de Kerkhof 2005b:203). By mid-1958, all but some 2,000 Dutch employees had left Indonesia (Meijer 1994:619).

British business and Malayanization/Malaysianization

The pivot of British economic presence in the colony of Malaya was a number of renowned management agencies such as Guthrie, Boustead and Harrisons & Crosfield.[24] Set up in Singapore in the first half of the nineteenth century as merchant firms, they greatly diversified their interests and by the 1920s controlled large segments of Malaya's economy, including the all-important rubber industry (Allen and Donnithorne 1957:52). As late as 1981, two historians of the British agency houses in Malaya could still claim that 'even a swift glance through the commercial directories and journals suffices to see that they are still an integral part of the economy'.[25]

The management agency houses were involved to varying degrees in the operation of the rubber plantations. They could be anything from plantation owners to mere secretaries of stand-alone estates. The estates were usually run by a handful of Europeans assisted by travelling agriculturalists, engineers and accountants in the service of the agency houses. Labour was provided by Indian and Chinese immigrants, the former carrying out routine tasks such as rubber tapping, whereas the latter performed more skilled operations such as the clearance of jungle areas. Very few Malays were involved in estate agriculture, not even as plantation labourers (Golay et al. 1969:345; Allen and Donnithorne 1957:112; Drabble and Drake 1981:309).

The other major destination of British private capital was tin mining, which, unlike rubber cultivation, was already a well-developed industry before Westerners became involved. As late as 1913, three-quarters of Malaya's tin production was in Chinese hands. However, the introduction of tin-dredging techniques in the 1910s led to an upsurge of British investment in the mining industry. The dredges were exclusively used by Western firms

24 The term 'Malaysia' is used here loosely (and sometimes a-historically) to denote the area once known as British Malaya (Straits Settlements and the Federated and Unfederated Malay States). Singapore was a separate political entity from 1948 except for a brief interval in 1963-65, when it formed part of the Federation of Malaysia, the successor of the Federation of Malaya which also included the two former British colonies Sabah and Sarawak.

25 Drabble and Drake 1981:299. Not all British management agency houses in Malaysia had the background described here. An important exception was Sime Darby & Co., itself the result of a merger in the plantation sector in 1902. For brief descriptions of the major agency houses, see Carter 2002.

on account of the large capital required both for the dredges and for the leasing of wide areas of mining land. Nevertheless, it was not until 1929 that tin production of Western firms exceeded that of Chinese enterprise (Helten and Jones 1989:164; Jones 2000:259; Kennedy 1993:189-96).

In addition, British merchants played an important role in the Singapore entrepot trade. The result was, in the words of Nicholas White, a 'highly incestuous system of interlocking directorships and shareholdings', which not only linked the rubber and tin companies, but also bound together several of the agency houses (White 1996:29). In turn, British firms were connected to Chinese wholesalers and through them to local retailers and the lower (Malay) bureaucracy.[26] The indigenous Malays, however, overwhelmingly continued their rural existence. At *Merdeka* (Independence) in 1957, three-quarters were still engaged in rice farming, smallholding and fishery (Golay et al. 1969:343).

The excessive dependence of the Malayan economy on only a few primary products, notably rubber and tin, proved a liability when prices for these commodities plummeted during the Great Depression of the 1930s. This experience assured that diversification of the economy would be one of the chief goals of Malaysian nationalists in the post-Independence period. Also, while drastic measures to restrict output succeeded in restoring commodity prices to profitable levels, the inequitable treatment of local smallholders as against European producers caused much resentment among the overwhelmingly rural Malays. The protective policy was also blamed for 'freezing' the colony's one-sided economic structure and hindering much-needed diversification (Lim 1977; Drabble 2000)

British wartime preparation for Malaya's 'liberation' centred on long-term planning and bureaucratic intervention to spur economic development, rationalize production structures in the major export industries and raise standards of living for all population groups, in particular the Malays (Harper 1999:247-50; White 1997:105). In this way, the British aimed to win the 'hearts and minds' of the people, prepare the Malays for Independence and, last but not least, restore the colony's pre-war capacity to earn foreign exchange.[27] In

26 The best-known intermediary figure was the comprador. The term initially referred to the Chinese managers of European firms in imperial China, but the system was later exported to other parts of Asia with large Chinese communities. In Malaysia, they enjoyed significant autonomy and often were businessmen on their own account rather than in the service of foreign firms. After the Second World War, the system disintegrated and the compradors became managers on the payroll of Western enterprise, although the reputable agency house Harrisons & Crosfield still had one in Singapore until the 1960s (Harper 1999:202; Jones 2000:231-3).

27 For Britain's economic designs for the post-war period, see Stockwell 1974.

1948, the Federation of Malaya Agreement explicitly recognized the 'special position' of the Malays.[28]

British colonial officials foresaw that the economic advance of the Malays, be it as businessmen, smallholders or civil servants, would put off more radical manifestations of economic nationalism, including the expropriation of British assets. Interestingly, during the negotiations about Independence, London did not demand formal guarantees for the continued operation of British business in a future independent Malaya nor was it sought by British firms. Such arrangements, it was held, might be viewed as limitations of Malaya's sovereignty and had failed in Burma, Pakistan and India, and Indonesia for that matter (White 1996:171 n. 52, 265).

Shortly after the Federation of Malaya was promulgated in 1948, the security situation deteriorated as a result of an insurgency mounted by the Malayan Communist Party (MCP), an organization whose membership was overwhelmingly Chinese. The Malayan government was able to defeat the insurgents with substantial British aid, although guerrilla fighting continued until 1960. It has been asserted that 'the Malayan Emergency was fought in large part to make Southeast Asia safe for British business' (Putchucheary 1960:23), but even if this is an oversimplification, it is clear that the British were very concerned about their investments in the peninsula.[29]

Outwardly, British business in Malaya adapted promptly to the new vocabulary of decolonization. As early as 1945, a director of Harrisons & Crosfield advocated 'the gradual promotion of Asiatic supervisors to the highest ranks of management' (Egmont-Hake 1945:101). In practice, however, British business responded grudgingly to calls for indigenization. Innate conservatism and the problems of incorporating indigenous employees into rather tradition-minded business organizations held back Malayanization of key functions. British executives feared that the Malays would not live up to the high moral standards which their new responsibilities required (Jones 2000:225).

Early initiatives focused on the training of talented young Malays in Britain to expose them intensely to British corporate culture.[30] In 1954,

28 The privileges extended to the Malays were exclusive titles to certain agricultural lands and preferential access to the civil service and branches of the bureaucracy such as medical services, education and the police force (Golay et al. 1969:360-1).

29 The Trade Advisory Committee of the Colonial Office signalled that 'there is, both in financial and commercial circles, a very severe lack of confidence in Malaya as a "good risk". This is so in the United Kingdom, in other capital exporting countries and in Malaya itself.' Public Record Office, London: Colonial Office (CO). Original correspondence, 1945-51: 6090, 17-5-1950 (Ministerial visits to Malaya: representations by business organizations. Memorandum of the Trade Advisory Committee).

30 In this respect an important difference may be observed between Indonesia and Malaysia. Whereas the personnel policies of Dutch companies in Indonesia focused on formal educational

Guthrie and Sime Darby were among the first British companies in Malaya to introduce a 'cadet scheme' to train Asians as assistant plantation managers. Other firms experimented with bringing local staff to work in Britain for a certain period of time, or making available scholarships for young Malays to study at universities and agricultural colleges. However, recruitment as well as retention of the most promising candidates proved no easy task, since many Malays resented being away from home (Drabble and Drake 1981:321-2; Jones 2000:225; White 2004:72).

The constitution of the independent Federation of Malaya (1957) reiterated the 'special position' of the Malays set out in the 1948 agreement (Siddique and Suryadinata 1981:671). The ruling Alliance Party coalition was the product of a 'bargain' between the three major ethnic groups in the country,[31] in which the Chinese and Indians accepted Malay political dominance in exchange for liberal citizenship regulations and guarantees that their economic interests would not be disadvantaged (Searle 1999:32). The Alliance aspired to uplift the Malays by providing social overhead services to backward rural areas. British firms were largely unaffected since the Malays recognized an interest in maintaining their presence in the economy as a bulwark against Chinese economic encroachment (Harper 1999:251-2).

Despite the absence of clear-cut policies to reduce the share of British interests in the economy, the 1950s and 1960s saw a gradual shift in patterns of ownership in favour of the domestic, principally Chinese, capitalist class.[32] For instance, the share of domestic (mainly Chinese) ownership in the tin mining industry rose from 22 per cent in 1954 to 64 per cent ten years later. However, since domestic participation was highly dispersed among a large number of individual investors, the British agency houses were able to retain a decisive vote in the selection of directors and senior management.[33] The transfer of ownership thus had only limited impact on the actual running of the companies involved.

The mounting costs of sending out expatriates in the 1950s and 1960s

merits, demonstrated by possession of diploma's, British firms in Malaysia (and elsewhere in Asia) above all stressed 'character' and social skills.

31 The Alliance consisted of the United Malays National Organization (UMNO), the Malay(si)an Chinese Association (MCA) and the Malay(si)an Indian Congress (MIC).

32 The absence of effective exchange controls, made possible by a foreign exchange position which was unique in Southeast Asia at the time, also facilitated repatriation of foreign capital and thus indirectly stimulated the transfer of ownership to Malaysian nationals (Golay et al. 1969:352-3).

33 White 2004:7; Yip Yat Hoong 1969:348-73. This transfer of property was not confined to the tin mining industry. For instance, Sime Darby, whose extensive interests in plantations and manufacturing made it into one of the largest foreign companies in independent Malaysia, estimated in 1976 that only 10 per cent of its shareholders were domiciled in Britain, compared to 48 per cent in Singapore and 36 per cent in Malaysia (Helten and Jones 1989:179).

offered a stimulus for British firms to recruit more domestic personnel, both *bumiputra* and non-indigenous. However, since it proved difficult to attract a sufficient number of competent candidates for key functions, there was tacit agreement between Kuala Lumpur and British enterprise that Malaysianization would not be rigidly enforced but achieved on the basis of natural wastage.[34] Consequently, indigenization of the higher echelons of British firms remained a slow process. In 1966, the Malaysian government noted that in several British companies practically no Malaysianization had taken place at all (Jones 2000:225; White 2004:74).

In the mid-1960s there were the first indications that Malaysia might become less considerate of British business interests.[35] The British Trade Commissioner in Kuala Lumpur predicted in 1964 that 'the happy position under which British firms have been able to employ virtually as many Europeans as they wished is coming to an end'. In November 1965, all trading and manufacturing enterprises were required to submit their Malaysianization schemes (Golay et al. 1969:385-6; White 2004:72-3). Managers of British companies were subsequently summoned before a standing committee and questioned about the number of Malays in their service and the qualifications of expatriate personnel.[36]

The Malaysian government used existing but until then scarcely enforced immigration restrictions to Malayanize/Malaysianize higher positions within British firms.[37] The issue of new working permits was taking much longer than before and especially junior expatriates had a hard time getting one at all. British firms, however, were still permitted to retain expatriates in 'key functions' as well as a 'pipeline' of junior recruits to fuel the top ranks.[38]

34 The scepticism of the British concerning the management skills of the Malaysians was demonstrated by the practice to split up estates previously managed by a single expatriate planter into smaller parcels managed by several Malaysian ones (White 2004:77).

35 According to Searle (1999:36), the Kongres Ekonomi Bumiputra (Economic Congress of Indigenous Peoples) of June 1965 may be viewed as a 'turning point' in this development. The congress made many recommendations to advance the indigenization of the economy, some of which were taken over by the Malaysian government.

36 Public Record Office, London: Commonwealth Relations Office, Economic relations, original correspondence 1960-66, 588 (Malaysia: employment of expatriates in business. Standing Committee of Officials on Malaysianisation in Commerce & Industry: Supplementary Information of Companies and Firms Submitting Malaysianisation Statement).

37 In 1959, the Malaysian government restricted work permits to foreigners earning over $1,200 a month and performing functions that could not be carried out by Malaysians. This policy, however, appeared to target Indian immigrant labour rather than Western firms, which were still able to bring in expatriate staff provided they had some technical or managerial qualification. Moreover, in bona fide cases permits for British managers were renewed automatically (White 2004:72-3).

38 In some industries, notably the plantation sector, the 'pipeline' concept was later abandoned in favour of a quota system for expatriate managers.

According to the British Commonwealth Office, the plantation industry was likely to suffer the consequences since 'it contains a large number of expatriates and it is difficult to claim that it contains many "key posts" [...] appropriate only for expatriates'.[39]

The British High Commissioner in Kuala Lumpur, Sir Michael Walker, argued that the indigenization measures had been prompted by the fact that 'many British firms have done nothing to take account of the Malaysianization objectives of the government [...] and have even adopted policies to frustrate them'.[40] He also maintained that 'a Malaysianization programme which does not require completion until twenty years after independence and even then leaves the safeguard of key posts and a continuing pipeline can hardly be regarded as unreasonable'. Significantly, in 1966 it was estimated that a mere 20 per cent of plantation managers were recruited locally (White 2004:75). Walker concluded 'that it is now up to them [British firms] to demonstrate a more constructively cooperative attitude [...] in this matter.'

In May 1969, fierce anti-Chinese riots broke out which brought to the fore the still vast disparities between the economic position of the Chinese and Malays. The Alliance's liberal economic policy turned out to be much more beneficial to the Chinese (and Indians) than to the indigenous population.[41] In response, the Malaysian government in 1970 introduced the New Economic Policy (NEP). The NEP was not directed primarily against British business, but aimed to reserve for *bumiputra* a share of the national economy commensurate with their numbers in the population.[42] The economic emancipation of the Malays, however, would inevitably require curtailment of the role of British firms in the economy.

In the 1970s and early 1980s, British business lost its key position in the Malaysian economy due to the rapid and government-sponsored build-up of Malaysian shareholding in British firms. Spectacular examples were the takeovers of the London Tin Company (1979), Guthrie (1981) and Harrisons

[39] Public Record Office, London: Commonwealth Relations Office 588, 28-7-1966 (G.S. Whitehead to J. Moreton).

[40] Public Record Office, London: Commonwealth Relations Office 588, Oct. 1966 (Internal memorandum).

[41] Between 1957 and 1970, average income per household grew by 33 per cent for Chinese, 31 per cent for Indians and 28 per cent for Malays. The welfare gap between the population groups actually widened (Searle 1999:34).

[42] Helten and Jones 1989:184-5; Searle 1999:66-78 .The NEP's purpose was to eradicate poverty 'irrespective of race' and to 'restructure Malaysian society to reduce and eventually eliminate the identification of race with economic function' (Searle 1999:14). The promulgation of the NEP followed a reconfiguration of Malaysian politics after the 1969 elections, which enhanced the position of those who favoured active indigenization.

& Crosfield (1982).[43] Such intricate share manoeuvres were accompanied by boardroom coups, perhaps the most spectacular being the capture of Sime Darby, one of Malaysia's largest foreign-owned companies, which in November 1976 was suddenly confronted with the suggestion of a Malaysian minority stockholder that four of the six British directors due for re-election be replaced by Malaysians. The 'revolt' was successful and there followed a process of rapid Malaysianization.[44]

The Malaysians had 'defeated British capitalists at their own games on their own home ground' (Helten and Jones 1989:184). Thus, what gentle appeals to the moral responsibility of British firms as well as immigration controls had failed to accomplish, became unavoidable once the British had lost formal control of their companies. One by one, the British directors and senior managers were withdrawn and replaced by Malaysians, turning Malaysia, despite heightened tensions with Britain in the mid-1980s, into one of the foremost examples of successful economic decolonization in Southeast Asia.

Conclusion

Analysis of the indigenization process within 'colonial' enterprise in independent Indonesia and Malaysia casts doubt on the often expressed supposition that Dutch firms in Indonesia were the agents of their own demise due to a lack of responsiveness to the new state's economic aspirations. British business in Malaysia was equally reluctant to vacate its privileged position yet was permitted a tardy retreat instead of an abrupt breakdown. The failure of Dutch firms to satisfy Indonesian national ambitions surely did not help matters when in 1957 temperatures reached fever pitch over West Irian. However, it does not adequately explain the exceedingly confrontational relationship between Dutch enterprise and independent Indonesia.

Comparison of the economic indigenization process in Indonesia and Malaysia reveals important similarities, which suggest that the posture of Dutch enterprise in Indonesia was not as exceptional as is often alleged. Both Dutch enterprise in Indonesia and British business in Malaysia outwardly responded constructively to calls for indigenization. Expatriate managers paid

43 Interestingly, it was a British financier, Jim Slater, who alerted the Malaysian government to the possibilities of share manoeuvres on the London Stock Exchange to advance the goals of the NEP. Slater played a major role in the Malaysian takeover of London Tin Company in the mid-1970s.

44 Harper 1999:363; Helten and Jones 1989:185-6. In 1978, Sime Darby's head office moved to Kuala Lumpur and in 1980, the company's legal domicile was transferred from Britain to Malaysia.

at least lip service to the new nations' desire for more indigenous employees in decision-making functions. In-company training, educational facilities and grants were made available to prepare young Indonesians and Malays for technical and managerial functions. These initiatives were voluntary and in large measure intended to create goodwill among the new ruling elites.

Such schemes, however, failed to produce the desired results. Several factors were at work here. The most important ones were the acute shortage of experienced and educated indigenous personnel to take over the functions of expatriates, and the conservative views, sometimes approaching racial prejudice, held by expatriate managers concerning the inaptness of Asians for positions requiring leadership skills and sense of duty. The result was that the top level functions in British and Dutch firms remained the exclusive domain of expatriate managers, while the lower and intermediate ranks underwent rapid indigenization.

The rising costs of sending out expatriates and the introduction of stringent immigration controls, in Indonesia in 1952 and in Malaysia in the mid-1960s, provided a strong incentive for Dutch and British enterprise to step up the pace of indigenization. 'Colonial' firms began to promote indigenous employees to decision-making positions which had in the past been out of their reach, even though their numbers remained very modest. British firms in Malaysia, moreover, were permitted to retain expatriates in 'key functions' and a 'pipeline' of junior recruits to fuel the top ranks. As a result, immigration restrictions had only limited effect in Malaysia.

Neither in Indonesia nor in Malaysia did indigenization of the top ranks occur as a result of voluntary initiatives of 'colonial' enterprise or immigration restrictions. Only direct interference in the companies' personnel policies accomplished that goal. In Indonesia, the takeover and subsequent nationalization of Dutch enterprise in 1957/1958 enabled the appointment of Indonesians at the apex of these firms to replace the repatriated Dutch managers. In Malaysia, British executives were removed from the scene in the late 1970s and early 1980s, when Malaysian investors used their combined majority share to impose the assignment of Malaysians to the board of directors and top management positions.

The most obvious difference between the indigenization process in Indonesia and Malaysia thus concerns not its end result, but the timing and the manner in which it was achieved. The British lost their hold of the Malaysian economy only after a series of spectacular boardroom coups and share manoeuvres on the London Stock Exchange in the late 1970s and early 1980s. Dutch business in Indonesia, however, collapsed a quarter of a century earlier in the face of labour union militancy and Jakarta's determination to prevail in the West Irian dispute. Dutch assets were nationalized in December 1958, although 'expropriated' is a better term, since full compensation was never paid.

Two factors may account for the very different patterns of indigenization followed in Indonesia and Malaysia. First, the fact that in Malaysia the politically dominant Malays barely outnumbered the economically powerful Chinese served to deflect Malay economic nationalism from British enterprise. The Malays for a long time saw the continued operations of British business as a safeguard against economic encroachment by other resident ethnic groups (Golay et al. 1969:346). Malaya's economic policies in the 1950s therefore centred on improving living conditions in the overwhelmingly Malay rural areas, followed in the 1960s by attempts to narrow the income gap between Malays and Chinese. The position of British enterprise in Malaysia was not seriously challenged until the 1969 anti-Chinese riots signalled the failure of this strategy to produce economic parity.

The situation in Indonesia was different in the sense that the comparatively small Chinese community did not constitute a separate political force (Siddique and Suryadinata:665-9). Political party formation in Indonesia in the 1950s generally cut across ethnic barriers, allowing widespread condemnation of Dutch enterprise as being intrinsically exploitative (Dick et al. 2002:182; Robison 1986:37). Indonesian nationalists resented the prominent economic position of the Chinese, yet they targeted above all Dutch control over the 'commanding heights' of the economy. Chinese business only came under serious attack once Dutch enterprise had been expelled in 1957/1958.

Second, there are important differences in the ideological orientation of the political leadership in both countries. As Bruce Glassburner has pointed out, 'the years 1950 and 1957 in Indonesia are best understood as years of a hopeless losing battle on the part of a very small group of pragmatically conservative political leaders against an increasingly powerful political opposition of generally radical orientation' (Glassburner 1971:71). The radical group advocated not mere reconstruction of the 'Dutch-dominated economy', but its downright eradication. This drift towards anti-Dutch militancy gained momentum when in February 1957 Sukarno proclaimed martial law, thus ending the democratic experiment, in an attempt to thwart uprisings in the Outer Islands.

In Malaysia, the pro-British sentiment of the ruling elites, consisting of Malay bureaucrats and aristocrats as well as non-Malay business leaders, survived until the late-1960s (Helten and Jones 1989:181). These groups were generally sympathetic towards free enterprise and an open capitalist economy, since they believed that the influx of foreign capital and expertise provided the stimulus for economic expansion that would facilitate the restructuring of capital ownership. It was not until the May 1969 anti-Chinese riots signalled the failure of this policy to close the gap between the Malays and the non-indigenous peoples that a forceful indigenization policy was adopted under a self-assured political leadership.

References

Allen, George and Audrey Donnithorne
1957 *Western enterprise in Indonesia and Malaya; A study in economic development.* London: Allen and Unwin.

Baudet, H. and M. Feddema et al.
1983 *Het Nederlands belang bij Indië.* Utrecht: Aula.

Breton, Albert
1964 'Economics of nationalism', *Journal of Political Economy* 72:376-86.

Carter, Lionel
2002 *Chronicles of British business in Asia, 1850-1960. A bibliography of printed company histories with short accounts of the concerns.* New Delhi: Manohar.

Dick, Howard W., Vincent J.H. Houben, J. Thomas Lindblad and Thee Kian Wie
2002 *The emergence of a national economy; An economic history of Indonesia, 1800-2000.* Crows Nest, NSW: Allen and Unwin.

Donnithorne, Audrey
1954 'Western enterprise in Indonesia today', *Pacific Affairs* 27:27-40.

Doorn, J.A.A. van
1994 *De laatste eeuw van Indië; Ontwikkeling en ondergang van een koloniaal project.* Amsterdam: Bert Bakker.

Drabble, John
2000 *An economic history of Malaysia, 1800-1990; The transition to modern economic growth.* New York/Basingstoke: Macmillan.

Drabble, John and Peter Drake
1981 'The British agency houses in Malaysia; Survival in a changing world', *Journal of Southeast Asian Studies* 22:297-328.

Egmont-Hake, H.B.
1945 *The New Malaya and you.* London: Lindsay Drummond.

Fieldhouse, David
1978 *Unilever overseas; Anatomy of a multinational, 1895-1965.* London: Croom Helm.

Glassburner, Bruce
1971 'Economic policy-making in Indonesia, 1950-1957', in: B. Glassburner (ed.), *The economy of Indonesia*, pp. 70-98. Ithaca, NY: Cornell University Press. [Reprint Jakarta: Equinox, 2007.]

Golay, Frank H., Ralph Anspach, M. Ruth Pfanner and Eliezer B. Ayal
1969 *Underdevelopment and economic nationalism in Southeast Asia.* Ithaca, NY: Cornell University Press.

Harper, Timothy
1999 *The end of empire and the making of Malaya.* Cambridge: Cambridge University Press.

Helten, Jean-Jaques and Geoffrey Jones
1989 'British business in Malaysia and Singapore since the 1870s', in: Richard Davenport-Hines and Geoffrey Jones (eds), *British business in Asia since 1860*, pp. 157-88. Cambridge: Cambridge University Press.

Hollandsch-Inlandsche Onderwijs Commissie
1931 *De werkgelegenheid in Nederlandsch-Indië voor Nederlandsch sprekenden.* Weltevreden: Landsdrukkerij.

Johnson, Harry
1965 'A theoretical model of economic nationalism in new and developing states', *Political Science Quarterly* 80:171-8.

Jones, Geoffrey
2000 *Merchants to multinational; British trading companies in the nineteenth and twentieth centuries.* Oxford: Oxford University Press.

Kahin, George McT.
1952 *Nationalism and Revolution in Indonesia.* Ithaca, NY: Cornell University Press.

Kennedy, J.
1993 *A history of Malaya.* Kuala Lumpur: Abdul Majeed

Keppy, Peter
2006 *Sporen van vernieling; Oorlogsschade, roof en rechtsherstel in Indonesië.* Amsterdam: Boom.

Kerkhof, Jasper van de
2005a '"Defeatism is our worst enemy"; Rehabilitation, reorientation and *Indonesianisasi* at Internatio and HVA, 1945-1958', *Lembaran Sejarah* 8-2:109-28.
2005b '*Indonesianisasi* of Dutch economic interests; The case of Internatio, 1930-1960', *Bijdragen tot de Taal-, Land- en Volkenkunde* 161:181-208.
2005c 'Onmisbaar maar onbemind; De Koninklijke Paketvaart Maatschappij en de Billiton Maatschappij in het onafhankelijke Indonesië (1945-1958)', *Tijdschrift voor Sociale en Economische Geschiedenis* 2-4:122-46.

Lim Teck Ghee
1977 *Peasants and their agricultural economy in colonial Malaya, 1874-1941.* Kuala Lumpur: Oxford University Press.

Meijer, Hans
1994 *Den Haag – Djakarta; De Nederlands-Indonesische betrekkingen 1950-1962.* Utrecht: Aula.

Paauw, Douglas
1963 'From colonial to guided economy', in: R.T. McVey (ed.), *Indonesia*, pp. 155-247. New Haven, CT: HRAF.

Puthucheary, J.J.
1960 *Ownership and control in the Malaysian economy.* Singapore: Eastern University Press.

Robison, Richard
1986 *Indonesia; The rise of capital.* Sydney: Allen and Unwin.

Round Table Conference
1950 *Round Table Conference; Results as accepted in the second plenary meeting held on 2 November 1949 in the Ridderzaal at The Hague. Djakarta: Kolff.*

Schmitt, H.O.
1962 'Foreign capital and social conflict in Indonesia, 1950-1958', *Economic Development and Cultural Change* 10:284-93.

Searle, Peter
1999 *The riddle of Malaysian capitalism; Rent-seekers or real capitalists?*. St. Leonards, NSW: Allen and Unwin.

Siddique, Sharon and Leo Suryadinata
1981 '*Bumiputra* and *pribumi*; Economic nationalism (indigenism) in Malaysia and Indonesia', *Pacific Affairs* 54:662-87.

Sluyterman, Keetie
2003 *Kerende kansen; Het Nederlandse bedrijfsleven in de twintigste eeuw*. Amsterdam: Boom.

Stockwell, A.J.
1974 'Colonial planning during World War II; The case of Malaya', *Journal of Imperial and Commonwealth History* 2:333-51.

Sutter, John O.
1959 *Indonesianisasi; A historical survey of the role of politics in the institutions of a changing economy from the Second World War to the eve of the general election, 1940-1955*. PhD thesis, Cornell University, Ithaca, NY.

White, Nicholas
1996 *Business, government, and the end of empire; Malaya, 1942-57*. Kuala Lumpur. Oxford University Press.
1997 'The frustrations of development; British business and the late colonial state in Malaya, 1945-1957', *Journal of Southeast Asian Studies* 28:103-19.
2004 *British business in post-colonial Malaysia, 1957-70; 'Neo-colonialism' or 'disengagement'?*. London: RoutledgeCurzon.

Yip Yat Hoong
1969 *The development of the tin mining industry of Malaya*. Kuala Lumpur: University of Malaya Press.

About the authors

Tri Chandra Apriyanto obtained his MA from the Department of History at Gadjah Mada University, Yogyakarta. He is presently teaching history at the University of Jember. His research focuses on the economic history of Jember.

Anne Booth is Professor of Asian Economics at the School of Oriental and African Studies of the University of London. She has published widely on the economic history of Southeast and East Asia, in particular Indonesia. Her most recent book is entitled *Colonial legacies; Economic and social development in East and Southeast Asia* (Honolulu 2007).

Jasper van de Kerkhof obtained his MA in economic history from the Department of History at Leiden University. He was affiliated with the Department of History and the International Institute of Asian Studies in Leiden and did research about Dutch business firms at the time of Indonesian decolonization. He is currently head of the economics section of the Gemeenschappelijke Pers Dienst in The Hague.

J. Thomas Lindblad is Associate Professor in Economic History and the History of Indonesia at Leiden University. He has published widely on the economic history of Southeast Asia, in particular Indonesia. His most recent book is entitled *Bridges to new business; The economic decolonization of Indonesia* (Leiden 2008).

Daan Marks obtained his PhD in economics at the University of Utrecht in 2009 with a dissertation entitled *Accounting for services; The economic development of the Indonesian service sector, ca. 1900-2000*. He is affiliated with the International Institute of Social History in Amsterdam and the University of Utrecht. His current research focuses on long-run economic development in Indonesia.

Peter Post is senior researcher at the Netherlands Institute for War Documentation in Amsterdam. He published widely on the history of Japan's economic relations with Indonesia and on Chinese business networks in Southeast Asia. He is general editor of the *Encyclopaedia of Indonesia in the Pacific War* (forthcoming).

Bambang Purwanto is Professor in History at Gadjah Mada University, Yogyakarta and also Extraordinary Leiden Professor for Relations between Indonesia and the Netherlands. He has published extensively on the economic and social history of Indonesia and on Indonesian historiography. His most recent book is entitled *Gagalnya historiografi Indonesiasentris?!* (Yogyakarta 2006).

Thee Kian Wie is retired senior research fellow of the Indonesian Academy of Science in Jakarta. He has published widely on the Indonesian economy and Indonesian economic history. He received several distinguished awards, including an honorary doctorate from the Australian National University. One of his foremost publications was *Recollections; The Indonesian economy, 1950s-1990s* (Singapore 2003).

Index